BLACK LEGACY PRESS™

WWW.BLACKLEGACYPRESS.ORG

SLAVE NARRATIVES

VOLUME II
ARKANSAS NARRATIVES
PART 6

By
United States.
Work Projects Administration

Copyright © 2024 by BLACKLEGACYPRESS.ORG

All rights reserved. No part of this publication may be reproduced or transmitted in any form or by any means electronic or mechanical, including information storage and retrieval systems without permission in writing from the publisher, except for student research using the appropriate citations.

ISBN: 978-1-63652-207-4

SLAVE NARRATIVES

A Folk History of Slavery in the United States.
From Interviews with Former Slaves

**UNITED STATES.
WORK PROJECTS ADMINISTRATION**

TYPEWRITTEN RECORDS PREPARED BY
THE FEDERAL WRITERS' PROJECT
1936-1938
ASSEMBLED BY
THE LIBRARY OF CONGRESS PROJECT
WORK PROJECTS ADMINISTRATION
FOR THE DISTRICT OF COLUMBIA
SPONSORED BY THE LIBRARY OF
CONGRESS

WASHINGTON 1941

VOLUME II
ARKANSAS NARRATIVES
PART 6

Prepared by
The Federal Writers' Project of
The Works Progress Administration
For the State of Arkansas

CONTENTS

Cecil Copeland 1
Doc Quinn 9
Henrietta Ralls 13
Irene Robertson 17
Senia Rassberry 21
Clay Reaves 25
Jane Reece 29
Frank Reed 31
James Reeves 33
Shepherd Rhone 45
Dora Richard 49
Jim Ricks 51
Charlie Rigger 53
Ida Rigley 57
Milton Ritchie 63
Alice Rivers 67
J. Roberts 69
George Robertson 71
Augustus Robinson 73
Malindy Robinson 79
Tom Robinson 81
Isom Rogers 87
Oscar James Rogers 89

Will Ann Rogers	93
William Henry Rooks	97
Amanda Ross	101
Cat Ross	107
Mattie Ross	109
Laura Rowland	113
Landy Rucker	117
Martha Ruffin	121
Thomas Ruffin	125
Casper Rumple	133
Henry Russell	139
Katie Rye	143
Bob Samuels	145
Emma Sanderson	151
Mary Scott	157
Mollie Hardy Scott	161
Sam Scott	165
Cora Scroggins	169
Sarah Sexton	171
Roberta Shaver	175
Mary Shaw	177
Violet Shaw	179
Frederick Shelton	181
Laura Shelton	185
Mahalia Shores	191
Rosa Simmons	195
Fannie Sims	197

Jerry Sims	199
Victoria Sims	201
Virginia Sims	205
Senya Singfield	209
Senya Singfield	211
Peggy Sloan	215
Arzella Smallwood	217
Sarah Smiley	219
Caroline Smith	221
Caroline Smith	225
Edmond Smith	227
Emma Hulett Smith	231
Ervin E. Smith	233
Frances Smith	239
Henrietta Evelina Smith	241
Henry Smith	245
J.L. Smith	249
John H. Smith	255
Maggie Snow and Charlie Snow	259
Robert Solomon	263
James Spikes	267
Kittie Stanford	269
Tom Stanhouse	271
Isom Starnes	273
Ky Hezekiah Steel	277
Maggie Stenhouse	281
Charlotte E. Stephens	285

William J. Stevens	293
Minnie Johnson Stewart	295
Liza Stiggers	297
James Henry Stith	299
Caroline Stout	307
Felix Street	309
Mary Tabon	317
Liza Moore Tanner	319
Fannie Tatum	323
Anthony Taylor	325
Lula Taylor	333
Millie Taylor	337
Sarah Taylor	341
Warren Taylor	343
Sneed Teague	353
Mary Teel	355
Wade Thermon	359
Dicey Thomas	361
Mandy Thomas	371
Omelia Thomas	373
Omelia Thomas	377
Tanner Thomas	383
Wester Thomas	385
Annie Thompson	387
Ellen Briggs Thompson	389
Hattie Thompson	397
Mamie Thompson	401

Mike Thompson ... 405
Laura Thornton ... 407
Emma TidwellBama? ... 417
Joe Tillman ... 421
J.T. Tims ... 423
Hannah Travis ... 435
Mark C. Trotter ... 443
Pernella Anderson ... 445
Mandy Tucker ... 449
Emma Turner ... 453
Henry Turner ... 457
Seabe Tuttle ... 465

Texarkana District
FOLKLORE SUBJECTS
Name of Interviewer: Cecil Copeland
Subject: Social Customs—Reminiscences of an Ex-Slave
Subject: Foods

This Information given by: Doc Quinn
Place of Residence: 1217 Ash Street, Texarkana, Arkansas
Occupation: None [TR: also reported as Ex-slave.]
Age: 93 [TR: also reported as 94.]
[TR: Information moved from bottom of first page.]
[TR: Repetitive information deleted from subsequent pages.]

CECIL COPELAND

Several months ago, I called at 1217 Ash Street, Texarkana, Arkansas where I had been informed a voluble old negro lived. An aged, gray-haired, negro woman came to the door and informed me her father was in the wood shed at the back of the house. Going around to the wood shed I found him busily engaged in storing his winter supply of wood. When I made known my mission he readily agreed to answer all my questions as best he could. Seating himself on a block of wood, he told this almost incredible story, along with lengthy discourses on politics, religion and other current events:

"I wuz born March 15, 1843, in Monroe County, Mississippi, near Aberdeen, Mah Mahster wuz Colonel Ogburn, one ob de bigges' planters in de state of Mississippi. Manys de time he raised so much cotton dat dem big steamers just couldnt carry it all down to N'Awlins in one year. But den along came de Civil War an' we didn't raise nothin' fo' several years. Why? Becase most uf us jined the Confederate Army in Colonel Ogburn's regiment as servants and bodyguards. An' let me tell yo' somethin', whitefolks. Dere never wuz a war like dis war. Why I 'member dat after de battle of Corinth, Miss., a five acre field was so thickly covered wid de dead and wounded dat yo' couldn't touch de ground in walkin' across it. And de onliest way to bury dem wuz to cut a deep furrow wid a plow, lay de soldiers head to head, an' plow de dirt back on dem."

"About a year after de war started de Mahster got one ob dese A.W.O.L.'s frum de Army so we could come to Miller County, where he bought de place on Red River now known as de Adams Farm."

"When we fust came here dis place, as well as de rest ob de Valley, wuz just a big canebrake—nothin' lived in dere but bears, wolves, and varmints. Why de Mahster would habe to round up de livestock each afternoon, put dem in pens, and den put out guards all night to keep de wolves and bears frum gettin' em. De folks didn't go gallivatin' round nights like dey do now or de varmints would get them. But den we didn't stay here but a few months until de Mahster's A.W.O.L. wuz up, so we had to go back and jine de army. We fought in Mississippi Alabama, Georgia, and South Carolina."

"When de war ended de Mahster moved us to Miller County, but not on de Adams farm. For de man whut used to own de farm said Uncle Sam hadn't made any such money as wuz paid him for de farm, so he wanted his farm back. Dat Confederate money wuzn't worth de paper it wuz printed on, so de Mahster had to gib him back de farm. Poor Massa Ogburn—he didn't live long after dat. He and his wife are buried side by side in Rondo Cemetery."

"Not long after de negroes wuz freed, I took 86 ob dem to de votin' place at Homan and voted 'em all straight Democratic. On my way back home dat evenin' five negroes jumped frum de bushes and stopped me. Dey 'splained dat I wuz too 'fluential wid de negroes and proceeded to string me up by de neck. I hollers as loud as I could, and Roy Nash and Hugh Burton, de election officers, just happen to be comin' down de road and hear me yell. Dey ran off de niggers and cut me down, but by dat time I had passed out. It wuz several weeks befo' I got well, and I can still feel dat rope 'round my neck. Iffen dey had known how to tie a hangmans knot I wouldn't be here to tell you about it."

"It wuzn't long after dis dat I jined Colonel' Baker's Gang for 'tection. 'Colonel' Baker wuz a great and brave man and did mo' fo de white folks of dis country den any other man. Why iffen it hadn't been fo' him de white folks couldn't hab lived in dis country, de negroes wuz so mean. Dey wuz so mean dat dey tied heavy plow shoes aroun' de necks ob two little white boys and threw dem in de lake. Yes suh. I wuz dere."

"And another time I wuz wid a bunch of niggers when dey wuz plannin' on killin a white man who wuz a friend ob mine. As soon as I could I slips away and tips him off. When I got back one ob dem niggers looks at me suspicious like and asks, "where yo been, nigger?" I wuz shakin' like a leaf in a storm, but I says: "I ain't been nowhere—just went home to get some cartridges to help kill dis white man."

"Not long after I jined Colonel Baker's Gang, we wuz comin' frum Fulton to Clipper through de Red River bottoms. De river wuz overflowin' an' as we wuz crossin' a deep, swift slough, Colonel Baker and his horse got tangled up in some grape vines. Colonel Baker yelled, and I turned my mule around and cut all de grape vine loose wid my Bowie knife. Dere ain't nothin' like a mule for swimmin'. Dey can swim circles aroun' any horse. As long as he lived, Colonel Baker was always grateful to me fo' savin' his life."

"De Colonel hated de sight ob mean niggers. We would ride up to a negro settlement, and tell de niggers we wuz organizing a colored militia to catch Cullen Baker and his gang. Most ob de negroes would join, but some ob dem had to be encouraged by Colonel Baker's big gun. De recruits would be lined up in an open field fo' drilling. And dey sho wuz drilled. Colonel Baker and his men would shoot them by the score. Dey killed 53 at Homan, Arkansas, 86 at Rocky Comfort, (Foreman) Arkansas, 6 near Ogden, Arkansas, 6 on de Temple place, 62 at Jefferson, Texas, 100 in North Louisiana, 73 at Marshall, Texas, and several others."

"All of de big planters wuz friendly to Cullen Baker. I have carried supplies many times frum de big plantations—Hervey, Glass, and others—to Cullen Baker. De Colonel always carried a big double-barrel shotgun. It must have been de biggest shotgun in de world, not less den a number eight size. He whipped 16 soldiers at Old Boston wid dis gun one time."

"I saw Colonel Baker killed. We had just arrived at his father-in-law's house and I wuz in the horse lot, about 50 yards from de house, when Joe Davis. Thomas Orr and some more men rode up."

"De Colonel wuz standin' by de chimney an did not see dem come aroun' de house. Dey killed him befo' he knew dey wuz aroun'. One ob de men asked Mr. Foster, "Where at dat d—n nigger?" I ducked down and crawled in under de rail fence and ran—I didn't stop 'til I wuz deep in the Sulphur River bottoms. Every minute my heart seemed like it wuz goin' to jump right out uv my mouth. I wuz the worst scared nigger that ever lived."

"I have lived many years since dat time. De times and ways of livin' have changed. I 'member killing deer where the Texarkana National Bank stands, way befo' Texarkana wuz even thought of. This place wuz one of my favorite deer stands. Nix Creek used to be just full ob fish. What used to be the best fishing hole aroun' here is now covered by the Methodist Church (Negro), in East Texarkana. Dr. Weetten had a big fine home out where Springlake Park is. He wuz killed when thrown by a buckin' horse. All of de young people I knew den have been dead many years."

- **Foods**

The question of eating special food on a particular day immediately brings in mind Thanksgiving Day, when turkey becomes the universal dish. Perhaps no other day in the year can be so designated, except among a few religious orders when the eating of meat is strictly prohibited on certain days.

The belief that negroes are particularly addicted to eating pork is well founded, as witness the sales of pork to colored people in most any meat market. But who could imagine that cotton-seed was once the universal food eaten in this vicinity by the colored people? That, according to Doc Quinn, a former slave, and self-styled exmember of Cullen Baker's Gang, was the custom before and shortly after the Civil War.

The cotton-seed would be dumped into a hugh pot, and boiled for several hours, the seed gradually rising to the top. The seed would then be dipped off with a ladle. The next and final step would be to pour corn-meal into the thick liquid, after which it was ready to be eaten. Cotton-seed, it must be remembered, had little value at that time, except as livestock feed.

"Yes suh, Cap'n," the old negro went on to explain. "I has never eaten anything whut tasted any better, or whut would stick to your ribs like cotton-seed, and corn-meal cake. Rich? Why dey's nuthin dat is more nutritious. You never saw a healthier or finer lookin' bunch of negroes dan wuz on Colonel Harvey's place."

"I 'member one time tho' when he changed us off cotton-seed, but we didn't stay changed fo' long. No suh. Of all de grumblin' dem niggers did, becase dey insides had got so used to dat cotton-seed and corn-meal dey wouldn't be satisfied wid nothing else."

"One mornin' when about forty of us niggers had reported sick, de Mahster came down to de qua'ters. 'Whut ailin' ye' lazy neggers?' he asked. Dem niggers los' about fifty pounds of weight apiece, and didn' feel like doin' anything. 'Mahster,' I say. 'Iffen you'll have de wimmen folks make us a pot full of dat cotton-seed and corn-meal, we'll be ready to go to work.' And as long as I work fo' Colonel Harvey, one uv de bes' men whut ever lived, we always had cotton-seed and corn-meal to eat."

United States. Work Projects Administration

Texarkana District
FOLKLORE SUBJECTS
Name of Interviewer: Mrs. W.M. Ball
Subject: Anecdotes of an Aged Ex-Slave.
Subject: Superstitious Beliefs Among Negroes. (Negro lore)
Story:—Information:

Information given by: Doc Quinn
Place of Residence: 12th & Ash Sts., Texarkana, Ark.
Occupation: None (Ex-Slave)
Age: 92
[TR: Information moved from bottom of second page.]
[TR: Repetitive information deleted from subsequent pages.]

DOC QUINN

"Mah young marster wuz Joe Ogburn. Me and him growed up togedder an' I wuz his body guard durin' de wahr. Many's de day I'ze watched de smoke ob battle clear away an' wait fo' de return ob mah marster. All de time I felt we wuz born to win dat wahr, but God knowed bes' an' you know de result.

"Three years ago I went to Little Rook wid Mr. Fisher. Lac' all folks whut goes to dis city, we wend our way to de Capitol to see de Governor. Gov. Futtrell sittin' bac' in his great fine office, saw me and jined me in conversation. De fus' question he axed me wuz 'whut party does yo' 'filiate wif?' I sez, 'de Democrat—de party whut's a frien' to de nigger.' De Governor axed me how does I lac' dis life? I sez 'very well, tho' things has changed since slavery days. Those wuz good ole days for de black man;

didn't hafter worry about nuthin'. Now, I sho' does mah share ob worryin'. I worries from one meal to de odder, I worries about whure I'ze gwine get some mo' clothes when dese wears out?'

"I tole de Governor mah 'sperience wif de Republican Party durin' de wahr. I been hung fo' times in mah life an' one ob de times by de Republicans. Long time ago, Mr. Roy Nash an' Mr. Hugh Sutton wuz a settin' ovah de ballot box on 'lection day, when I voted 80 Democrats. Yas, suh; I jus' marches 'em in an' tells 'em how to cas' dey vote. Dat night, on mah way home frum de votin', goin' down de lonely road, I wuz stopped an' strung up to a tree by de neck. Dey 'splained dat I wuz too 'fluential wid de niggers. When I wuz hangin' dere I did some manful howlin'. Dat howlin' sho brought de white folks. When dey see mah distres' dey 'leased de rope an' I wuz saved. Dat is when I 'pealed to Col. Baker for 'tection. He wuz mah frien' as long as he lib, and he wuz a good frien' ob de South 'cause he saved lots ob white folks frum de wrath ob de mean niggers."

(Note: The Col. Baker referred to was Cullen Baker, the leader of a ruthless gang of bushwhackers that operated in this section shortly after the Civil War.)

Doc Quinn tells a "ghost story" connected with the old church at Rondo, built in 1861.

"De Masonic Hall wuz built up ovah dis buildin' an' ever month dey had dey meetin'. One night, when dey was 'sembled, two men wuz kilt. Dat sho' did scatter dat lot ob Masons and frum dat time on de spirits ob dese men roamed dis chu'ch. Sometime in de dead ob night, dat bell wud ring loud an' clear, wakin' all de folks. Down dey wud come, clos' like, to de chu'ch,—but scared to go closer. Mr. Bill Crabtree, a rich man an' a man whut wuz scared too, offered anybody $100.00 to go inside dat chu'ch an' stay one hour. Didn't nobody need dat $100.00 dat bad!"

The old negro tells the following grave yard story:

"One dark, drizzly night, de niggers wuz out in de woods shootin' craps. I didn't hab no money to jine in de game. One nigger say, "Doc, effen you go down to de cemetey' an' bring bac' one ob dem 'foot boa'ds' frum one ob dem graves, we'll gib yo' a dollar." I ambles off to de cemete'y, 'cause I really needed dat money. I goes inside, walks careful like, not wantin' to distu'b nuthin', an' finally de grave stone leapt up in front ob me. I retches down to pick up de foot boa'd, an' lo! de black cats wuz habin' a meetin' ovah dat grave an' dey objected to mah intrudin', but I didn't pay 'em no mind; jus' fetched dat boa'd bac' to dem niggers, an'—bless de Lawd,—dey gib me two dollars!"

- **Superstitious Beliefs Among Negroes**

Some aged Negroes believe that many of the superstitious ideas that are practiced by their race today had their origin in Africa. A practice that was quite common in ante bellum days was for each member of the family to extract all of their teeth, in the belief that in doing so the family would never disagree. Fortunately, this and similar practices of self mutilation have about become extinct.

An old custom practiced to prevent the separation of a husband and wife was to wrap a rabbit's forefoot, a piece of loadstone, and 9 hairs from the top of the head in red flannel, and bury it under the front door steps.

As a preventitive against being tricked or hoo-dooed, punch a hole through a dime, insert a string through the hole, and tie it around the left ankle.

To carry an axe or hoe into the house means bad luck. An itching nose indicates some one is coming to see you, while an itching eye indicates you will cry.

Interviewer: Bernice Bowden
Person interviewed: Henrietta Ralls
1 Fluker St.
Pine Bluff, Ark.
Age: 88

HENRIETTA RALLS

"Yes ma'am, I was here in slavery times. I was born in Mississippi, Lee County, March 10, 1850. Come to Arkansas when I was ten years old. Had to walk. My old master was Henry Ralls. Sometimes we jump up in the wagon and he'd whip us out.

"My old mistes name was Drunetta. She was good to us. We called her Miss Netta. Old master was mean. He'd whip us. One day he come along and picked up sand and throwed it in my eyes. He was a mean old devil. He thought I was scared of him. Cose I was. That was before the war.

"I recollect when the Yankees come. I knowed they was a'ridin'. White folks made me hide things. I hid a barrel of wool once—put meal on top. They'd a'took it ever bit if they could have found it. They wanted chickens and milk. They'd take things they wanted—they would that. Would a'taken ever bit of our wool if they could have found it.

"They wouldn't talk to old mistes—just talk to me

and ask where things was. She didn't notice them and they didn't notice her.

"I reckon the Lord intended for the Yankees to free the people. They was fightin' to free the people.

"I hear em say war is still goin' on in the world.

"The owners was tryin' to hide the colored people. Our white folks took some of us clear out in Texas to keep the Yankees from gettin' em. Miss Liza was Miss Netta's daughter and she was mean as her old daddy. She said, 'Oh, yes, you little devils, you thought you was goin' to be free! She had a good brother though. He wanted to swap a girl for me so I could be back here with my mammy, but Miss Liza wouldn't turn me loose. No sir, she wouldn't.

"After freedom I hired out—cooked, milked cows and washed and ironed.

"I went back to Mississippi and stayed with my father. Old Henry Ralls sold my father fore we come to Arkansas.

"I never been married. I could have married, but I didn't. I don't know hardly why.

"I been makin' my own livin' pretty much since I left my father.

"Biggest majority of younger generation looks like they tryin' to get a education and tryin' to make a livin' with their brain without usin' their hands. But I'd rather use my hands—cose I would.

"I went to school some after the war, but I had to pay for it.

"I been disabled bout five or six years. Got to have somethin' to take us away, I guess."

United States. Work Projects Administration

Interviewer: Miss Irene Robertson
Person interviewed: Diana Rankins, Brinkley, Arkansas
Age: 66

IRENE ROBERTSON

"I was born at Arlington, Tennessee but when I was a chile the depot was called With. My parents' name Sarah and Solomon Green. There was seven girls and one boy of us. My sister died last year had two children old as I was. I was the youngest chile. Folks mated younger than they do now and seem like they had better times when there was a big family.

"Adam Turnover in Charleston, South Carolina owned my papa. When he died they sold him. He was one year and six months old when he was sold.

"I think S.C. Bachelor, around Brownsville, Tennessee, owned mama first. She said they put her upon the block and sold her and her mother was crying. The man after he sold her ask her if she didn't want him to sell her. She said she didn't care but said she knowed she was afraid to say she cared cause she was crying. She never seen her mama no more. She was carried off on a horse. She was a little girl then. General Hayes bought her and he bought papa too. They played together. General Hayes made the little boys run races so he could see who could run the fastest.

"Papa said they picked him up and carried him off. He said they pressed him into the breastworks of the war. He didn't want to go to war. Mr. Hayes kept him hid out but they stole him and took him to fight. He come home. He belong to Jack Hayes, General Hayes' son. They called him Mr. Jack or Mr. Hayes when freedom come. Mr. Jack sent him to Como, Mississippi to work and to Duncan, Arkansas to work his land. I was fifteen years old when we come to Arkansas. Mr. Walker Hayes that was president of the Commercial Appeal over at Memphis lost his land. We been from place to place over Arkansas since then. Mr. Walker was General Hayes' grandson. We worked field hands till then, we do anything since. I nursed some for Mr. Charles Williams in Memphis. I have done house work. I got two children. My son got one leg off. I live with him. This little gran'boy is the most pleasure to us all.

"The Ku Klux never did interfere with us. They never come to our house. I have seen them.

"When papa come from war it was all over. We knowed it was freedom. Everybody was in a stir and talking and going somewhere. He had got his fill of freedom in the war. He said turn us all out to freeze and starve. He stayed with the Hayes till he died and mama died and all of us scattered out when Mr. Walker Hayes lost his land.

"Ladies used to be too fine to be voting. I'm too old now. My men-folks said they voted. They come home and say how they voted all I know about voting.

"Walker Avenue in Memphis is named for Mr. Walker Hayes and Macremore was named for him or by him one.

"We never was give a thing at freedom but papa was

buying a place from his master and got in debt and sold it. I don't own a home.

"I have high blood pressure and the Welfare gives me $8 a month. I'm not able to work. When you been used to a good plenty it is mighty bad to get mighty near helpless."

United States. Work Projects Administration

Interviewer: Mrs. Bernice Bowden
Person interviewed: Senia Rassberry
810 Catalpa Street, Pine Bluff, Arkansas
Age: 84

SENIA RASSBERRY

"Yes'm, I know what I hear em say. Well, in slavery times I helped make the soldiers' clothes.

"I was born on the old Jack Hall place on the Arkansas River in Jefferson County.

"I know I was 'leven years old when peace declared. I reckon I can member fore the War started. I know I was bastin' them coats and pants.

"My old master's name was Jack Hall and old mistress' name was Priscilla. Oh, yes'm, they was good to me—just as good to me as they could be. But ever' once in awhile they'd call me and say, 'Senia.' I'd say, 'What you want?' They say, 'Wasn't you out there doin' so and so?' I'd say, 'No.' They say, 'Now, you're tellin' a lie' and they'd whip me.

"I was the house girl, me and my sister. My mammy was the cook.

"Old master had two plantations. Sometimes he had a overseer and sometimes he didn't.

"Oh, they had plenty to eat, hog meat and cracklin'

bread. Yes ma'am. I loved that, I reckon. I et so much of it then I don't hardly ever want it now. They had so much to eat. Blackberry cobbler? Oh Lawd.

"How many brothers and sisters? Me? My dear, I don't know how many I had but I heard my mother say that all the chillun she did have, that she had 'leven chillun.

"Our white folks took us to Texas durin' of the War. I think my old master said we stayed there three years. My mother died there with a congestive chill.

"We come back here to Arkansas after freedom and I think my father worked for Jack Hall three or four years. He wouldn't let him leave. He raised my father and thought so much of him. He worked on the shares.

"After freedom I went to school. I learnt to read and write but I just wouldn't do it. I learnt the other chillun though. I did that. I was into ever'thing. I learnt them that what I could do. Blue Back? Them's the very ones I studied.

"In slavery times I had to rise as early as I could. Old master would give me any little thing around the house that I wanted. They said he was too old to go to war. Some of the hands run off but I didn't know where they went to.

"Some of the people was better off slaves than they was free. I don't study bout things now but sometimes seems like all them things comes before me.

"I used to hear em talkin' bout old Jeff Davis. I didn't know what they was talkin' bout but I heered em.

"I was sixteen when I married and I had eleven chillun. All dead but four.

"Yes'm, I been treated good all my life by white and black. All of em loved me seemed like.

"I been livin' in Arkansas all my life. I never have worked in the field. I always worked in the house. I always was a seamstress—made pants for the men on the place.

"After I come here to Pine Bluff I worked for the white folks. Used to cook and wash and iron. Done a lot of work. I did that.

"I been blind 'leven years but I thank the Lord I been here that long. Glory to Jesus! Oh, Lord have mercy! Glory, glory, glory to Jesus!"

United States. Work Projects Administration

Interviewer: Miss Irene Robertson
Person interviewed: Clay Reaves, (light mulatto, large man)
Palestine, Arkansas
Age: 80

CLAY REAVES

"I will be eighty years old my next birthday. It will be July 6th. Father was bought from Kentucky. I couldn't tell you about him. He stayed on the Reaves place that year, the year of the surrender, and left. He didn't live with mother ever again. I never did hear no reason. He went on Joe Night's farm. He left me and a sister older but there was one dead between us. Mother raised us. She stayed on with the Reaves two years after he left. The last year she was there she hired to them. The only thing she ever done before freedom was cook and weave. She had her loom in the kitchen. It was a great big kitchen built off from the house and a portico joined it to the house. I used to lay up under her loom. It was warm there in winter time. I was the baby. I heard mother say some things I remember well.

"She said she was never sold. She said the Reaves said her children need never worry, they would never be sold. We was Reaves from back yonder. Mother's grandfather was a white man. She was a Reaves and her children are mostly Reaves. She was light. Father was about, might be a little darker than I am (mulatto). At times she worked in the field, but in rush time. She wove all the clothes on the place. She worked at the loom and I lay up under there all day long. Mother had three girls and five boys.

"Mr. Reaves, we called him master, had two boys in the army. He was a real old man. He may have had more than two but I know there was two gone off. The white folks lived in sight of the quarters. Their house was a big house and painted white. I've been in there. I never seen no grand parents of mine that I was allowed to claim kin with.

"When I got up some size I was allowed to go see father. I went over to see him sometimes. After freedom he went to where his brothers lived. They wanted him to change his name from Reaves to Cox and he did. He changed it from James Reaves to James Cox. But I couldn't tell you if at one time they belong to Cox in Kentucky or if they belong to Cox in Tennessee or if they took on a name they liked.

"I kept my name Reaves. I am a Reaves from start to finish. I was raised by mother and she was a Reaves. Her name was Olive Reaves. Her old mistress' name was Charlotte Reaves, old master was Edmond Reaves. Now the boys I come to know was John, Bob; girls, Mary and Jane. There was older children. Mother was a sensible, obedient woman. Nobody ever treated her very wrong. She was the only one ever chastised me. They spoiled me. We got plenty plain rations. I never seen nobody married till after the surrender. I seen one woman chastised. I wasn't close. I never learned what it was about. Old Master Reaves was laying it on.

"Mother moved to New Castle, Tennessee from Mr. Reaves' place. We farmed—three of us. We had been living southeast of Boliver, Tennessee, in Hardeman County. I think my kin folks are all dead. Father's other children may be over in Tennessee now. Yes, I know them. Mother died over at Palestine with me. She always lived with me. I married twice, had one child by each wife. Both wives are dead and my children are dead.

"Mother said I had three older brothers went to the Civil War and never come back home. She never heard from them after they went off. I don't know but it was my understanding that they was to be soldiers. I don't recollect them.

"Mother got so she wasn't able to work in the field several years before she died. She worked in the field long as she was able. She lived with me all my whole life till she died. But I farmed. Some years we done well and some years we jess could live. I farmed all my life but a few years. I love farm life. It is independent living. I mean you are about your own man out there. I work my garden out at my shop now. I make baskets and bottom chairs at Palestine. A few years I kept Mrs. Wilkerson's yard and garden. Her husband died and she moved off to Memphis. They did live at Palestine.

"I heard it said that Reaves said he could keep his own farm. The Ku Klux never bothered us. I have heard a lot of things but I am telling you what I know. I don't know nothing about the Civil War nor the Ku Klux. I was most too small a boy at that time to know much.

"I used to vote. Can't write my name. Don't fool with it.

"I went to school on rainy days. I went a few other

days. People used to have to work. I always wanted to work. I piddle around all the time working now. I went to colored teachers all together. I can read a little.

"I had a brother-in-law in Arkansas. I heard a lot of talk. I come on a visit and stayed three months. I went back and moved here. I come to this State—over at Palestine—March 11, 1883 on Sunday. I have a good recollection, or I think I have for my age. I've lived a pretty sensible life, worked hard but had good health. If I had another life to live now I would go to the farm. I love farm life.

"I chop wood, garden, go in the woods get my splints for baskets, chairs. I live by myself. I eat out some with I call them kin. They are my sister's children. I get some help, $10 and commodities.

"When I did vote I voted Republican or I thought I did. But now if I did vote, I might change up. Times have changed.

"I don't know much about the young generation. I do talk with them—some. They are coming up in a changed time. I wouldn't talk against the colored race of people. Some of them work—are good. Some don't. I think some will not work. Maybe they would. I come to know mighty little about them—no more than I know about the white girls and boys. I see them on the streets about as much as I ever see colored folks anywhere."

Interviewer: Mrs. Bernice Bowden
Person interviewed: Jane Reece
819 W. Ninth Street, Pine Bluff, Arkansas
Age: 85

JANE REECE

"I know this—I'm 85. I was born in North Carolina.

"Oh, yes'm, I 'member the War.

"I'm three thousand miles from my home.

"Old John Blue (Belew?) was my white folks.

"I did have good white folks. Yes ma'am, I'll say that. Stayed there a long time after we was sot free. They was good to us.

"My mother was the mother of twelve chillun—she was a fast breeder.

"I was the onliest girl and old missis was just wild about me. I had good owners. I don't remember no hard treatment among 'em.

"I 'member she used to have me runnin' from house to house totin' a little note. That's the reason I had such a good time. Heap of times I slept up at the big house with old missis.

"I got a good memory. We was allowed to sing and

pray. I know our white folks was good that way. I'll say that for 'em. I won't go back on 'em.

"Our folks stayed right on there a long time.

"My father died three years after ever'thing had done got quiet and peaceful.

"I left my husband back there and come here to Arkansas with my mother.

"The bigges' work I done—I used to be terrible 'bout cookin', washin' and ironin', and field work. Ever'thing a man ever done I've done—cut wood, cut down sprouts, barn brush—I've done ever'thing.

"Oh yes, I went to school a whole lot. Got so I could read. Used to write too, but all that done left me.

"I'm gwine tell you the truth, lady. I don't know whether the folks is better off free or not. They is better off in one way—they is free—but this young race is the devil."

Interviewer: Mrs. Bernice Bowden
Person interviewed: Frank Reed,
1004 Missouri Street, Pine Bluff, Arkansas
Age: 78

FRANK REED

"I was a little boy pickin' up chips and helpin' feed the hog in slavery times for old master. Name was George Houston. That was in Alabama.

"I reckon I do remember George Houston. As far as I know he was good to us. I remember when he died.

"Our people stayed right there after freedom. My mother was a Houston till she married.

"I reckon I do remember the paddyrollers. I remember the hounds runnin' too. I never thought I would remember that no more.

"They didn't get after me 'cause I was too little. It didn't last long enough for 'em to get after me.

"I'm sick and not able to help myself. I got run over by a wagon.

"I'm livin' here with my daughter. Her husband is a preacher and they got eight children, so you can imagine how much they can do for me.

"One word of the white folks is worth a thousand of ours."

Interviewer: Samuel S. Taylor
Person interviewed: James Reeves
2419 W. Twentieth Street, Little Rock, Arkansas
Age: 68
Occupation: Preacher

JAMES REEVES

"I was born in 1870 down in Ouachita County about fourteen miles south of Camden going on toward El Dorado. They didn't have no railroad then. I was a young man when they put the branch through. You see, I was born five years after slavery, but I remember my mother, my grandmother, and my great-grandmother. They taken me and talked to me freely and I know everything they knew.

• **Great-Grandmother on Mother's Side**

"My great-grandmother belonged to the Goodmans. Her master was named Bob Goodman. She lived to get one hundred thirteen years old. From the children of the old master, I got the information concerning her age. I looked it up after emancipation. One of old master's sons was named Frank Goodman, and another was named Norphleet Goodman, and there was another whose name I don't recall.

"My grandmother, great-grandmother, was named

Frankie Goodman. I wasn't here in slavery time, but I knew her after emancipation.

• Grandmother on Mother's Side

"My grandmother was named Hannah Goodman. These were different Goodmans but they were kin to these others. There was a large family of them. I don't know the correct age of my grandmother but she was up in the eighties when she died.

• Mother

"My mother was born a Goodman, but she married Reeves, my father. The record of their marriage I ain't got. Back there, they didn't keep up like you and I do, and we don't keep up like these younger folks do. Near as I could get it, she lived to be about seventy-one years old.

• Father

"My father was named Adam Reeves. His master was named Rick Reeves. My father was born in Union County about ten miles from El Dorado. You might say north of El Dorado because he lived south of Camden. He lived there all his life. I have known him to move out of Ouachita County into Union, and from Union back to Ouachita.

• Grandfather on Mother's Side

"My grandfather on my mother's aide was Henry Goodman. His mistress was a woman by the name of Lucy Goodman. She was the same woman who owned my mother. There was a big family of them Goodmans.

"His age—he lived to be about eighty years old. He died in Hot Spring County.

• Grandmother on Father's Side

"My grandmother on my father's side was named Hetty. Her master was named Sam Abbott. She lived right close to seventy-four or seventy-five years. She been gone quite a while now. She used to live with papa.

• Other Ancestors

"I don't know so much about another of my ancestors.

• Wife

"My wife didn't have many people. She knows her mother, her mother's mistress, and all. Her ma was named Martha Henson. That was her married name. Her mistress' last name was Stribling. Martha Henson was a well-treated slave. The Striblings lived in Rockport, Arkansas, but their native home was Georgia. I don't know where the Striblings are now. The old man died before the Civil War broke out. I guess they are all dead and in torment. My wife's grandmother and grandfather on her mother's side were gone so far back that neither she nor I know anything about them.

• Whippings

"My great-grandmother on my mother's side was in Union County when I knew anything of her—close to El Dorado. I was about twenty-two years old when she died. She was tall and spare built, dark ginger cake color. Coarse straight black hair that had begun to mingle with gray. She never did get real gray, and her hair was never white. Even when she died, at a hundred and thirteen years, her hair was mostly black mingled with gray.

"The overseer knocked her in the head in slavery times, and they had to put a silver half-dollar in her head to hold her brains in. I have seen the place myself. When I was a little fellow she used to let me feel the place and she would say, 'That's where the overseer knocked granny in the head, son. I got a half-dollar in there.' I would put her hair aside—my but she had beautiful hair!--and look at the place.

"My wife could tell you what my mother told her. She has seen the marks on my mother's back and has asked, 'Mama, what's all these marks on your back?' And mama would say, 'That's where I was whipped in slavery times, daughter.' She never did like to tell the details. But the scars were awful.

"My grandmother was roughly treated and she had pretty near lost her eyesight from the ill treatment. She got so before she died that she could hardly see to go nowhere. I don't know what it was they done to her that made her eyesight bad, but she insisted that it was due to bad treatment in slavery time.

• Patrollers

"I have heard that the pateroles used to run the slaves if they didn't have a pass from their mistress and master. The pateroles would run them and catch them and whip them.

• How Freedom Came

"All my mother knew was that it got out that the Negroes were free. The day before the old woman told them that they were free, my grandfather, Henry Goodman who was a teamster, old mis' called him and told him to tell all the darkies to come up to the house the next day.

"Next morning, she said, 'Henry, you forgot what I told you. I want you to call all the darkies up here this morning.' Henry had a voice like a fog-horn. He started hollering. I wish I could holler the way he did, but I got to consider the neighbors. He hollered. 'Tention, 'tention, hey; Miss Lucy says she wants you all up to the big house this morning. She's got somepin to tell you.'

"They all come up to the yard before the house. When they got there, she says to him—not to them; she wouldn't talk to them that morning; maybe she was too full—'Henry, you all just as free now as I am. You can stay here with Miss Lucy or you can go to work with whomsoever you will. You don't belong to Miss Lucy no more.'

"She had been sick for quite a bit, and she was just able to come to the door and deliver that message. Three weeks after that time, they brought her out of the house feet foremost and took her to the cemetery. The news killed her dead. That's been seventy years ago, and they just now picking up on it!

- **Slave Time Amusements**

"The old people say they used to have breakdowns in slave time—breakdown dances with fiddle and banjo music. Far after slavery, they had them. The only other amusement worth speaking about was the churches. Far as the churches was concerned, they had to steal out and go to them. Old man Balm Whitlow can tell you all about the way they held church. They would slip off in the woods and carry a gang of darkies down, and the next morning old master would whip them for it. Next Sunday they would do the same thing again and get another whipping. And it went on like that every week. When old man Whitlow came out from slavery, he continued to preach. But the darkies didn't have to steal out then. He's dead now, him and the old lady both.

• Houses

"The slaves lived in old log houses. Some of them would be hewed and put up well. I have seen lots of them. Sometimes they would dob the cracks with mud and would have box planks floors, one by eight or one by ten, rough lumber, not dressed. Set 'em as close together as they could but then there would be cracks in them. I can carry you to some old log houses down in Union County now if they haven't been torn down recently.

"One old log house there used to be old lady Lucy Goodman's home. It has four rooms. It has a hall running through it. It was built in slave times. There is a spring about two hundred yards from it. That is about ten or twelve feet deep. There is a big cypress tree trunk hollowed out and sunk down in it to make a curbing. That cypress is about two or three feet across. The old man, Henry Goodman, sunk that cypress down in there in slavery time. He drove an ox team all the time. That is all the work he done. She would tell all the overseers,

'Now, don't you fool with Henry because we ain't never whipped him ourselves.'

"I don't know who it is that is living now. It's been fifty years ago since I was there.

• Right After Freedom

"Right after freedom, when the surrender came, my mother was just a girl 'bout fifteen or sixteen. She married after freedom. Her and her husband farmed for a living—you know, sharecropped.

• Ku Klux Klan

"The Ku Klux and the pateroles were the same thing, only the Klan was more up to date. It's all set up with a hellish principle. It's old Pharaoh exactly.

"The Ku Klux Klan didn't have no particular effect on the Negro except to scare him.

"When the emancipation came about, the people of the South went to work to see what they could do about it. The whole South was under martial law. Some of the people formed the Ku Klux Klan to keep the Negro down. I never remember that they bothered any of our family or the people in our house. But they scared some and whipped more, and killed some.

• Political Trouble about 1888

"The darkies and the white folks in Union County had an insurrection over the polls about the year 1888. In them days, when you wanted to put a Republican man in, you didn't have to do much campaigning. They just went to the polls and put him in. Everybody that could vote was Republican. In the fall of 1888 they had a great trouble down there, and some of them got killed. They went around and commanded the Negroes not to go to the polls the next day. Some of the Negroes would tell them, 'Well, I am going to the polls tomorrow if I have to crawl.' And then some of them would say, 'I'd like to know how you goin' to vote.' The nigger would ask right back, 'How you goin' to vote?' The white man would say, 'I'm goin' to vote as I damn please.' Then the nigger would say, 'I'm going to do the same thing.' That started the trouble.

"On Sunday before the election on Monday, they went around through that county in gangs. They shot some few of the Negroes. As the Negroes didn't have no weapons to protect theirselves, they didn't have no chance. In that way, quite a few of the Negroes disbanded their homes and went into different counties and different portions of the state and different states. Henry Goodman, my grandfather, came into Hot Spring County in this way.

• **Opinions**

"Roosevelt has got himself in a predicament. They are drunk and don't know what to do. The whole world is stirred up over why one-fourth of the world should rule the other three-fourths. One-fourth of the world is white. The Bible says a house divided can't stand. The people don't know what to do. Look how they fight the Wage Hour Bill. Look at the excitement they raised when it was first suggested that the Union and Confederate veterans meet together.

"We were savages when we came over here. Everything we got and everything we know, good and bad, we got from the white folks. Don't know how they can get impatient with us when everything we do they learnt us.

"Roosevelt has done more than any Democrat that has ever been in the Chair. He had to do something to keep down a rebellion. Then we like to had one as it is through the labor question.

"The poor white man always has been in a tight [HW: place]. He was almost as much oppressed as the Negro.

"The young people of today ain't got no sense. They don't give no thought to nothing. They don't know how to think at all. All the schools and education they give don't make them think. If I had as much education as they have, I would be able to accomplish something. The teachers don't press down on them and make them know what they go over. There is a whole lot of things happening now.

• Old People in Pulaski County

"Out in Pulaski County, going west out the Nineteenth Street Pike till you strike the Saline County line, there are quite a few old colored people. I guess you would find no leas than twenty-five or thirty out that way. There is one old man named Junius Peterson out that way who used to run a mill. If you find him, he is very old and has a good memory. He is a mulatto. You could get out to him by going down till you come to a place that is called the Henderson Lane. You turn to the right and go off the pike less than a mile and you come to a big one-story house settin' on a hill where Peterson lives. Right on beyond that about three-fourths of a mile on the right side of the road, you come to George Gregory's. The mother of my church is about eighty-one years old but she is over in Saline County. Her name is Jane Joyner.

"There are quite a few old persons around Woodson that can give you information. But that is in Saline County, I think. Sweet Home, Wrightsville, Toltec—all of them have a few old colored persons on the farm that was here in slavery times."

• Interviewer's Comment

Reeves' story was taken because of his clear memories of his parents and grandparents. He described to me an old log house still standing in Union County.

I got all agog with excitement. I asked him for the exact location. He gave it. Then I suggested that maybe he would go down with me sometime to visit it. He agreed. Then at the last moment caution began to assert itself, and I said, "When was the last time you saw the cabin?"

He reflected a moment; then he said, "Waal, I guess it was a little more 'an fifty years ago."

I lost my enthusiasm.

Reeves told the Phill-la-me-york story which was told by Austin Pen Parnell. You will find it in his story. The only difference between his story and Parnell's is that Reeves had the conclusion. He claimed that the old master got in a fight with one of the slaves present and yelled out his identity when he was getting badly beaten. The story sounds like it came from the Arkansas folklore collection or from someone who contributed it to that collection.

An aftermath of Reeves' story is finding out that most people consider Henry Banner, whose story has been previously given and whose age was given as eighty-nine, is considered by many persons to be ninety-four.

Neely, one of the adult school-teachers, says that he has gone over Banner's life carefully with him, and that he must have been twenty-one or twenty-two at the close of the War because during slavery, he had experience at logging, or rather at logrolling, a work so difficult that only full-grown men were used at it. Since Banner is slightly built, there is scarcely a possibility that he did such work before the normal time.

[HW: Cf. 30715 for interview with Parnell.]

United States. Work Projects Administration

Interviewer: Bernice Bowden
Person Interviewed: Shepherd Rhone
10th and Kentucky
Pine Bluff, Ark.
Age: 75

SHEPHERD RHONE

"Yes ma'am, I was bred and born in 'sixty-three in Phillips County, Arkansas, close to Helena, on old Judge Jones' plantation. Judge Jones, he was a lawyer. Remember him? I ought to, he whiped me enough. His wife's name was Caroline Jones. She used to smack my jaws and pull my ears but she was a pretty good woman. The old judge was a raw one though. You had to step around or he'd step around for you.

"I stayed right there till I was grown. My mother was named Katie Rhone and my father was named Daniel Rhone. My mother was born in Richmond, Virginia and my father in Petersburg, Virginia.

"Judge Jones brought em here to Arkansas. My father was a bodyguard for old Judge Jones' son Tom in the War. My father stuck with him till peace declared—had to do it.

"They was thirteen of us chillun and they is all gone but me, and I'll soon be gone.

"I know when the Yankees come I run from em. When

peace declared, the Yankees come all through our house and took everything they could get hold of to eat.

"The only reason the Yankees whipped the South was they starved em.

"I know one time when peace declared I caught afire and I run and jumped in a tub of water and I had sense enough not to tell my mother. A girl I was raised up with went and told her though.

"After freedom I worked for old Judge Jones on the half system. He give me everthing that was due me. When he was eighty years old, he called all his old tenants up and give em a mule and twenty-five dollars. He was pretty good to em after all.

"I went to free school in the summertime after the crops was laid by, I can read and write pretty good.

"I came here to Jefferson County in 'eighty-six and I put in thirty-six years at the Cotton Belt Shops. When that strike come on they told us colored folks to quit and I never went back. I worked for em when she was a narrow gauge.

"I worked in the North three years. I nightwatched all over St. Louis and Madison, Illinois. I liked it fine up there—white folks is more familiar up there and seems like you can get favors. If I don't get somethin' here, I'm goin' back up there.

"When I got big enough I voted the Republican ticket and after they got this primary. I think the colored people ought to vote now cause they make em pay taxes.

"I'll tell you right now, the younger generation is

goin' to the dogs. We'll never make a nation of em as long as they go out to these places at night. They ought to be a law passed. When nine o'clock comes they ought to be home in bed, but they is just gettin' started then.

"I belong to the Catholic Church. I think it's a pretty good church. We have a white priest and I'll tell you one thing thing—you can't get a divorce and marry again and stay in the Catholic Church."

United States. Work Projects Administration

Interviewer: Mrs. Bernice Bowden
Person interviewed: Dora Richard
3301 W. 14th Avenue, Pine Bluff, Arkansas
Age: 76

DORA RICHARD

"I was born in South Carolina and I was my mother's baby chile.

"Jacob Foster was our old master and he sold my mother over in east Tennessee. Now of cose she wasn't put upon the block and sold. She was the house woman and spin and wove. After they sold her my father run off. Oh sure, they caught him and I know old mistress said, 'Now, Jacob, if you want to go where Lydia is, you can go.' So they sold him near her.

"I stayed with the Fosters till peace was declared and ever'thing was declared free. Then my father come after me.

"I can just sketch things. I try to forget it. My mother and father was pretty agreeable when they was set free.

"In Tennessee we stayed at the foot of Lookout Mountain and I can remember seein' the cannon balls.

"Here's the way I want to tell you. Some of the white people are as good to the colored people as they could be and some of em are mean. My own folks do so bad I'm ashamed of em.

"So many of the colored of the South have emigrated to the North. I have lived there and I don't know why I'm here now.

"Some of my color don't like that about the Jim Crow Law, but I say if they furnish us a nice comfortable coach I would rather be with my own people. And I don't care to go to the white folks' church.

"My mother used to tell me how they used to hide behind trees so the boss man couldn't see em when they was prayin' and at night put out the light and turn the pot down.

"I went to school in Tennessee. I never will forget it. I had a white teacher. He was in the War and he had a leg shot off. I went through the sixth grade and was ready for the seventh Ray's Arithmetic. I walked four miles there and four miles back—eight miles a day.

"I can remember too when my mother and father was baptized. I know mama come out of the water a shoutin'. Oh, that was good times then. I felt better when I was under my mother cause when I married my life was over. I raised about ten children.

"I remember when the Ku Klux come to my sister's house lookin' for her husband. I know I was in the bed and I raised up. I was scared you know.

"When I hear some colored folks say they wish the old slavery times was back, I just knows they is lazy. They don't want any responsibility."

Interviewer: Mrs. Bernice Bowden
Person interviewed: Jim Ricks
517 E. 22nd Avenue, Pine Bluff, Arkansas
Age: 79

JIM RICKS

"I was born in slavery times. I 'member runnin' from the Yankees when they wanted to carry me off. Just devilin' me, you know. You know how little chillun was 'bout white folks in them days.

"I went to school three weeks and my daddy stopped me and put me to work.

"Old master was named Jimmie Ricks. They named me after him, I think.

"My mother said he was a mighty good master. Didn't 'low his niggers whipped.

"Yes'm, I was born and raised in Arkansas, down here in Calhoun County.

"I had a chance to learn but I was a rowdy. I wanted to hunt. I was a mighty huntsman.

"I was a good worker too. White folks was all stuck on me 'cause I was a good worker.

"I did farm work and then did public work after the crops was laid by. But now I got too old to work.

"I seen the Ku Klux once or twice when they was Ku Klukin' around. Some of 'em would holler 'Kluk, kluk, kluk.' I was quite small, but I could remember 'am 'cause I was scared of 'em.

"I farmed all my life till year before last. I was a good farmer too.

"I used to vote years ago. I voted Republican. Yes ma'am.

"Younger generation ain't near like they was when I was young. I was well thought of. Couldn't be out after sundown or they'd bump my head. My stepfather would give me a flailin'. I thought he was mean to me but I see now he done right by whippin' me.

"I know in slavery times they got plenty of somethin' to eat. Old master fed us well."

Interviewer: Miss Irene Robertson
Person interviewed: Charlie Rigger
R.F.D., three miles, Palestine, Arkansas
Age: 85 plus, doesn't know age

CHARLIE RIGGER

"I was born six miles from Mounticellar close to the line of Morgan and Jasper County. Mother belong to the Smiths. Her father was part Creek (Indian). They all was sold to Floyd Malone. His wife was Betsy Malone. They had five children.

"When I was a child I lay under the loom day after day picking up the sickle. Ma was a cook and a weaver too.

"Malone was a good man but his wife was one of 'em. She was a terrible piece of humanity. Father was a farm hand. They had a gin, a shoe shop, and a blacksmith shop all on Floyd Malone's place. I picked a little cotton before 'mancipation. Floyd Malone had to buy my mother to git her where my father was.

"Some of the boys wore dresses till they was twelve or fifteen years old. One fellar rode a mule or cow one the other to preaching. While he sit talking to his gal at the window a steer cone up and et off his dress tail. Boys got to courting before they got to take off their long shirts.

"They wasn't so good to mother. She run off several times. She went 'bout one and one-half miles to her mother on the Compton place. They didn't whoop her. They promised her a whooping. They whooped her and me too but I never knowed 'em to whoop my father. When they whoop my mother I'd run off to place we lived and crawl under the house.

"We chillun had nothing to do wid coffee. We drunk milk out little bowls. We'd turn it up or lap it out which one could do the best. They fed us. We'd ask for more till we got filled up.

"I recollect the soldiers come by in July 1863 or 1864 and back in December. I heard talk so long 'fore they got there I knowed who they was. They took my oldest brother. He didn't want to go. We never heard from him. He never come back. My white master hid out. He didn't go to war. One son went and come back. It was the Yankees made my oldest brother go. The first crowd in July swapped their wore-out scrub stock for our good stock. That second crowd cleaned them out, took our hogs. Miss Betty had died 'fore they come in July. That second crowd come in December. They cleaned out everything to eat and wear. They set the house 'fire several times with paper and coal oil (kerosene). It went out every time. One told the captain. He come up behind. It went out every time. He said, 'Let's move on.' They left it clean and bare. We didn't like them. We had meat hid in the cellar. We got hungry that spring sure as you born.

"The old man married pretty soon after freedom. He married young to what he was.

"I didn't find much fault to slavery 'cepting the abuse. We et three times a day and now if I get one piece I do well. Mother cooked, washed, ironed and spun four cuts a day. We all et at the master's kitchen three times a day. We had thirty-two families. I've heard that ag'in time and ag'in so as I recollect it till now. We didn't have to work no harder 'en we do now if you have a living.

"Master waited till all there. He had a horn made sorter like a bugle for that business. Called us to our meals. We stayed a year. Went to his brother's one year, then to Major Lane's big farm. We had to work about the same as b'fore freedom. Not much change.

"The Ku Klux come 'round right smart. Some had on skin coverings, cow heads and horns. Some wore white sheets and black dresses on white horses. They was scary looking. They would whoop and kill too. I was too scared to get caught off at night.

"Mother died. I was traveling about. I spent thirteen months in Mississippi. Three winters right in Memphis. I married in Mississippi. I left two daughters in Georgia. My wife died. I come to Arkansas in 1902. I live all alone.

"This present generation is traveling too fast. It-is-to-be. Fast traveling and education. Times not good as it always have been b'fore that last war (World War). When the white folks start jowing we black folks suffers. It ain't a bit our fault. Education causes the black man to see he is bit (cheated) but he better not say a word. It very good thing if it is used right. Fast traveling is all right in its place. But too many is traveling and they all want to be going. We got into pretty fast time of it now. It-is-to-be and it's getting shoved on faster."

Interviewer: Miss Irene Robertson
Person interviewed: Ida Rigley, Forrest City, Arkansas
Age: 82

IDA RIGLEY

"I was born in Richmond, Virginia. Colonel Radford and Emma Radford owned my mother. They had a older girl, Emma and Betty and three boys. I called her Miss Betty.

"My mother was Sylvia Jones and she had five children. Bill Jones was my father. He was a born free man and a blacksmith at Lynchburg, Virginia in slavery times.

"He asked Colonel Radford could he come to see my mama and marry her. They had a wedding in Colonel Radford's dining room and a preacher on the place married them. They told me. My father was a Presbyterian preacher. I heard papa preach at Lynchburg. He had a white principle but no white blood. I never knew him very much till long after freedom.

"Miss Betty Radford was raising me for a house girl. I was younger than her children. Mother was a weaver for all on the place. Old aunt Caroline was the regular cook but my mother helped to cook for hands he hired at busy seasons of the year. My sisters lived in the quarters and mama slept with them. She helped them. They worked in the field some. They was careful not to overwork young hands. They cooked down at the quarters. They had a real old man and woman to set about and see after the children and feed them. The older children looked after the babies. When Miss Betty went off visiting she would send me down there. I did love it.

"Emma and Betty went to school at Richmond in a buggy. They had a colored boy driver. He was the carriage driver. Emma and Betty would play with me too. Miss Betty fed me all the time. She made me a bonnet and I can't get shed of my bonnet yet. I got four bonnets now.

"When the white folks had a wedding it lasted a week. They had a second day dress and a third day dress and had suppers and dinner receptions about among the kin folks. They had big chests full of quilts and coverlets and counterpanes they been packing back. Some of them would have big dances. A wedding would last a week, night and day.

"They had a farm right. We had peacocks, white guinea and big black turkeys, cows, sheep, goats, hogs; he had deer. He kept their horns cut off and some of the cow's horns were off. We had a acre in a garden and had roses and all kinds of flowers. I like flowers now. Tries to have 'em. They had a gin on the place. He raised corn, rye, cotton, and tobacco. The hands got their supplies on Saturday. On rainy days all the women would knit, white and colored both. Miss Betty knitted some at night in winter. They had a shop to sharpen and keep all the tools in. A particular old man made the brooms and rakes.

"It seem like there wasn't so many flies. Miss Betty mixed up molasses and flour and poison and killed flies sometimes. She spread it on brown paper. We had fly weed tea to set about too sometimes. We didn't have to use anything regular. We didn't have no screens. We had mighty few mosquitoes. We had peafowl fly brushes. They was mighty pretty.

"One thing we had was a deep walled well and an ice-house. They cut ice in blocks and put it up for winter[HW:?]. We had one spring on the place I know.

"They kept hounds. Colonel Radford's boys and the colored boys all went hunting. We had 'possum and potatoes all along in winter; 'possum grease won't make you sick. Eat all you want. I'd hear their horn and the dogs. They would come in hungry every time. I never seen no whiskey. He had his cider and vinegar press and made wine. We had cider and wine all along. Colonel Radford was his own overseer and Charlie his oldest boy. They whooped mighty little. They would stand up and be whooped. Some of the young ones was hard-headed and rude. He advised them and they minded him pretty well.

"Our yards was large and beautiful; some had grass and some clean spots about in the shade. Friday was wash day. Saturday was iron day. Miss Betty would go about in the quarters to see if the houses was scrubbed every week after washing. They had to wear clean clothes and have clean beds about her place. She'd shame them to death.

"Colonel Radford had a colored church for us all. It was a log house and he had a office for his boys to read and write and smoke cob pipes in. The white folks' church was at the corner of his place. I went there most. They shouted and pat their hands. Colonel Radford was a Baptist.

"Nearly every farm had a fiddler. Ever so often he had a big dance in their parlor. I'd try to dance by myself. He had his own music by the hands on his place. He let them have dances at the quarters every now and then. Dancing was a piece of his religion.

"I don't think our everyday frocks was stiffened but our dress up clothes was. It was made out of flour—boiled flour starch. We had striped dresses and stockings too. We had checked dresses. We had goobers and a chestnut grove. We had a huckleberry patch. We had maple sugar to eat. It was good. We had popcorn and chinquapins in the fall of the year, I used to pick up chips to use at the pot. I had a little basket. I picked up corn cobs. They burnt them and made corn cob soda to use in the bread and cakes. We parched peeled sweet potatoes slice thin and made coffee.

"The Civil War was terrible. One morning before we was all out of bed the Yankees come. It was about daylight. He and the three boys were there. They didn't burn any houses and they didn't hesitate but they took everything. They took all Miss Betty's nice silverware. They took fine quilts and feather beds. That was in the fall of the year. They drove off a line of our slaves (a block long) fer as from me to that railroad. Made them go. They walked fast in front of the cavalrymen. They took mama and my sisters. She got away from them with her girls and found her way back to papa at Lynchburg.

"Colonel Radford went and took some of the slave men and his boys. They brought home plenty beds and a barrel of salt. He brought back plenty. He sent his slave man to town any time. They had no notion leaving.

"One time some Yankees come. I run hid around Miss Betty's long dress. She was crying. They was pulling her rings off her fingers. I told them to quit that. One of the mean things said, 'Little nigger, I shoot your head off.' They took all her nice clothes. They said they took all niggers. I sassed them. They went in another room. I shot under Miss Betty's big skirt. They looked about for me but they thought I run off to my mama. She was gone but they didn't know it. I seen my best times then. We had a good time there. Miss Betty was good and kind to me. Good as I wanted. I wish I had that good now.

• Freedom

"The soldiers come and I knowed it was the Yankees I hated. They took all they could find and wasted a lot of it. I was scared. I kept hid about. The slaves put their beds and clothes up on the wagons and went off behind them and some clumb up in the wagons. I heard Miss Betty say, 'They need not follow them off, they are already free.' The way she said it, like she was heart broken, made me nearly cry and I remember her very words till this day. She was a good woman.

"Mama come and got me long time after that and I didn't want to go nor stay neither. It was like taking me off from my own home. Papa was freeborn and freedom I couldn't understand till I was long grown. I never got a whooping in my life. I was taught politeness.

"During slavery we bought mighty little. Flour in barrels, salt. We had Maple sugar and sorghum molasses in bounty. We was happy and had plenty to eat and wear.

"I learned to make the fine cakes from a Jew woman

(Jewess), Mrs. Isaac. I've been called a cook here in Forrest City. I was taught by Mrs. Isaac to make angel food, coffee cake, white bread and white cakes. From that I made the other kinds my own self."

- **Interviewer's Comment**

People in Forrest City send for Ida and keep her a week or two baking Christmas and wedding cakes.

Interviewer: Miss Irene Robertson
Person interviewed: Milton Ritchie
R.F.D., Brinkley, Arkansas
Age: 78

MILTON RITCHIE

"I was born in Marietta Hotel at Marietta, Georgia. The hotel belong to Milton Stevens. He had two sons. One died fo I was born and Pink was in the war. Mistress Thursday was old moster's wife. We all had to refugee. My sister was down in the bottoms with all the slaves and cattle when she died. She took sick and died suddenly. They heard the soldiers was coming to Atlanta and knowed they would come by Marietta. Moster Stevens sold the hotel just at the beginning of the war. He moved to the country. Mama cooked at the hotel and in the country both. The hotel was a brick house on the railroad where they fed a lot of people every day. Moster Milton used to take me bout where he went, rode me on his foot when I was a baby. After they went to the farm every evening Mistress Thursday come get me, take me to the house. She got bread and butter, sugar, give it to me and I slept on a pallet in her room. I never did know why she done that. Mama had a little house she slept in. She cooked. They never whooped me. They never whooped mama.

"One time the Federal army camped not a great ways from us. One time I was playing in a gully—big red ditch.

I spied the Federals coming. I flew out the ditch up the hill and across the field. They was calvary men camped back of our field. We all left that place and refugeed to another place. They didn't burn the house but they sent two bullets through the walls or that house. 'Old Granny' was too old to refugee. She kept living by herself in a house on the place. They never bothered her. She wasn't kin to us but Moster Milton owned her and kept her fed. We raised sugar-cane, hogs, corn, and goobers. The sugar-cane had no top. I got a whooping every Monday. Mama whoop me. We go drink sugar-cane juice in the trough at the mill. We got up in there with our feet. They had to wash out the troughs. It was a wood house. It was a big mill. He sold that good syrup in Atlanta. It wasn't sorghum. The men at the mill would scare us but we hid around. They come up to the house and tell on us.

"We had moved from the farm when they burned Atlanta. From the place where Moster Milton refugeed I could hear a roaring all the time nearly, sometimes clearer, and the roaring was broke sometimes.

"Moster Milton ran the farm when he run the hotel cept I was born at the hotel and Mistress Thursday lived there then too. He had all Negro overseers. Each overseer had a certain lot of hands to do what he told them. He didn't have no trouble. He told them if they made something for them and him too it would be fine, if they didn't work they would have to do without. They had plenty they said.

"My mama was sold on the block in Virginia when she was twelve years old. She and her little brother sold the same day. Moster Milton Stevens bought her. The same man couldn't buy them both, didn't have money enough. They had a little blanket and she and her brother cut it into and put it around their shoulders. They been sleeping together and Moster Milton brought her home on his horse up behind him. Her mama was crying when she left her. She never heard nor seen none of her folks no more she told me. (The old Negro cried.)

"My mama and papa was dark but both was mixed. They never told me if it was white or Indian. Papa was a tall, big bony man. Mama wasn't so big and stouter. He never tried to get away from his owners. He belong to Sam Ritchie five or six miles away. I never beard much about them. They had Negro overseers. Papa was a foreman. He tanned the cow hides and made shoes for all the hands on Ritchie's place. He made our shoes over there too. They said Stevens and Ritchies didn't keep bad dogs. Mistress Eliza Ritchie was a Stevens before she married. Papa never was sold. He said they was good to them. Mama was named Eliza too and papa George Ritchie.

"When freedom was on papa went to Atlanta and got transportation to Chattanooga. I don't know why. He met me and mama. She picked me up and run away and met him. We went in a freight box. It had been a soldier's home—great big house. We et on the first story out of tin pans. We had white beans or peas, crackers and coffee. Meat and wheat and cornbread we never smelt at that place. Somebody ask him how we got there and he showed them a ticket from the Freedmans bureau in Atlanta. He showed that on the train every now and then. Upstairs they brought out a stack of wool blankets and started the rows of beds. Each man took his three as he was numbered. Every night the same one got his own blankets. The room was full of beds and white guards with a gun over his shoulder guarded them all night long. We stayed there a long time—nearly a year. They tried to get jobs fast as they could and push em out but it was slow work. Mama got a place to cook at—Mrs. Crutchfield's. She run a hotel in town but lived in the country. We stayed there about a year. Papa was hired somewhere else there.

"Papa got us on a farm in middle Tennessee after that. We come to Mr. Hooper's place and share cropped one year, then we went to share crop for Wells Brothers close to Murfreesboro. I been on the farm all my life since then.

"The Ku Klux never pestered us. I heard about them.

"The Welfare helps me and I would do work if I could get work I can do. I could do light work. Times is hard. Hard to get a living. I don't mind work. I couldn't do a day's work now.

"The young generation is beyond me. I don't be about them much."

Interviewer: Mrs. Bernice Bowden
Person interviewed: Alice Rivers
W. 17th, Highland Addition, Pine Bluff, Arkansas
Age: 81

ALICE RIVERS

"Yes'm, I remember when the Yankees come. I ricollect when they throwed out all the meat from old master's smokehouse. The colored folks was tryin' to ketch it and I know I tried to ketch it too.

"Don't I look like I been here in Reb. time? I was born in Mississippi on Colonel Reed's place in 1857.

"I just know the Yankees come through. Had on blue coats with gold lookin' buttons. I never will forget it 'cause it was so frightening.

"I can ricollect way back there.

"I don't know whether the white folks was good or not, we hardly ever saw 'em. Had a old woman that cooked for the chillun at the quarters. I ricollect they had a big old kittle and she'd cook that full of somethin'. I know the old lady give us plenty of somethin' to eat.

"All the white folks didn't treat their hands mean. Some of 'em was a fool 'bout them little niggers.

"Old woman what cooked for the chillun was old Aunt Henie and she walked half bent with a stick.

"I went to school some after freedom. Learned how to spell and read but not much writin'.

"I can't tell you 'bout no whippin's 'cause if they whipped the folks they didn't do it at the quarters where the chillun was.

"I been farmin' all my life till I come to Arkansas in 1916. Since then I first cooked and washed. I ain't worked out in three years now.

"I gets a little pension from the Welfare and I make out on that. My granddaughter lives with me. She will finish high school in May and then she can take care of herself.

"I used to own this place but it was sold for taxes. Don't make any difference if you is as old as Methuselah you got to pay them taxes. Old Caeser started 'em and we've had to pay 'em ever since.

"Younger generation ain't mannerly now like they was when I was young. Chillun used to be obedient but they got to have their way now. Old folks done put the chillun where they is now and they ought to take care of 'em.

"I don't know where the world gwine come to in the next five years. I reckon they'll all be dead way they're gwine now. Storms takin' 'em away here and war in them other countries."

Interviewer: Miss Irene Robertson
Person interviewed: J. Roberts, Brinkley, Arkansas
Age: 45 or 50
Occupation: Methodist preacher

J. ROBERTS

"My father was a Federal soldier in the Civil War. He was from Winston, Virginia. He went to war and soon after the end he came to Holly Grove. He was in Company "K". He signed up six or seven papers for men in his company he knew and they all got their pensions. Oh yes! He knew them. He was an awful exact honest man. He was a very young man when he went into the war and never married till he come to Arkansas. He married a slave woman. She was a field woman. They farmed. Father sat by the hour and told how he endured the war. He never expected to come out alive after a few months in the war.

"John Roberts Collins was his owner in slavery. I never heard why he cut off the Collins. I call my own self J. Roberts."

"The present times are hard times. Sin hath caused it all. Machinery has taken so much of the work."

"The present generation are fair folks but wild. Yes, the young folks today are wilder than my set was. I can't tell you how but I see it every way I go."

United States. Work Projects Administration

Interviewer: Miss Irene Robertson
Person interviewed: George Robertson? or George Robinson?
Brinkley, Arkansas
Age: 81

GEORGE ROBERTSON

"My papa named Abe Robertson. His owner named Tom Robertson. I was born in middle Tennessee. My mama named Isabela Brooks. Her master named Billy Brooks. His wife name Mary Brooks. My master boys come through here six years ago wid a tent show. My papa went off wid the Yankees. Last I seed of him he was in Memphis. They took my mama off when I was a baby to Texas to keep the Yankees from gettin' her. My grandma raised me. We stayed on the big plantation till 1880.

"I don't want no Sociable Welfare help till I ain't able to work. I don't want none now."

(To be continued)
[TR: no continuation found.]

Interviewer: Samuel S. Taylor
Person interviewed: Augustus Robinson
2500 W. Tenth Street, Little Rock, Arkansas
Age: 78

AUGUSTUS ROBINSON

"I was born in Calhoun County, Arkansas in 1860, January 15th. I am going according to what my daddy told me and nothing else. That is all I could do.

• How the Children Were Fed

"My grandmother on my mother's side said when I was a little fellow that she was a cook and that she would bring stuff up to the cabin where the little niggers were locked up and feed them through the crack. She would hide it underneath her apron. She wasn't supposed to do it. All the little niggers were kept in one house when the old folks were working in the field. There were six or seven of us.

• Sold

"My daddy was a white man, my master. His wife was so mean to me that my master sold me to keep her from beating me and kicking me and knocking me 'round. She would have killed me if she could have got the chance. He [HW: My daddy] sold me to a preacher who raised me as though I were his own son. Whenever he sat down to the table to eat, I sat down. He made no difference at all. He raised me in El Dorado, Arkansas. His name was James Goodwin. He sent me to school too.

• Visited by Father

"When Harrison and Cleveland ran for President, my [HW: white] father came to Little Rock. Some colored people had been killed in the campaign fights, and he had been summoned to Little Rock to make some statements in connection with the trouble. He stopped at a prominent hotel and had me to come to see him. When I went up to the hotel to meet him, there were a dozen or more white men at that place. When I shook hands with him, he said, 'Gentlemen, he's a little shady but he's my son.' His name was Captain I.T. Robinson. He lived in Lisbon, Arkansas.

• Mother

"My mother's name was Frances Goodwin. She belonged to Captain Robinson. I don't know but I think that when they came to Arkansas, they came from Georgia. They were refugees. When the War started, people that owned niggers ran from state to state to try to hold their niggers.

• House

"I lived right in the yard. We had four houses in the yard and three of them was made of logs and one was made out of one-by-twelve planks. I lived in the one made out of planks. It had one big room. I reckon it was about twenty by fifteen, more than that, I reckon. It was a big room. There [HW: were] two doors and no windows.

We had old candlesticks for lights. We had old homemade tables. All food was kept in the smokehouse and the pantry. The food house and the smokehouse were two of the log cabins in the yard.

• Schooling

"Goodwin schooled me. [TR: First sentence lined out.] He had a teacher to come right on the place and stay there teaching. He raised me and brought me up just as though I was his own child.

"I remember getting one whipping. I didn't get it from Mr. Goodwin though. His brother gave it to me. His brother sent me to get a horse. An old hound was laying in the way on the saddle and the bridle. He wouldn't move so I picked up the bridle and hit him with it. He hollered and master's brother heard him and gave me a whipping. That is the only whipping I ever got when I was small.

• Ku Klux

"I heard of the Ku Klux Klan but I don't know that I ever seen them. I never noticed what effect they had on the colored people. I just heard people talking about them.

• Occupational Experiences

"The first work I did was farming—after the War. I farmed,—down close to El Dorado, about six miles away from there. I kept that up till I was about seventeen or eighteen years old or somewheres about there. That was on James Goodwin's place—my last master, the man who raised me. Then I left him and came to Little Rock.

I don't remember in what year. I went to school here in Little Rock. I had already had some schooling. My grandmother sent me. The school I went to was called the Union School. It was down on Sixth Street. After I left there, I went to Capitol Hill School. I was going to school during the Brooks-Baxter War. The statehouse was on Markham Street and Center. My grandmother's name was Celie Robinson. She went by the name of her owner.

"After I had gone to school several years—I don't remember just how many—I worked down town about ten or eleven years. Then I went to railroading. First I was with the Iron Mountain and Southern. Later, it changed its name to the Missouri Pacific. I worked for them from 1891 to 1935. On August 29th I received my last pay check. I have tried ever since to get my railroad pension to which my years of service entitle me but have been unable to get it. The law concerning the pension seems to have passed on the same day I received my last check, and although I worked for forty-four years and gave entire satisfaction, there has been a disposition to keep me from the pension. While in service I had my jaw broken in two pieces and four front teeth knocked out by a piece of flying steel.

"Another man was handling the steam hammer. I was standing at my regular place doing my regular work. When that happened, I was cut down like a weed. There wasn't a man ever thought they would see me in that job again after that piece of steel cut me down.

"Also, I lost my right eye in the service when a hot cinder from the furnace flew in it while I was doing my regular work. Then I was ruptured because of the handling of heavy pieces of iron at my work. I still wear the truss. You can see the places where my jaw was broke and you can see where my teeth were knocked out.

"Out of all the ups and downs, I stuck to the company just the same until they retired me in 1935 because of old age. The retirement board wanted to know when I asked for a pension, why did I think I was entitled to a pension? I told them because I had been injured through service with the company and had honorably finished so long a period of service. It is now admitted that I am eligible to a railroad pension but there seems to still be a delay in paying it for some reason or other.

• Support Now

"I get a little assistance from the Welfare, and I get some commodities. If it wasn't for that, I would be broke up."

[HW: Brooks-Baxter War was about 1872-74.]

Interviewer: Miss Irene Robertson
Person interviewed: Malindy Robinson
8th Street, West Memphis, Arkansas
Age: 61

MALINDY ROBINSON

"I was born in Wilkerson County, Mississippi. My ma never was sold, She said she was eleven years old when peace was declared. Master Sims was grandma's owner. Grandpa was never sold. He was born in Mississippi. He was a mulatto man. He was a man worked about the house and grandma was a field woman. She said she never was whooped but worked mighty hard. They was good to grandma. She lived in the quarters. My parents b'long to the same owner. But far as I ever knowed they married long after freedom. They was raised close to Woodville, Mississippi."

United States. Work Projects Administration

Interviewer: Mary D. Hudgins
Person interviewed: Tom Robinson
Aged: 88
Home: Lives with his son on outskirts of Hot Springs

TOM ROBINSON

As I entered Goldstein Grade school for colored I passed an old fellow sitting on the sidewalk. There was somthing of that venerable, dignified, I've-been-a-slave look about him, so much of it that I almost stopped to question him. Inside I entered a classroom, where a young woman was in conference with a couple of sheepish youngsters who had been kept in after school.

Did she know the whereabouts of any ex-slaves? She beamed. Only the other day an old man had appeared on the school grounds. She appealed to her charges. Didn't they remember that she had told them about him and about what slavery had meant. Sheepish looks were gone. They were agog with interest. Yes 'um, they remembered. But none of the three knew his name or where to find him.

Another teacher entered the room. No, she couldn't remember the name. But the old man often came up to watch the children at play. He said it made him happy to see them getting opportunities he never could have had.

Wait a minute—he might be outside at this very moment. A clatter of heels and calls of triumph. "Yes! Yes! Here he is!"

Outside I dashed to drop flat on the sidewalk[HW:?] beside the aged man I had passed a few minutes before. Out came my smile and a notebook. With only a few preliminaries and amenities the interview was in full swing. It neither startled nor confused him, to have an excited young woman plant herself on a public sidewalk at his side and demand his life's story. A man who had belonged to three different masters before the age of 15 was inured to minor surprises. Tom Robinson long since learned to take life as it came.

He is quite deaf in one ear and hears poorly with the other. Nobody within a quarter of a block could have been in doubt of what was going on. A youth moved closer. The kept-after-school pair emerged from the building and stood near us, goggle-eyed thruout the interview. When we were finished, Robinson turned to the children and gave them, a grandfatherly lecture about taking advantage of their opportunities, a lecture in which the white woman sitting beside him joined heartily—drawing liberally on comments of ex-slaves in recent interviews concerning the helplessness felt in not being able to write and read letters from well loved friends.

"Where was I born, ma'am? Why it's my understanding that it was Catawba County, North Carolina. As far as I remember, Newton was the nearest town. I was born on a place belonging to Jacob Sigmens. I can just barely remember my mother. I was not 11 when they sold me away from her. I can just barely remember her.

"But I do remember how she used to take us children and kneel down in front of the fireplace and pray. She'd pray that the time would come when everybody could worship the Lord under their own vine and fig tree—all of them free. It's come to me lots of times since. There she was a'praying, and on other plantations women was a'praying. All over the country the same prayer was being prayed. Guess the Lord done heard the prayer and answered it.

"Old man Sigmens wasn't a bad master. Don't remember so much about him. I couldn't have been 11 when he sold me to Pickney Setzer. He kept me for a little while and then he sold me to David Robinson. All three of them lived not so far apart in North Carolina. But pretty soon after he bought me old men Dave Robinson moved to Texas. We was there when the war started. We stayed there all during the war. I was set free there.

"We lived in Cass County. It was pretty close to the Arkansas border, and 'twasn't far from Oklahoma—as is now. I remember well when they was first gathering them up for the war. We used to hear the cannon often. Was I afraid? To be sure I was scared, right at first. Pretty soon we got used to it. Somebody even made up a song, 'Listen to the Home-made Thunder'. They'd sing it every time the cannon started roaring.

"No, ma'am, there never was any fighting right around us. I never really saw any fighting. Old man Dave Robinson was good to me. He didn't have a big farm—just owned me. Treated me almost like I was one of his own children. Course, I had to work. Sometimes he whipped me—but no more than he had to. I was just a child and any child has got to be made to mind. He was good to me, and old Miss was good to me. All my masters was pretty good to me—lots better than the usual run. Which one I like the best. Well, you might know. I kept the name Robinson, and I named my son Dave. You might know which one I think the most of.

"One day I was out milking the cows. Mr. Dave come down into the field, and he had a paper in his hand. 'Listen to me, Tom,' he said, 'listen to what I reads you.' And he read from a paper all about how I was free. You can't tell how I felt. 'You're jokin' me.' I says. 'No, I ain't,' says he. 'You're free.' 'No,' says I, 'it's a joke.' 'No,' says he, 'it's a law that I got to read this paper to you. Now listen while I read it again.'

"But still I wouldn't believe him. 'Just go up to the house,' says he, 'and ask Mrs. Robinson. She'll tell you.' so I went. 'It's a joke,' I says to her. 'Did you ever know your master to tell you a lie?' she says. 'No,' says I, 'I ain't.' 'Well,' she says, 'the war's over and you're free.'

"By that time I thought maybe she was telling me what was right. 'Miss Robinson,' says I, 'can I go over to see the Smiths?'—they was a colored family that lived nearby. 'Don't you understand,' says she, 'you're free. You don't have to ask me what you can do. Run along child.'

"And so I went. And do you know why I was a'going? I wanted to find out if they was free too." (a chuckle and toothy smile) "I just couldn't take it all in. I couldn't believe we was all free alike.

"Was I happy? Law Miss. You can take anything. No matter how good you treat it—it wants to be free. You can treat it good and feed it good and give it everything it seems to want—but if you open the cage—it's happy.

"What did I do after the war was over? I farmed. I farmed all my life, 'til I got too old. I stopped three—four years ago. I lives with my son—Dave Robinson—the one I named for my master.

"How did I farm? Did I share crop? No, ma'am!" (Sharply as tho repramanding the inquirer for an undeserved insult.) "I didn't share crop, except just at first to get a start. I rented. I paid thirds and fourths. I always rented. I wasn't a share-cropper.[A]

[A: Socially and economically sharp distinctions are drawn between the different classes of renters, both by owners and tenants themselves. Families whom ambition and circumstances have allowed to accumulate enough surplus to buy farm implements and have food for a year ahead look with scorn on fellow farmers who thru inertia or bad luck must be furnished food and the wherewithall to farm. In turn, families that have forged ahead sufficiently to be able to pay cash rent on farms they cultivate look down On both of the other groups.]

"It was awful hard going after the war. But I got me a place—had to share-crop for a year or two. But I worked hard and saved all I could. Pretty soon I had me enough that I could rent. I always raised the usual things—cotton and corn and potatoes and a little truck and that sort of thing—always raised enough to eat for us and the stock—and then some cotton for a cash crop.

"My first wife, well it was kind of funny; I wasn't more than 19. She had 11 children. Some of them was older than

I was. No ma'am it wasn't so hard on me. They was all old enough to take care of themselves. I lived with that woman for 17 years. Then she died.

"I been married five times. Three of my children are living. One's here—that's Dave. Then there's one in Texarkana and there's one in Kansas City. Two of my children's dead. The youngest died just about last year. All my wives are dead.

"Almost every day I comes up to sit here and watch the children. It does me good to see 'em. Makes me feel good all over to think about all the fine chance they has to get a good education. Sonny, you hear me? You pay attention too, sonny. I'm watching you—you and all the other little boys. You mind me. You learn all you can. You ought to be so thankful you allowed to learn that you work hard. You mind me, sonny. When you're grown up, you'll know what I'm talking about—and know I'm right. Run along, sonny. No use hanging around the school yard too long."

Interviewer: Miss Irene Robertson
Person interviewed: Isom Rogers, Edmondson, Arkansas
Age: 67

ISOM ROGERS

"I was born in Tunica County, Austin, Mississippi. I been in Edmondson, Arkansas ten years. I come to do better. Said farming was good here. My folks' owners was Master Palmer and George Rogers. My parents was never sold. They was young folks in slavery time and at time of freedom. They was farm hands. Their names was Pat and Ely Rogers.

"I heard him say he made palings and went 'round mending the fences when the ground was froze. He made boards to cover the houses with too—I heard him say. He was strong and worked all the time at some jobs. Never heard mother say very much.

"I been farming and I have worked on quarter-boat and back farming. I been here ten years."

Interviewer: Miss Irene Robertson
Person interviewed: Oscar James Rogers, Wheatley, Arkansas
Age: Up in 70's

OSCAR JAMES ROGERS

"I come to dis state in 1885. I run off from my parents back in North Carolina. They was working in a turpentine forest there.

"When freedom was declared my folks heard 'bout a place where money was easy to make. So they walked from down close to Charleston up there and carried the children. I was 'bout nine or ten years old. I liked the farm so I left the turpentine farm. I got to rambling round and finally got to Arkansas. I run off from my folks cause they kept staying there. I was a child and don't recollect much 'bout slavery. I was at the quarters wid all the children. My mother b'longed to Bob Plat and my father to a man named Rogers. My father could get a pass and come to see us every Sunday providin' he didn't go nowhere else or stop long the road. He came early and stay till bedtime. We all run to meet him. He kiss us all in bed when he be leavin'.

"I heard them say they 'spected a home and freedom but when the time come they master forgot 'bout home cause they just took the few clothes in bundles and left. Then they had a hard time 'cause they never thought how freedom would be. They never axed for nothin' and they never got nothin'. They didn't understand how to hustle lest somebody tell them what to do next. They did have a hard time and it was cold and rocky up in North Carolina to what they had been used to down close to Charleston.

"When I got out to Arkansas I like it better than any country I seed and I say 'I'm stayin' here.' I meant to go back but I married and didn't get no money ahead for a long time. Then I had a family of 11 children. Jes' 'fore I married I got to go to school four months' close to Cotton Plant, where I married.

"When I was young I sho could knock off de work. I cummulated 80 acres land in Lee County. I paid $900 for it, got in debt and had let it fur 'bout ($247.50) Two hundred forty-seven and a half dollars. All I got outen it. I had a bad crop and had a little provision bill. I made on time, man agreed to run me on then took it 'bout all.

"Then I still was a strong man an' we bought 40 acres 14 miles from Cotton Plant and I had it 27 years. Then lost it.

"My second wife owned a house and garden at Wheatley half a mile or so from town. We live over there. Our children all gone. She say she cooked and washed and farmed for it. It cost $100.00.

"I could do heap work if I could get it. Old man can't get 'nuff regular work to cover my house or buy me a suit closes. The Government gives me $10.00 a month. That's a help out but it don't go fir high as provisions is. Me an' the old woman both too feeble to do much hard work. I gets all the odd jobs the white folks give me. Misses, I ain't lazy, I jess gettin' old and not able to hold out to do much. Whut I could do they give it to the young fellows cause they do it in a hurry.

"I used to vote right smart when they needed me to help out. I voted for Hoover. Don't think it right the way the men settin' round and deir wives workin' fer livin' and votin'. The women can vote if they want to but I don't think it right. Seems lack the cart in front ob de horse now.

"It wouldn't do no more good to vote in the Primary than it do in the General election. It don't do much good nohow.

"Fur as I ever knowed the slaves had no uprisin's. They thought well enough of their masters. Everybody worked then hard as they could. The master he worked all time in the shop making things jess like he needed, boards and handles, plows and things. Missus, everybody worked hard dem days, both black and white, and that is the reason folks had plenty. The old grandmas done work whut suited them and helped out. Now lack me, I can't get the right work whut I able to do 'nuff to keep me livin'. It is bad.

"If times was bad as they was few years ago all old folks done been rotten, starved to death. Times is better but they sho ain't all right yet.

"This young generation livin' so fast they stop thinkin'. They do well to keep livin' their selves. They wastes a heap they outer save fur rainy days. They ain't takin' no advice from old folks. I don't know whut goiner become of them."

Interviewer: Miss Irene Robertson
Person interviewed: Will Ann Rogers
R.F.D., Brinkley, Arkansas
Age: 70

WILL ANN ROGERS

"I was born three years after the surrender. I was born at Fryers Point, Mississippi. The reason I ain't got the exact date when I was born, my ma put it down in the Bible and the house burned up and everything in it burned to ashes. No mam she got somebody what could write real nice to write all the names and ages for her.

"When ma was a young woman, she said they put her on a block and sold her. They auctioned her off at Richmond, Virginia. When they sold her, her mother fainted or drapped dead, she never knowed which. She wanted to go see her mother lying over there on the ground and the man what bought her wouldn't let her. He just took her on. Drove her off like cattle, I recken. The man what bought her was Ephram Hester. That the last she ever knowed of any of her folks. She say he mated 'em like stock so she had one boy. He livin' down here at Helena now. He is Mose Kent. He was born around Richmond, Virginia jes' lack dat she say.

"When it nearly 'bout time for freedom a whole army of Yankees come by and seed Mose working. They told him if he come go wid them they give him that spotted horse and pair red boots. He crawled up on the horse an' was gone wid 'em for a fact she said. She started right after them, following him. She followed them night and day. She nearly starved, jess begged 'long the road all she could. I heard her say how fast she have to walk to keep on trail of 'em and how many nights. She say some nights when they camped she would beg 'round and try to fill up. But she couldn't get to Mose without them seein' her. When they got to Fryers Point she went an' got him. They jess laughed and never give him nuthin'. They left that army fast as they could she say.

"She married at Fryers Point. She had jes' one boy and I had four or five sisters. They all dead but me and Mose. He think he 'bout ninety years old. He come here to see me last year. He sho is feeble.

"How come I here? When I was fourteen years old my family heard how fine this State was and moved to Helena. I lived at Moro and Cotton Plant. Then, the way I come here was funny. A man come up there and say a free train was comin' to go back to Africa. All who wanted to go could go. My pa sold out 'bout all we had an' we come here lack they say. No train come yet goin' to Africa as I seed. My pa give the white man $5.00 to pay fer the train. Tom Watson was one of 'em too. He was a sorter leader 'mong 'em wantin' to go back. Well when the day come that the train due to start everybody come to the depot whar the train going to stop. There was a big crowd. Yes mam, dressed up, and a little provisions and clothes fixed up. Jes' could take along a little. They say it would be crowded so. We stayed around here a week or two waitin' to hear somethin' or be ready to go. Most everybody stayed prutty close to the depot for two or three days. Yes mam there sho was a crowd—a whole big train full from here 'sides the other places. I jes' stayed here an' been here ever since. The depot agent, he told 'em he didn't know 'bout no train going to Africa. The tickets was no good on his trains.

"How I owns this place, I'll tell you. A man here had all dis land 'round here (Negro town) laid off. He couldn't sell none of his lots. They wouldn't buy his lots. So he got after me. We had made a good crop, so I got up the money and bought this place. One hundred dollars is what I give him. Others then started to settlin' in and about close to my place.

"I guess it was Spotsells in Virginia what raised her. She say her name was Lizzie Spotsell Johnson. Then when Ephram Hester bought her they learned her to do about in their house. She cooked and swept and knocked flies and tended to the children. She stayed with 'em a pretty long time till she run off and went to Fryers Point.

"She may have told us about the Nat Turner rebellion but I don't remember it. They sung a lot in my mother's time. Seemed lack they was happier than we are somehow. She sung religious songs and one or two field songs. I don't recollect 'em now.

"I never did vote. I never cared nuthin' about it. Some of 'em 'round here wouldn't miss votin' for nothin'.

"Lawd me, chile, the times is done run ahead of me now. I'm so fur behind I never expect to catch up. I don't pay no more attention to the young folks, the way they act now, 'an I do my little dog there. They don't want no advice and I would be afraid I would 'vise 'em wrong.

When my children come I tell 'em you are grown and you knows right from wrong. Do right. That's all I know to say.

"The way I am supported is my husband gets all the jobs he able to do and can and the governmint give me an' him $10 a month. We has a little garden."

Interviewer: Miss Irene Robertson
Person interviewed: William Henry Rooks
Baptist Preacher; Brinkley, Arkansas
Age: 84

WILLIAM HENRY ROOKS

The slaves didn't spect nothing but freedom. Jes freedom! In Africa they was free as wild animals and then they was so restricted. Jes put in bondage for no reason at all.

No plantations was divided. I was born a slave and I remembers right smart how it was.

My master was John Freeman and his wife's name was Fannie. I went to Como, Mississippi twice a week to get the mail all durin the war. It was eight miles. I rode a pony.

If you go to church you have to have a pass from the master. The pattyrollers see you and you have to show it to them. It was just a note. If you didn't have it they take or send you home. If they catch you any more without a pass they whip you. They come to the church and in all public places like the police stands around now. They rode around mostly. Sometimes they went in droves.

They would let you go visiting sometimes and exchange work. Some masters was good and some was mean jess like they are now and some slaves good and some bad. That is the way they are now.

Some of the white men had a hundred slaves and had plenty money. The war broke nearly all of them. The very worse thing I ever knowed about it was some white men raised hands to sell like they raise stock now. It was hard to have your child took off and never see or hear tell of it. Mean man buy it and beat it up. Some of them was drove off to be sold at auction at New Orleans. That was where some took them cause they could get big money for them.

I never knowed of a master to give the slaves a dime when they become free. They never promised them nothing. The Yankees might have to toll them off. The hands all stayed on John Freeman's place and when it was over he give them the privilege of staying right on in their houses. Some left after awhile and went somewhere they thought they could do better.

They didn't have the Ku Klux but it was bout like it what they had. They wore caps shine de coons eye and red caps and red garments. Red symbolize blood reason they wore red. They broke up our preaching. Some folks got killed. Some was old, some young—old devlish ones. They was like a drove of varments. I guess you be scared. They run the colored folks away from church a lot of times. That was about equalization after the freedom. That was the cause of that.

There was uprisings like I'm telling you but the colored folks didn't have nothing to go in a gun if he had one. White folks make them give up a gun.

The first votin I done I was workin for young Henry

Larson back in Mississippi. He give my mother $120 a year to cook for his young wife and give her what she eat and I worked on his farm. He told me to go vote, it was election day. I ask him how was I going to know how to vote. I could read a little. I couldn't write. The ballot box was at Pleasant Mount. Ozan set over the box. He was a Yankee. He was the only one kept the box. It was a wooden box nailed up and a slit in the top. A.R. Howe and Captain Howe was two more Yankee white men there watching round all day. Ozan was the sheriff at Sardis, Mississippi soon after the war. Some more colored folks come up to vote. We stood around and watched. We saw D. Sledge vote; he owned half of the county. We knowed he voted Democrat so we voted the other ticket so it would be Republican. I voted for President Grant. I don't believe in women voting. They used to have the Australian Ballot System. It's a heap more the man that's elected than it is the party. We all voted for Hoover; he was a Republican and foe he got one term served out we was about on starvation. I ain't voted since. That President claim to be a Democrat. He ain't no Democrat. I don't know what he be.

I been farming and preaching. I started preaching in Mississippi. I joined the conference in Arkansas in 1886 and started preaching at Surrounded Hill (Biscoe). I come here in 1884 from Pinola County. Mississippi. I had some stock and they was fencing up everything over there. I had no land so I come to an open country. It wasn't long before they fenced it in. I come to Brinkley and worked for Gun and Black sawmill and I been here forty or fifty years. I don't know jess how long. I couldn't starve to death in a whole year here. The people wouldn't let me. I got lot of friends, both black and white, here.

I married December 17, 1874 in the Baptist church. Glasco Wilson was the preacher married me. My wife died here in dis house nine years ago. We had ten children but jes two livin now. My girl married a preacher and live at Hope. Arkansas. My son preaches in Parson, Kansas.

I supports my own self. I works and I preaches a little yet. I saved up some money but it nearly give out. The young generation, some of them, do mighty bad. Some of them is all right. Some of them don't do much and don't save nothing. I owns this house and did own another one what burned down. A lamp exploded and caught it while I was going off up the road but I never looked back or I would have seen it. It seem lack now it takes more money to do than it ever did in times before. Seems like money is the only thing to have and get. Folks gone scottch crazy over money, money! Both is changing. The white folks, I'm speaking bout, the white folks has changed and course the colored folks keeping up wid them. The old white and colored neither can't keep up wid the fast times. I say it's the folks that made this depression and it's the folks keeping the depression. The little fellow is squeezed clear out. It out to be stopped. Folks ain't happy like they used to be. Course they sung songs all the time. Religious choruses mostly.

Interviewer: Samuel S. Taylor
Person interviewed: Amanda Ross
817 Schiller Street, Little Rock, Arkansas
Age: 82

AMANDA ROSS

"I was nine years old in the time of the surrender. I know I was here in that time. I don't know nothin' 'bout their carryin'-on. I know they whipped them with hobble rods. You don't know what hobble rods is!!! Ain't you seen these here long thin hick'ry shoots? They called hobble rods. I don't know why they called 'em hobble rods. I know they made you hobble. They'd put 'em in the fire and roast 'em and twist 'em. I have seen 'em whip them till the blood run down their backs. I've seen 'em tie the women up, strip 'em naked to their waist and whip 'am till the blood run down their backs. They had a nigger whipper, too.

"I was born in Salem, Alabama. I came up here about twenty-five years ago.

"Isaac Adair was the name of the old man who owned me. He owned my mother and father too, Hester and Scip. Their last name was Adair, the same as their master's.

"I don't remember the names of my grandfather and grandmother, 'cause we was crossed up, you see, One of my grandmothers was named Crecie and the other was named Lydia. I don't remember my grandfather's name. I spect I used to call 'im master. I used to remember them but I don't no more. Nobody can't worry me 'bout them old folks now. They ast me all them questions at the Welfare. They want to know your gran'pa and your gran'ma. Who were they, what did they do, where did they live, where are they now? I don't know what they did. That's too far back for me.

"My mother and father had nine children. I have only one sister living. All the others done gone to heaven but me and her.

"My mother and father lived in a log cabin. They had one-legged beds nailed to the wall. They had benches and boxes and blocks and all sich as that for chairs. My daddy made the table we used. He made them one-legged beds too. They kept the food in boxes and gourds. They had these big gourds. They could cut holes in the top of them and put things in them. My mammy had a lot of 'em and they were nice and clean too. Wisht I had one of them now.

"Some folks didn't have that good. We had trundle beds for the children that would run under the big bed when they wasn't sleeping in it. We made a straw mattress. You know the white folks weren't goin' to let 'em use cotton, and they didn't have no chickens to git feathers from; so they had to use straw. Oh, they had a hard time I'm tellin' you. My mother pulled greens out of the garden and field, and cured it up for the mattress.

"For rations, we'd eat onions and vegetables. We et what was raised. You know they didn't have nothin' then 'cept what they raised. All the cookin' was done at one house, but there was two cooks, one for the colored folks and one for the white folks. My grandma cooked for the white people. They cooked in those big old washpots for the colored people. We all thought we had a pretty good master.

"We didn't know nothin' about a master.

"I ain't positive what time the hands ate breakfast. I know they et it and I know they et at the same time and place. I think they et after sunrise. They didn't have to eat before sunrise.

"When they fed the children, they cook the food and put it in a great big old tray concern and called up the children, 'Piggee-e-e-e-e, piggee-e-e-e-e.' My cousin was the one had to go out and call the children; and you could see them runnin' up from every which way, little shirt tails flyin' and hair sticking out. Then they would pour the food out in different vessels till the children could git around them with those muscle-shell spoons. Many of them as could get 'round a vessel would eat out of it and when they finished that one, they'd go to another one, and then to another one till they all got fed.

"My master worked seventy hands they said. He had two colored overseers and one white one. He didn't allow them overseers to whip and slash them niggers. They had to whip them right. Didn't allow no pateroles to bother them neither. That's a lot of help too. 'Cause them pateroles would eat you up. It was awful. Niggers used to run away to keep from bein' beat up.

"I knowed one gal that ran away in the winter time and she went up into the hollow of a tree for protection.

When she came in, she was in sich a bad condition they had to cut off both her legs. They had froze out there. They taken care of her. They wanted her to work. She was jus' as nice a seamstress as you ever saw. And she could do lots of things. She could get about some. She could go on her knees. She had some pads for them and was just about as high as your waist when she was goin' along on her hands and knees, swinging her body between her arms.

- **Ate in the Big House**

"The cooks and my mother stayed in the white folks' yard. They weren't in the quarters. My mother was seamstress and she was right in the house all the day long sewing. The children like me and my sister, they used us 'round the house and yard for whatever we could do. They didn't never whip none of my father's children. If we done something they thought we ought to been whipped for, they would tell father to whip us, and if he wanted to, he would; and if he didn't want to, he wouldn't. They made a big difference for some reason.

- **Marriage**

"They married in that time by standing up and letting someone read the ceremony to them. My master was a Christian. There wasn't no jumpin' over a broomstick on my master's place. The white folks didn't have no nigger preacher for their churches. But the colored folks had 'em. They preached out of these little old Blue Back Spellers— leastways they was little blue back books anyhow.

- **Freedom**

"My folks was on the road refugeeing from Magnolia, Arkansas to Pittsburg, Texas when the news came that the colored folks was free. And my master came 'round and told the niggers they was free as he was. I didn't hear him. I don't know where I was. I'm sure I was out playin somewheres.

• Slave Wages and Experiences after the War

"My father worked in a blacksmith shop right after the War. Before the War, he went far and near to work for the white folks. They'd risk him with their money and everything. They would give him part of it; I don't know how much. He brought money to them, and they sure give him money.

"We didn't have to wear the things the other slave children had to wear. He would order things for his family and my father would do the same for us. When old master made his order, my father would put his in with it.

• Family

"I am the mother of fifteen children—ten girls and five boys. That was enough for me. I am willing to quit off. My husband is dead. He's been dead for thirty-five years.

• Opinions

"I don't know what to say about these young people. Mine are pretty good. So, I'm 'fraid to say much about the others.

"Lord, I don't know what we'll do if we don't get some rain.

• Vocational Experiences

When I was able I washed and ironed. I didn't have to do nothin' till after my father and husband died. Then I washed and ironed and cooked till the white folks set me out. They said I was too old. That is one thing I hates to think of. They had the privilege to say I couldn't work; they ought to a seen that I got somethin' to live on when I wasn't able to work no more."

• Interviewer's Comment

You can't get the whole story by reading the words in this interview. You have to hear the tones and the accents, and see the facial expressions and bodily movements, and sense the sometimes almost occult influence; you have to feel the utter lack of resentment that lies behind the words that sound vehement when read. You marvel at the quick, smooth cover-up when something is to be withheld, at the unexpected vigor of the mind when the bait is attractive enough to draw it out, and at the sweetness of the disposition. Some old people merely get mellowed and sweetened by the hardships through which they have passed. Sometimes, you wonder if some of the old folk don't have dispositions that they can turn off or on at will.

It is not hard to realize the reason why Amanda was treated better than other children when you remember that she called her grandpa "Master".

Interviewer: Miss Irene Robertson
Person interviewed: "Cat" Ross
Brassfield, Ark.
Age: Born 1862

CAT ROSS

"I was born in Releford County on old Major Ross place. I was born durin' a battle between the North and South at Murfreesboro. The house was on the battle ground. Mama had five children. Her name was Susanna Wade. Papa's name was Amos Ross. He belong to Major Bill Ross. Major Ross had ten houses houses—one at the edge of the thicket, two on Stone river, and they was scattered around over his land. Major Ross never went to war. Papa went with Major Billy to bury his gold. It stayed where they put it till after the war they went and dug it up. I seen that. When they brought it to the house, it was a pot—iron pot—full of gold. I didn't know where they had it buried nor how they fixed it.

"My folks was all field hands. They muster been blessed cause they didn't get mixed up with the other nations. Grandfather's mother—Grandma Venus—come from Africa. She'd been in bondage about a hundred years. I recollect her well. My folks all lived to be old people, over a hundred years old. They was all pretty well, all Africans.

"I have seen the Ku Klux quarter mile long and two breasted on horses. They scared me so bad I never had no experiences with them. They run my uncle in. He was a big dancer. One time they made him dance. He cut the pigeon-wing for them. That was the name of what he danced.

"I never was sold. I was give way. One of the Wades married into the Mitchell family. Mama belong to the Wades. They give me and Mama and Aunt Sallie—she wasn't my aunt but I called her that—to Wade's daughter. She was the young mistress. The Wades wasn't so good to their slaves. When freedom was declared, Papa come and got me and Mama and took us on over to his place agin. We started sharecroppin' at Major Ross's place. In 1881 Chick McGregor paid my way. I come to Arkansas. I farmed all my life till 1922 to 1933 I been here in Brassfield sawmilling. They took the mill away from here. I cain't plough, I'm not able. I pick and hoe cotton. I work day labor. I never have got on the Welfare."

Southfield
FOLKLORE SUBJECTS
Name of Interviewer: Pernella Anderson
Subject: Centennial Snow—Spring in St. Louis addition

Name: Mattie Ross
Occupation: Gardening
Residence: South Field, Oil Field.
Age: 74
[TR: Information moved from bottom of second page.]

MATTIE ROSS

Ah wuz born aftuh surrender. Ah guess ah'm about 74 years ole. Mah pa wuz er slave an mah ma wuz too. Dey moster wuz name Green Traylor an dey lived right down dar at Tula Creek. Mah mistess wuz named Martha Traylor an dey name me aftuh huh. Mah name is Martha Lee Traylor. Aftuh she mahried huh name wiz Martha Tatum. We worked down dar. Oh! Mah Lawd! How we did work—all ovah dat bottom. De puttiest fiel' ah evah did see. De Traylor's owned hit den. Later on de Tatums bought hit fum dem and years aftuh dat de Nash's bought hit fum de Tatums. But new all uv dat place is growed up. Nothing but er pine thicket and er black berry thicket. Ye caint hardly walk through de place. Later on de Cobbs owned us. George Cobb wuz his name. He lived down in de Caledonia settlement. Ah went behin' him er many er day wid de hoe or he'd crack mah haid. He use tuh be de sheriff here de years uv de boom an his nephew is de sheriff now—Grady Wosley. Later en while ah wuz a gull ah werked fuh de Swilleys an wuz partly raised on dey plantation. De ole man wuz name Lawson Swilley. His wife, Margaret Swilley, and I clare dem two people treated me white. She mammied me er many er day. Ah wuz bred and born right down dar er-round Caledonia. Ah wuz a big gull durin de time uv de centennial snow. Dis snow wuz called dat cause hit wuz de bigges snow dat evah been. Hit wuz ovah yo haid. We had tuh spade our way evah whah we went. Tuh de wood gitting place, tuh de sping, tuh de hoss lot, and evah whah. De anow wuz warm an soft. We piled up so much snow till hit took hit er half er year tuh melt. Dat snow stayed on de groun two months.

Ah am de muthah uv five gulls and fo' boys. Didn nairy one uv mah gulls come in de pen till dey wuz mahried. Ah use tuh fish in er big ole fish pond rat down whah de wesson depot is now. Years ergo people come fum Camden an othuh places tuh fish in dat fish pond.

Mr. Sam Austin sole old man Burgy (Burgiss?) er piece uv groun' to bury folks in and he wuz de first man tuh die an be buried dar. So dey name hit de Burgy Cemetery.

Down dar in Memphis Addition atah the colored Prof. Dykes place dar use tuh be one uv de bes' springs. Course at dat time hit wuz er big ole fiel' den and de watuch wuz jes lak ice watuh.

Dat make me think. Mah pa sed he went tuh de wah tuh cook fuh his ole moster, Green Traylor. Well pa said dar wuz er spring whar dey got watuh. Said he went tuh git watuh outen de sping and had tuh pull dead men outn de spring an dat day drinked of'n dem dead men all while de wah wuz going on.

United States. Work Projects Administration

Interviewer: Miss Irene Robertson
Person Interviewed: Laura Rowland
(Bright Mulatto)
Age: 65?
Address: Brinkley, Arkansas

LAURA ROWLAND

"My parents name was Mary Ann and Sam Billingslea. Mother's father lived with us when I first remember. His name was Robert Todd. He was a brown skin Negro. They said he was a West Indian. He talked of olden times but I don't remember well enough to tell you. Father owned a home that we was living on when I first remember. Mother was bright color, too. Vaden, Mississippi was our trading post. Mother had twenty children. She was a worker. She would work anywhere she was put. My folks never talked much about slavery. I don't know how they got our place.

"I know they was bothered by the Ku Klux. One night they heard or saw the Ku Klux coming. The log house set low on the ground but was dug out to keep potatoes and things in—a cellar like. The planks was wide, bout a foot wide, rough pine, not nailed down. They lifted the planks up and all lay down and put the planks back up. The house look like outside nothing could go under it, it was setting on the hard ground. When they got there and opened the doors they saw nobody at home and rode off.

"Another time, one black night, a man—he must have been a soldier—strided a block step with his horse and ordered supper. She told him she didn't have nothing cooked and very little to cook. He cursed and ordered the supper. Told her to get it. She pretended to be fixing it and slipped out the back door down the furrows and squatted in the briers in a fence corner. Long time after she had been out there hid, he come along, jumped the fence on his horse, jumped over her back, down into the lane and to the road he went. If the horse hadn't jumped over her and had struck her he would have killed her. Now I think he was a soldier, not the Ku Klux. I heard my father say he was a yard boy.

"I married in Mississippi and came to Malvern and Hot Springs. He was a mill hand. I raised three children of my own and was a chamber maid. I kept house and cooked for Mrs. Bera McCafity, a rich woman in Hot Springs. My husband died and was buried at Malvern. I married again, in Hot Springs, and lived there several years. We went to the steel mill at Gary, Indiana. He died. I come back here and to Brinkley in 1920. One daughter lives in Detroit and one in Chicago. The youngest one is married, has a family and a hard time; the other makes her living. It takes it all to do her. I get $8.00 on the P.W.A.

"They all accuse me around here of talking mighty proper. I been around fine city folks so much I notice how they speak.

"I don't fool with voting. I don't care to vote unless it would be some town question to settle. I would know something about it and the people.

"I don't know my age. I was grown when I married

nearly sixty years ago. We have to show our license to get on the W.P.A. or our age in the Bible you understand."

United States. Work Projects Administration

Interviewer: Mrs. Bernice Bowden
Person interviewed: Landy Rucker
2315 W. Fourth Avenue, Pine Bluff, Arkansas
Age: 83

LANDY RUCKER

"I was born in 1854 in the State of Georgia, Elbert County.

"I member some about the war. I went to the field when I was twelve. Pulled fodder, picked peas and tended to the cow pen. I had to go then. We had a good master. Our mistress wasn't good though. She wouldn't give us enough to eat. Old master used to ask if we had enough to eat and he'd pull out great big hams and cut em all to pieces and give em to us. Old mistress would cry and say, 'You're givin' away all my good dinner.' But she repented since the war. She said she didn't do right.

"We got here to Pine Bluff in '61.

"Oh yes, I remember comin' here on the train and on the boat.

"Old mistress whipped us when she thought we needed it. I been pretty good all my life.

"My father was a blacksmith and one day when I was six or seven I was takin' his dinner when some dogs smelled the dinner and smelled me too and they got after me. I had to climb a tree and they stayed around till they heard some other dogs barkin' and ran off. I come down then and took my bucket and left. Nother time some hogs chased me. They rooted all around the tree till they heard somethin' crackle in the woods and run off and then I'd come down.

"After the war I went to school three days and the teacher whipped me. I went home and I didn't go back. I went home and went to the field. I had a mother and a sister and I tried to make a living for them.

"I went to school a little while after that and then went to the field. Most I know I learned by myself.

"Yes'm, I seen the Yankees bout a year fore the war ceasted. They come to get somethin' to eat and anything else they could get. Got the mules and things and took my two brothers and put em in the war. One come back after surrender and the other one died in the war. They said they was fightin' to free the niggers from being under bondage.

"I seen the Ku Klux. Looked like their horses could fly. Made em jump a big high fence. They come and took my father and all the other men on the place and was goin' to put em in the Confederate army. But papa was old and he cried and old mistress thought a lot of him so they let him stay. I just lay down and hollered cause they was takin' my brothers, but they didn't keep em long. One of my brothers, six years older than me, come up here to Pine Bluff to jine the Yankees.

"We could hear the guns at Marks Mill.

"I been married twice. There was about eleven years betwixt the two marriages.

"I worked on the farm till about '85. Then I worked in the planing mill. I got hit by a car and it broke my hip so I have to walk on crutches now. Then I got me a little shoe shop and I got along fine till I got so I couldn't set down long enough to fix a pair of shoes. I bought this house and I gets help from the Relief so I'm gettin' along all right now."

United States. Work Projects Administration

Interviewer: Samuel S. Taylor
Person interviewed: Martha Ruffin
1310 Cross Street, Little Rock, Arkansas
Age: 80

MARTHA RUFFIN

"I was born in North Carolina, and I was seven years old when the Surrender was. Every one of my children can tell you when they was born, but I can't. My mother, Quinettie Farmer was her name. Brother Robert Farmer is my cousin. He is about the same age as my husband. He got married one week and me and my husband the next. My father's name was Valentine Farmer. My grandmother on my mother's side was Mandy Harrison, and my grandfather's name on my mother's side was Jordan Harrison. My grandpa on my father's side was named Reuben Farmer, and his wife was Nancy Farmer. I have seed my grandpa and grandma on my father's side. But my mother didn't see them on my mother's side.

"I 'members my daddy's white folks' names, Moses Farmer. My father never was sold. My daddy, Valentine Farmer, was a ditcher, shoemaker, and sometimes a tanner. My mother was a house girl. She washed and ironed. I couldn't tell exactly what my grandparents did. My grandparents, so my parents told me, were mostly farmers. I reckon Moses Farmer owned about three hundred slaves.

"I was born on Robert Bynum's place. He was my mother's owner. He married one of the Harrison girls and my mother fell to that girl. My mother done just about as she pleased. She didn't know nothin' about workin' in the field till after the Surrender.

"The way my mother and father happened to meet—my old master hired my daddy to do some work for him and he met my mama that way.

"The way my folks learned they was free was, a white school-teacher who was teaching school where we stayed told my mother she was free, but not to say nothing about it. About three weeks later, the Yankees come through there and told them they was free and told my old boss that if he wanted them to work he would have to hire them and pay them. The school-teacher stayed with mother's folks—mother's white folks. The school-teacher was teaching white folks, not niggers. She was a Yankee, too. My mother was the house girl, and the school-teacher stayed with her folks. The War was so hot she couldn't git no chance to go back home.

"My daddy farmed after the War. He farmed on shares the first year. The next year, he bought him a horse. He finally owned his own farm. He owned it when he died. He had about one hundred acres of land.

"I have pretty fair health for an old woman like I am. I am bothered with the rheumatism. The Lawd wouldn't let both of us git down at the same time. (Here she refers to her husband who was sick in bed at the time she made the statement. You have his story already. It was difficult for her to tell her story, for he wanted it to be like his—ed.)

"I belong to the Primitive Baptist Church. I haven't changed my membership from my home.

"I got married in 1882, in February. How many years is that? I got so I can't count up nothin'. Fifty-six years. Yes, that's it; that's how long I been married. I had a little sister that got married with me. She didn't really git married; she just stood up with me. She was just a little baby girl. They told me I was pretty near twenty-three years old when I married. I have a daughter that's been married twenty-five years. We had older daughters, but that one was the first one married. I have got a daughter over in North Little Rock that is about fifty years old. Her husband is dead. We had ten children. My daughter is the mother of ten children too. She got married younger than I did. This girl I am living with is my baby. I have four children living—three girls and one boy. A woman asked me how many children I had and I told her three. She was a fortuneteller and she wanted to tell me my fortune. But I didn't want her to tell me nothin'. God was gittin' ready to tell me somethin' I didn't want to hear. I've got five great-grandchildren. We don't have no great-great-grandchildren. Don't want none."

• Interviewer's Comment

The old lady's style was kind of cramped by the presence of her husband. Every once in a while, when she would be about to paint something in lurid colors, he would drop in a word and she would roll her phrases around in her mouth, so to speak, and shift and go ahead in a different direction and on another gear.

Very pleasant couple though—with none of the

bitterness that old age brings sometimes. The daughter's name is Searles.

Interviewer: Samuel S. Taylor
Person Interviewed: Thomas Ruffin
1310 Cross Street, Little Rock, Arkansas
Age: 82 or 84

THOMAS RUFFIN

"I was born in North Carolina, Franklin County, near Raleigh. My father's name really I don't know. Folks said my master was my daddy. That's what they told me. Of course, I don't know myself. But then white folks did anything they wanted to in slavery times.

"My mother's name was Morina Ruffin. I don't know the names of my grandparents. That is too far back in slavery for me. Of course, old man Ruffin my father's father, which would have been my grandfather, he died way back yonder in slave times before the war. My father gotten kilt in the war. His name was Tom Ruffin. I was named after him. He died trying to hold us. That man owned three hundred slaves. He never married. Carried my mother round everywhere he went. Out of all his niggers, he didn't have but one with him. That was in slavery time and he was a fool about her.

"I couldn't tell you exactly when I was born. Up until the surrender I couldn't tell how old I was. I am somewheres around eighty-two years old. The old lady is just about the same. We guesses it in part. We figure it on what we heard the old folks say and things like that. I remember plenty of things about slavery that I saw.

"I never did much when I was a boy. The biggest thing I remember is a mule got to kicking and jumped around in a stall. She lost her footing and fell down and broke her neck right there in the stall. I remember her name as well as if it was yesterday. Her name was Bird. That was just before the war. I know I must have been at least four years old then. You can figure that up and see what it comes to.

"I never did any work when I was a child. I jus went to the spring with the young Mistress and danced for them sometimes. But they never did give me any work to do,— like they did the others. I lived right in the biggest house the biggest portion of my time.

"That day and time, they made compost heaps. Mixed dirt with manure. They hoed cotton and crops. They didn't know what school was. They helped with washing and ironing. Did every kind of work they had strength enough to do till they got big enough to go to the field. That was what the children did.

"When they were about seven years old, to the best of my recollection they would go to the field. Seven or eight. They would pick up corn stalks and brush. And from that on when they were about eight or nine, they would pick cotton.

"My mother never did have to do anything round the farm. She lived about seventy-five miles from it, there where the master had his office. He was a lawyer. After I was born, she didn't come out to see me but once a year that I recollect. When she did come, she would bring me some candy or cakes or something like that.

"I didn't see the soldiers during the time of the war. But I saw plenty of them afterwards—riding round and telling the niggers they were free. They had some of the finest saddles I ever seed. You could hear them creaking a block off. No, I didn't see them while they was fighting. We were close enough to hear the guns crash, and we could see the light from them, but I didn't actually see the fightin. The Yankees come through on every plantation where they were working and entered into every house and told us we was free. The Yankees did it. They told you you were free as they were, that you didn't have to stay where you was, that you didn't have no more master, that you could go and come as you pleased.

"I got along hard after I was freed. It is a hard matter to tell you what we could find or get. We used to dig up dirt in the smokehouse and boil it and dry it and sift it to get the salt to season our food with. We used to go out and get old bones that had been throwed away and crack them open and get the marrow and use them to season the greens with. Jus plenty of niggers then didn't have anything but that to eat.

"Even in slavery times, there was plenty of niggers out of them three hundred slaves who had to break up old lard gourds and use them for meat. They had to pick up bones off the dung hill and crack them open to cook with. And then, of course, they'd steal. Had to steal. That the bes way to git what they wanted.

"They had a great big kitchen for the slaves. They had what you call pot racks they could push them big pots in and out on. They cooked hog slop there. They had trays and bowls to eat out of that were made out of gum wood. It was a long house used as a kitchen for the hands to go in and eat. They et dinner there and for supper they would be there. But breakfast, they would have to eat in the field. The young niggers would bring it out to them. They would bring it about an hour after the sun rose and the slave hands would eat it right out in the field; that was the breakfast. You see the hands went to the field before sunup, and they didn't get to eat breakfast in the kitchen and it had to be et in the field. Little undergrowth of children—they had plenty of them on the place—had to carry their meals to them.

"They would usually give them collars [HW: collards] in green times, potatoes in potato time. Bread,—they didn't know what that was. White folks hardly knew theirselves. They didn't have butter and they didn't have no sugar. Didn't know much about what meat was yet. They would give the little bits of children pot liquor. That's the most I ever seed them git. Of course I was treated differently. You couldn't judge them by me. I was the only half-white youngun round there, and they said I was half-brother to ol Marse's chillun. And the white chillen would git me up to the house to dance for them and all like, and they would give me biscuits or anything good they had. I never seed the others eatin nothin but pot liquor.

"Most of the slaves lived in log cabins. You know they never had but one door. In general where they had large families, they would have two rooms with a chimney in the middle of the house. The chimney was built out of mud and straw. I can remember them sawin the timber.

Two pulled a big ol crosscut saw. Didn't have no saw mills then. This world has come from a long ways. They used to didn't have no plows. It was without form. You made it at home.

"They had ol homemade bedsteads to sleep in. They had a little rope that ran back and forth instead of slats. That was called a corded bed. Cheers were all made at home and were split bottoms.

"They didn't many of the slaves have food in their homes. But when they did, they would jus have a little wooden box and they would put their food in it.

"It seems like the white people got to burying their money during the time of the war. That never come out till after the war. Then they got to wantin that money and started looking for it. There never was any talk of buried treasure before the war.

"My folks didn't give me any schoolin before the surrender. I never got any before the surrender and a mighty little afterwards. No nigger knowed anything. I started to farming when I was thirteen years old. I used to be a fertilizer, and then a cotton sower. That was the biggest I knowed about farming when I was a boy. My mother lived about fifteen years after slavery. I reckon.

"In the time of slavery, you couldn't marry a woman. You just took up with her. Mother married the same man she had been going with after freedom. She had four children after the surrender as fer as I can tell—three girls and two boys.

"I moved from North Carolina to Louisiana. Stayed there one year and then moved here. Bought forty acres of land. Bought it after I'd been here a year. It took me four years to pay for that. Then next time I bought eighty acres and paid for them. Paid them out in two years. Then I bought eighty acres more and paid for them in two years. Couldn't pay for them cash at first, but could have paid for the last eighty when I bought them if I had a wanted to. Then I bought eighty more and then I bought eighty again and then forty and on till I had five hundred and three acres of farm land. I got the three over when I got the sorghum mill.

"I left my farm and come to the city for doctor's treatment. My old lady and I worked out five hundred and three acres of land. I got five children living. I gave each one of them forty acres of land. Most of the rest I sold. I got a fellow here that owes me for one of the places now. He lives over on Third and Dennison. His name is Wright. My old lady an me held on to that and didn't lose it even in all these hard years.

"My daughter kept after me to come here and she built this little house out here where I could holler or do anything I wanted to do and not disturb nobody. I couldn't feel at home up in a big house with other people. Four or five months ago it would take two people to put me to bed. I would get off from home and have to carry me back. But I am gettin along fine now. This high blood pressure keeps me from remembering so well. Ol lady where's my pipe? You didn't find it up to daughter's? Ain't it in the kitchen? Can't you find it nowheres? What didju do with it? Well, you needn't look for it no longer. It's here in my pocket. That's my high blood pressure workin. That whut it does to you.

"I belong to the Primitive Baptist Church and have

been belonging to it altogether about sixty-three years. I used to be a Missionary. I been a member of the church a long time.

"I think times are jus fulfilling the Bible. The people are wiser now than we ever known them to be and wickeder. I don't believe the times you see now will be always. People are getting so wise and so wicked that I think the end is near at hand. You notice the Germans now are trying to make slaves out of the Jews. There's the Japans that is jus slaughtering up the Chinese like they was nothin but dumb brutes. The world is wickeder than it ever has been before.

"The young people today! I'd hate to tell you what I do think of them. The business is going to fall."

United States. Work Projects Administration

Interviewer: Miss Irene Robertson
Person interviewed: Casper Rumple, De Valls Bluff, Arkansas
Age: 78

CASPER RUMPLE

"I will be, providin' the good Lord spare me, 79 years old the first day of January. I was born in Lawrence County, South Carolina. The Big road was the dividing line between that and Edgefield County. My mother belonged to John Griffin. His wife named Rebecca. My father was a Irishman. Course he was a white man—Irishman. Show I did know him. He didn't own no slaves. I don't guess he have any land. He was a overseer in Edgefield County. His name was Ephraim Rumple. What become of him? He went off to fight the Yankees and took Malaria fever and died on Red River. I could show you bout where he died.

"My mother had a big family. I can't tell you much bout them. I was the youngest. She cooked up at John Griffins. He was a old man and the land was all his wife's. She was old too. She had some grown girls. He had no children. They called him Pa and I did too. I stayed round with him nearly all the time helping him.

"He had a room and she had a room. I slept on a bed—little bed—home-made bed—in the room wid him and she slept in the room with her two girls and my mother slept in the kitchen a whole heap so she be there to get breakfast early. They riz early every mornin'. John Griffins wife owned four plantations more than 160 acres in each one, but I couldn't say how much.

"My mother was a field hand in busy times too. Miss Rebecca had all the slaves clothes made. She seed to that. She go to the city, Augusta, and bring back bolts cloth. One slave sewed for Miss Rebecca and her family. She didn't do all the sewing but she sewed all the time. One woman done all the weavin'. At night after they work in the field Miss Rebecca give em tasks—so many bats to card or so much spinnin' to do.

"Master John didn't want em to work at night but she made em work all the same. They b'long to her. Another thing the women had to do was work in the garden. It was a three acre garden. They always had plenty in thar. Had it palinged so the young chickens couldn't squeeze through the cracks.

"They had plenty stock and made all the fertilizer needed in the garden and patches. They had goober patch, popcorn patch, sorghum patches, several of em, pea patches but they was field cabbage patch and water-mellon patch. They had chicken house, goose house, duck house and way off a turkey pen. It had a cover on it. They had to be cleaned and all that manure moved to the garden and patches. Old man John Griffin was a good man. Things went on pretty quiet bout the place. They had to do their own cooking. They got for the grown ups 3 pounds meat, 1 pk.[TR:?] meal a week. They fed the young chaps plenty so they wouldn't get stunted. They keep em chunky till they get old nough to grow up tall and that make big women and big men. They stunt em then when they start runnin' up, it cause em to be low. The owners was mighty careful (not)[HW: ?] to feed the chaps nough to eat so they make strong hands.

"Men come long the road peddlin' from out the cities, men come long with droves of horses and mules. They was called horse traders. Then once in a while they come long tradin' and selling slaves. Nother way they sell em was at public auction. Iffen a slave steal from another master, like go in his smoke house or crib and steal, the sheriff have to whip him. They would have public whippin'.

"How'd they know was freedom? How'd they not know it was freedom? Everybody went wild. They was jes' crazy cause they was free. Way I knowd for certain it was freedom Mr. John Griffin had all the slaves that hadn't done went off come to the house and he told them they was all free. Some of em just started walking the roads till they nearly starved. The government didn't start feeding the slaves till so many nearly starved. My mother cooked on nearly a year. Then she went to work for Vaughn in Edgefield County.

"They didn't give them no land. The white folks was land pore.

"They didn't have no money. When the masters had money they give the slaves a little spending money. Nearly all the slaves had a little money long. They get a pass to split rails for a neighbor and make money. That was befo freedom. After freedom nobody had money but the Yankee soldiers. They keep it closer than the folks you been livin' with.

"Mr. Griffin, he was called General by all the young men. He was too old to fight so he trained soldiers. He didn't wear a uniform but they did. They met certain days every week. They wore gray uniforms.

"They had a battle at Lawrence. It was 17 miles. The soldiers passed long the Big road. I didn't see the battles. I heard plenty talk about that conflict at Lawrence though.

"I heard the slaves was goin' to get 40 acres and a mule. I tell you they didn't wait to see if they was going to get another meal. They went wild, walking and hooping up and down the road. They found out when they nearly starved they had got the bad end of the game somehow. Then to keep em from starvin' they had certain days to go to Lawrence and get a little rations. Not much I tell you. They started stealin' and the Ku Klux started up bout that.

"The President got killed (Abraham Lincoln). Then they knowed the gig was up. They had to go to work hard as ever and mighty little to eat. The slaves did vote. It was the color of the paper they used way they knowed how to vote. The Republican government had full sway 12 years. All the offices at Edgefield nearly was Negroes cept the sheriff. The Yankees tell em what to do way they knowed how. Butler went to Congress. He was a Negro—(???). That was what the Ku Klux was mad bout. They run the Yankees out and took holt of the offices soon as they could.

"Our master had no Ku Klux comin' on our place. He protected us, It wasn't no different than slavery till I was nearly grown and a drove was walking going west to better place. I got in with them and come on. The Ku Klux had killed several Negroes. That scared them all up. I remember Tuscaloosa, Alabama when we cone through there. We was walking—a line a mile long—marching and singing. They was building back in a hurry seemed like to me. The town had been burned up. Some dropped out to get work along. Some fell out sick. Some so weak they died long the road. Had to keep up. Some stopped; they never caught up no more. Mostly old folks or half starved folks couldn't keep going. The Ku Klux whoop and shoot you down for any little thing. They started at night, fraid of the Yankees but they whooped and run them out and the Negroes left. The Ku Klux got so bold they didn't dress up nor go at night neither. At first they was careful then they got bold. The Yankee soldiers bout all they was afraid of. The Negroes found out who some of the Ku Klux was and told the Yankees but it didn't do much good. After bout twelve years all the Yankees gone back home. The white folks down in Carolina thought bout as little of them as Negroes. They wouldn't let them have no land if they did have money to pay any price for it. They didn't want them living amongst them. They say they rether have a Negro family.

"The biggest Negro uprisin' I ever seed was at freedom. They riz up in a hurry.

"I had to stop and work all along. I got to Arkansas in 1881. I never went no further. I been all my life farmin'. I cut and sell wood, clear land. The best living was when I farmed and sold wood. I bought a 10 acre farm and cleared it up graduly, then I sold it fer $180.00 cause I got blind and couldn't see to farm it. I had a house on it. I own this here house (a splendid home). My daughter and her husband come to take care me. They come from Cincinatti here. She made $15.00 a week up there three years. I get $8.00 a month now from the Social Welfare. If I could see I could make money.

"I never seen times like this. Sin is causin' it. Unrest and selfishness. No neighborly spirit. I don't bother no young folks. I don't know how they will come out. If they caint get a big price they won't work and the white folks are doing their own work, and don't help like they did. I could get along if I could see. I had a light stroke keeps me from talkin' good, I hear that."

Interviewer: Thomas Elmore Lucy
Person interviewed: Henry Russell, Russellville, Arkansas
Age: 72

HENRY RUSSELL

"My father's name was Ed Russell, and he was owned by Dr. Tom Russell, de first pioneer settler of Russellville—de' man de town got its name from.

"My name is Henry, and some folks call me 'Bud.' I was born at Old Dwight de 28th of October, 1866. Yes suh, dat date is correct.

"I was too young to remember much about happenings soon after de War, but I kin ricollect my father belongin' to de militia for awhile during de Reconstruction days. Both Negroes and whites were members of de militia.

"My folks come here from Alabama, but I don't know much about them except dat my grandmother, Charlotte Edwards, give me an old wash pot dat has been in de family over one hundred years. Yes suh, it's out here in de ya'd now. Also, I owns an old ax handle dat I keep down at de store jist for a relic of old days. It's about a hundred years old, too.

"My wife was Sallie Johnson of Little Rock, and she was a sister of Mrs. Charley Mays, de barber you used to know, who was here sich a long time.

"For a long time I worked at different kinds of odd jobs, sometimes in de coal mines and sometimes on de farms, but for several years I've run a little store for de colored folks here in Russellville. Ain't able to do very much now.

"I remember very well de first train dat was ever run into Russellville. Must have been 68 or 69 years ago. A big crowd of people was here from all over de country. Of course dere was only a few families living in de town, and only one or two families of colored folks. People come in from everywhere, and it was a great sign. Little old train was no bigger dan de Dardanelle & Russellville train. (You remember de little old train dey used to call de 'Dinkey' don't you?) Well, it wasn't no bigger dan de Dinkey, and it didn't run into de depot at all, stopped down where de dump is now. Sure was a sight. Lot of de folks was afraid and wouldn't go near it, started to run when two men got off. I saw only two man working in front of it, but I remember it very plain. Dey was working with wheelbarrows and shovels to clear up de track ahead.

"Another thing I remember as a boy was de 'sassination of President Gyarfield. I can't read or write but very little, but I remember about dat. It was a dull, foggy mornin', and I was crossin' de bayou with Big Bob Smith. (You remember 'Big Bob' dat used to have the merry-go-'round and made all de county fairs.) Well, he told me all about de killing of de President. It was about 1881 wasn't it?

"I think times was better in de old days because people was better. Had a heap more honor in de old days dan dey have now. Not many young folks today have much character.

"All right. Come back again. Whenever I kin help you out any way, I'll be glad to."

NOTE: Henry Russell is quite proud of the fact that his ancestors were the first families of Russellville. He is a polite mulatto, uneducated, and just enough brogue to lend the Southern flavor to his speech, but is a fluent conversationalist.

United States. Work Projects Administration

Interviewer: Miss Sallie C. Miller
Person interviewed: Katie Rye, Clarksville, Arkansas
Age: 82

KATIE RYE

"We lived in Greenbrier, Faulkner County, Arkansas. All stayed at home and got along very well. We had enough to eat and wear. Mistress was awful mean to us but we stayed with them until after the war. After the war master moved us off to another place he had and my father farmed for his self, master and his pa and ma, and mistress' pa and ma. They awful good to us, but mistress was so high tempered she would get mad and whip some of the slaves but she never whipped any of us. She worried so over the loss of her slaves after the war she went crazy. We had two white grand pas and grand mas. We colored children called them grandpa and ma and uncle and aunt like the white children did and we didn't know the difference. The slaves was only allowed biscuit on Christmas and sometimes on Sundays but we had beef and plenty of honey and everything after we moved from the big house. Mistress used to come down to see us an' my mother would cook dinner for her and master. He was such a good man and the best doctor in the State. He would come in and take the babies up (mother had nine children) and get them to sleep for my mother. His mother would come to the kitchen and ask for a good cup of coffee and mother would make it for her. The master and his family were Northern people and my mother was given to the mistress by her father and mother when she married.

"After my father bought his own farm about ten miles from the big house, father would put us all in an ox wagon and take us back to see our white folks.

"The mistress claimed to be a Christian and church member but I don't see how she could have been she was so mean.

"I think the present day generation mighty wicked. Seems like they get worse instead of better, even the members of the church are not as good as they used to be. They don't raise the children like they used to. They used to go to Sunday School and church and take the children, now the children do as they please, roam the streets. It is sad to see how the parents are raising the children, just feed them and let them go. The children rule the parents now.

"We sang the old hymns and 'Dixie', 'Carry Me Back to Old Virginia', 'When You and I Were Young, Maggie'."

STATE—Arkansas
NAME OF WORKER—Miss Hazel Horn
ADDRESS—Little Rock, Arkansas
DATE—Last of April, 1936
SUBJECT—Ex-slave
[TR: Repetitive information deleted from subsequent pages.]

BOB SAMUELS

• Circumstances of Interview

1. Name and address of informant—**Uncle Bob Samuels**, Washington, Arkansas

2. Date and time of interview—Last of April, 1936

3. Place of interview—Washington, Arkansas

4. Name and address of person, if any, who put you in touch with informant—J.C.W. Smith.

5. Name and address of person, if any, accompanying you—J.C.W. Smith

6. Description of room, house, surroundings, etc.

• Personal History of Informant

1. Ancestry—Grandmother, Spanish; Grandfather, Negro; father, Negro.

2. Place and date of birth—Born about 1846

3. Family—

4. Places lived in, with dates—

5. Education, with dates—

6. Occupations and accomplishments, with dates—

7. Special skills and interests—

8. Community and religious activities—

9. Description of informant—Tall and straight. He is blind. Clean in appearance, dressed in slightly faded overalls. He has short, clean, grey beard. Speaks with a clear accent.

10. Other points gained in interview—Ancestors were in De Soto expeditions.

• Text of Interview (Unedited)

"From my mother's mother I learned that on my mother's side my ancestor came with De Soto from Spain where she was educated at Madrid. From Spain she came to Havana, Cuba, and from there to Tampa, Florida. From Florida she came to some point in Alabama. From this place she came to the Mississippi river and the East Bank and crossed where it is called Gaines Landing. After they crossed the river they went ten kilometers from there, traveled north from there to where Arkansas County is close to the mouth of the Arkansas River. Here they camped awhile. When they broke camp there they traveled northeast to Boiling Springs. Making their way from here they crossed the Ouachita River on the other side of Arkadelphia. They traveled on, crossing Little Missouri River below Wallaceburg. Here they found some Indian mounds. Then they traveled on a trail from there to Washington, turned into Washington and took a trail toward Columbus and turned off to the right (Uncle Bob not sure of the name of this trail) and crossed what is known as Beard's Lake. They crossed Little River at Ward's Ferry and crossed the Saline river. Traveling northwest they reached White Oak shoals where Index is now and crossed over into what was Mexico and traveled to a place called Kawaki located where [TR: ?] now is.

"After camping here for a while they came back into Arkansas to some point near Rando, crossed Red River at Dooley's Ferry, went to Coola Fabra(?) and back to Boiling Springs. [Here a gold mine was found and a quarrel ensued, and in a fight De Soto was killed.] They carried his body overland and buried him in the Mississippi River between Grensville[HW:sp.] and Vicksburg. [TR: Moved from end of interview: De Soto was buried at the junction of the Mississippi and [??] Rivers, about 100 miles south of Vicksburg.] The remaining forces of the expedition returned to Spain.

"Sometime in 1816 my mother's mother was born. My mother's mother was Spanish. My mother says she was well educated. Mother and her mother have Spanish mixed with Negro blood. I had a sister named Mary and a brother named John.

"Armarilla, my grandmother came here from Cuba through to Gaines Landing. Her son Edmin and her husband were with her. They crossed the Mississippi River and she said they stopped at the old De Soto camp. A short distance west of this place they met two men— Nick Trammel and John Morrow who profited (dealt) in Negro slaves. My grandfather and mother employed these men to guide them to Coola Fabre(?) Camden?. From Little River to Dooley's Ferry these men carried them to Waco, Texas. They killed my grandfather and kept my grandmother forcing her to marry either a half-breed Mexican, an Indian or a Negro. It was near Waco in Hickman[HW:sp.] Prairie that mother was born. The boy Edmin was returned to Dooley's Ferry and remained in the vicinity until he was about seventeen years of age. He then lived in the vicinity of Little Rock about six months before returning to Mexico. My grandmother said that Mr. Trammel and Mr. Morrow probably thought he might cause trouble and killed him as she never saw him after he returned from Little Rock. Mother was held in Lafayette County at a point where the river crossed and joined Bowie County (Texas) and where Louisiana bounded the south.

"De Soto traveled by land, not by boat. He had a force of about 550 persons. The women dressed as men. My grandmother was with her husband.

"My mother was a slave. She was held in Bowie County, Hickens[HW:sp.] Prairie, by Bob Trammel. They kept her locked up and I have heard mother say that she used whale bone, card bats and a spinning wheel. Finally they got so hot behind the Trammels in 1847-48, they pulled up stakes and went down on the Guadalupe River and carried my mother's mother down there. Before they left Dave Block went on Trammel's bond and got my mother. He made my mother head housekeeper slave. She had been taught Spanish. She was tall and fair with straight black hair. She was married to Dick Samuels, my father.

"After the war my father was elected [HW: Hempstead]

County Clerk in 1872 on the Republican ticket. He could neither read nor write, so was clerk in name only securing one of the white men to attend to the office. By trade he was a blacksmith."

• Interviewer's Comment

Uncle Bob Samuels is the son of Richard Samuels and Mary. He was a slave of David Block. After freedom he came to Little Rock with a sister and a brother, John. Uncle Bob said he often heard his mother speak of a gold mine. She had a trunk of maps and charts which her mother had given to her. In this was supposed to be the papers regarding De Soto's legendary gold mine. The trunk had been lost as Uncle Bob has no idea where the gold mine is. He tells the story the same way, never varying a point. He does not claim to remember Indian trails or names.

Uncle Bob is tall and straight. He is blind. Was clean in appearance dressed in slightly faded overalls. He has a short, clean grey beard. He talks with a clear accent, no Negro accent. During Reconstruction days he served as County Clerk of Hempstead County under Carpetbagger rule. During those days he was a political power to be reckoned with. He was a national as well as a state figure in the "Lily White Republican" organization. [His wife was a Negro, good looking, but showed little trace of much white blood.]

United States. Work Projects Administration

Interviewer: Mary D. Hudgins
Person Interviewed: Emma Sanderson
Home: 617 Wade Street, Hot Springs.
Aged: 75

EMMA SANDERSON

"Emma Sanderson"—"Wade Street". That was all the prospective interviewer could learn. "Emma Sanderson—ex-slave!" "Wade Street"—"Why it's way off that way. You go sort of thatta way, and then thatta way."

A city map disclosed no Wade Street. Maps belonging to a local abstractor helped not a whit. "Insurance maps are in more detail." someone advised, "Wade Street," mused the young woman at the desk, "I've heard of it. We have written a policy for someone there." The head of the department was new to the city, but he was eager to help. After about five minutes search—from wall maps to bound volumes of blocks and back again it appeared that "Wade Street" more frequently known as "Washington Street" meanders wanderingly from Silver Street, in the colored section out to the "Gorge addition" inhabited by low economic level whites.

Down Malvern Avenue (Hot springs' Beale Street) went the interviewer. On she went past the offices of a large Chicago packing house. For better then a block she trudged by dilapidated shops which a few seasons back had housed one of the key transient centers of the U.S.A. Down the street she walked, pausing for a moment to note that coffee colored faces decorated the placards in the beauty shop window—two well groomed mulatto girls sitting inside, evidently operators. Her course took her past sandwich joints and pool halls. Nails, she noted as she drifted along, had been driven into the projection beneath the plate glass window of the brick bank (closed during the depression—a building and bank built, owned and operated by negro capital) to keep loungers away. The colored theater (negroes are admitted only to the balconies of theaters in Hot Springs—one section of the balcony at the legitimate theater) she noticed was now serving as a religious gathering place. The well built and excellently maintained Pythian Bath house (where the hot waters are made available to colored folk) with the Alice Eve Hospital (45 beds, 5 nurses, 2 resident physicians—negro doctors thruout the town cooperating—surgical work a specialty) stood out in quiet dignity. For the rest, buildings were an indiscriminate hodgepodge of homes, apartment houses, shacks, and chain groceries. At the corner where "the street turns white" the interviewer turned east.

The Langston High School (for colored—with a reputation for turning out good cooks, football players and academicians) stands on Silver Street. A few paces from the building the interviewer met a couple of plump colored women laughing and talking loudly.

"I beg your pardon," was her greeting, "can you tell me where Wade Street is?" They could and did. They were so frankly interested in knowing why the white women wanted Emma Sanderson that she told them her mission.

They were not taken aback—there was no servility—no resentment they were frankly charmed with the idea. Their directions for finding Mrs. Sanderson became even more explicit.

When the proper turn off was found the question of Wade versus Washington Street was settled. A topsy-turvy sign at the intersection announced that Wade Street was ahead. Emma Sanderson's grandson lived a couple of blocks down the road.

Only the fact that she could hear someone inside moving about kept the interviewer hammering on the door. Finally she was rewarded by a voice. "Is that somebody a' knockin'?" In a moment the door opened. The question, "Were you a slave" no matter how delicately put is a difficult one to ask, but Mrs. Sanderson was helpful, if doubtful that her story would do much good. "I was just so little when it all happened." But the interviewer was invited in and placed in a chair near the fire.

"No ma'am. He ain't my grandson—I's the third grandmother. No son, you ain't three—you's five. Don't you remember what I told you? Yes, he stays with me, ma'am. I take care of him while the rest of 'em works.

"It's hard for me to remember. I was just so little. Yes, ma'am, I was born a slave—but I was so little. Seems to me like I remember a big, big house. We was sort of out in the country---out from Memphis. I know there was my father and my mother and my uncles and my aunts. I know there was that many. How many more of us old man Doc Walker had—I just don't know. They must have took good care of us tho. My mother was a house nigrah.

"When the war was ready to quit they gave us our pick. We could stay on and work for wages or we could go. The folks decided that the'd go on in to Memphis. My Mother and Father didn't live together none after we went to town. First I lived with Mother and then when she died my Father took me. My mother died when I was 9. She worked at cooking and washing. When I was big enough I went to school. I kept on going to school after my Father took me. He died when I was about 15. By that time I was old enough to look out after myself.

"What did I do? I stayed in folkses houses. I cooked and I washed. Then when I was about 16, I married. After that I had a man to take care of me. He was a carpenter.

"We been here in Hot Springs a long time—you maybe heared of Sanderson—he took up platering and he was good too. How long I been in Hot Springs—law I don't know—'cept I was a full grown women when we come.

"I's had four children—all of 'em is dead. I lives with my grandson. The little fellow, he'll be old enough to go to school in a year or two. A dime for him ma'am—an' 2 cents besides? Now son you keep the dime and you can spend the pennies. I always tries to teach him to save. Then when he gets big he'll know what to do."

Dining room and living room joined one another by means of a high and wide arch. The stove was sensibly set up in this passage. Both rooms were comfortably furnished with products which had in all probability been bought new. The child stood close by thruout the entire conversation. There was no whit of timidity about him, nor was he the least impertinent. He was frankly interested and wanted to know what was being said. He received the dime and the pennies with a pleasant grin and a (grandmother prompted) "Thank you". But the gift didn't startle him. Dimes must have been a fairly usual part of his life. But a few minutes before the interviewer left she dropped her pencil. It was new and long and yellow. The child's eyes clung to it as he returned it. "Would you like to have it." the young woman asked, "would you like a pencil of your very own, to draw with?" Would he! The child's whole face beamed. Dimes were as nothing compared to shiney new pencils. The third grandchild was overjoyed with his new plaything. Ella Sanderson was delighted with her great grandchild's pleasure. The interviewer received a warm and friendly "Good-bye".

United States. Work Projects Administration

Interviewer: Miss Irene Robertson
Person Interviewed: Mary Scott
DeValls Bluff or Biscoe
Age:

MARY SCOTT

"I said if ever I seed you agin I'd show you dis here scar on my head. See here [a puffed-out, black, rusty, not quite round place, where no hair grew]. Dat dar what my young mistress put on me when I was a chile. Dock Hardy hired me. He was rich and married a pore gal. It went to her head. He was good to me. She was mean. She had him whoop me a time or two for nothin'. They had two little babies, I stayed round wid. I loved em. I churned, brought in all the wood mighty near, brought bout all the water from the spring. Master Dock be coming horseback from Franklin, Tennessee. I knowed bout time I take the babies to meet him. He'd wait at a big stump we could climb on his horse, take the baby in front and us up behind him, and put us off on the back piazza at the house. I wrapped up the churn and quit. She ax me what I quit churnin' for. I say the butter come. She say it ain't had time. I say it ready to take up anyhow. She got so mad she throwed a stick of stove wood, hit me on my head. I run out crying, the blood streamin' down. I started to the spring, come back and got the water bucket. I got me some water and brought back a fresh bucket full. I washed my head in cool water where it was bleedin'. It bled all way back. She say, 'Where you been?' I say I been to the spring, brought some cool water to the babies. I give em some I told her. When I got water I always give them some. She took the bucket, made me go wid her, poured the water out in the path under a shade tree, and made me take 'nother bucketful home. I thought she was so mean; I didn't know what she was doing that about. Got to the house she put me on a clean chemisette. I slipped off down to the feed house, lay down, my head on the cotton seeds, and went to sleep.

"When Master Dock come he woke me up, wanted to know why I didn't meet him. He seen that blood. Went on to the house. He ask her what done my head that way. She say, 'She went to the spring, fell down, spilled the water, and hurt it on a rock.' I told him that wasn't so—not so! I told him all bout it. He told her she ought to be 'shamed treat good little nigger chap mean. He was so sorry for me. She didn't care. They had been goin' to old missis house every week. It was three weeks 'fo she would go. I got to see my mama, 'fo she died.

"Old Mistress Emily was a doctor woman. Dock told her, 'Mama, Scrubbs jumps and screams bout a hour late every evening wid her head.' When it got late it hurt and I screamed and jump up and down. Mistress Emily come got me in her arms, put me to sleep. When I woke up Dock and Kitty gone home with the babies. I cried bout being from the babies; I loved em, never been away from em 'fo. She got three maggots and says, 'Scrubbs, see what I got out your little head.' Mama had died then. She say, 'Your mama would want me to keep you here wid me.' She kept me till it healed up. Them maggots big as a sage broom straw. We swept the floor wid sage straw tied together then. Mistress Emily kept me a month with her and doctored my head every day. I slept on a pallet and on a little bed she had in the room. When I went back to Kitty's she wasn't as mean to me as she been—but mean nough then.

"My mama named Amy Hardy. She had five boys, three girls. She died with a young baby. I reckon they had different papas. I was my papa's only chile. They all said that. Bout a month after I went to Dock and Kitty's, it was surrender. He (the little Negro girl's father) come, stayed all night, and took me wid him to live. Dock wanted me to stay; I love Dock and the children. Every year till a few years ago my head get sore and run. We tried all kinds medicine on it. Don't know what cured it.

"The week 'fo I left there I had a task to make a cut of thread every night, a reel. When I heard papa was coming to git me, I put cotton bats under the reels and kivered em up. Good thing papa got me—Kitty would killed me when she went to spin next week. She been so mean why I done that way.

"They never sold any of our set but some on the place was sold. The mothers grieve and grieve over their children bein' sold. Some white folks let their slaves have preachin', some wouldn't. We had a bush arbor and set on big logs. Children set round on the ground. 'Fo freedom I never went to preachin'. I kept Kitty's babies so she went. Mothers didn't see their children much after they was sold.

"Fo freedom they would turn a wash pot upside-down at the door and have singin' and prayer meetin'. The pot would take up the noise. They done that when they danced too. I don't know how they found out the iron pot would take up the noise. They had plenty of em settin' round in them days. Somebody found it out and passed it on."

Interviewer: Miss Irene Robertson
Person interviewed: Mollie Hardy Scott, R.F.D., DeValls Bluff, Arkansas
Age: 90

MOLLIE HARDY SCOTT

"I was born at Granville, Georgia in Franklin County. I don't know my age cept I was big enough to plow when young master lef and went to war. My mother died bout time the war started. We belonged to Miss Eliza and Master Jim Hardy. He had two boys bout grown, Jim and John. My father belong to the Linzys. I don't know nuthin much bout them nor him neither. When the war was done he come and got me and we went to Barton County, Georgia. When I lef they give me my feather bed, two good coverlets and my clothes. White folks hated fo me to leave. We all cried but I never seen em no more. They said he take me off and let me suffer or die or something. I was all the child my father had but my mother had ten children I knowed of. We all lived on the place. They lived in a little log house and I stayed wid em some an up at white folks house mostly. No I never seed my folks no more. We had plenty to eat. Had meat and garden stuff. We had pot full of lye hominy. It last several days. It was good. I seed em open up a pot full of boiled corn-on-the-cob. Plenty milk and butter. We had wash pot full of collards or turnip salad. Maybe a few turnips on top and a big piece of fresh meat. We had plenty to eat and wear long as I lived wid the white folks. We had goobers, molasses candy to pull and pop corn every now and then. They fill all the pockets, set around the fire an eat at night. Sometimes we bake eggs and sweet potatoes, cracklin hoe cake covered up in the ashes. Bake apples in front of the fire on de hearth. Everybody did work an we sho had plenty to eat an wear.

"I had plenty when I stayed at my father's an we worked together all the time. When he died I married. I've had a hard time not able to work. There ain't no hard time if yous able to get bout. I pieces quilts an sells em now. Sells em if I can. For $150 piece (has no idea of money value). Some women promised to come git 'em but they ain't come yet. I wanter buy me some shoes. I could do a heap if they send fo me. I can nurse. I kept a woman's children when she teached last year (Negro woman's children).

"I brought four or five when I come to Arkansas of my own. They all dead but my one girl I lives wid.

"Seemed lack so many colored folks coming out West to do better. We thought we come too. We come on immigrate ticket on the train. All the people I worked for was Captain Williams, Dr. Givens. Mr. Richardson right where Mesa is now but they called it 88 then (88 miles from Memphis). Mr. Gates. I farmed, washed and ironed. I nursed some since I'm not able to get about in the field. I never owned nothing. They run us from one year till the next and at the end of the year they say we owe it bout all. If we did have a good crop we never could get ahead. We couldn't get ahead nuff not to have to be furnished the next year. We did work but we never could get ahead. If a darky sass a white land owner he would be whooped bout his account or bout anything else. Yes siree right here in dis here county. Darky have to take what the white folks leave fo em and be glad he's livin.

"I say I ain't never voted. Whut in de world I would want er vote for? Let em vote if they think it do em good.

"I seen a whole gang of Ku Kluxes heap of times when I was little back in Georgia. I seed paddyrollers and then they quit and at night the Ku Kluxes rode by. They would whoop or shoot you either if you didn't tend to yo own business and stay at home at night. They kept black and white doing right I tell you. I sho was afraid of them but they didn't bother us. If you be good whose ever place you lives on would keep 'em from harmin you. They soon got all the bad Yankies ran back North from Georgia. They whip the black men and women too but it was mostly the men they watched and heap of it was for stealing. Folks was hungry. Couldn't help stealin if they seed anything. I seed heap of folks having a mighty hard time after the war in them restruction (Reconstruction) days. I was lucky.

"My daughter would do mo than she do fo me but she is a large woman and had both her legs broke. They hurt her so bad it is hard fo her to do much. She good as she can be to everybody. The Welfare give three of us $10.00 a month (daughter, husband, and Mollie). We mighty glad to get that. We sho is. I am willin to work if I could get work I could do. That's my worst trouble. Like I tell you, I can nurse and wash dishes if I could get the jobs.

"I don't see much of the real young folks. I don't know what they are doing much. If a fellow is able he ought to be able to do good now if he can get out and go hunt up work fo himself. That the way it look like. I don't know."

Interviewer: Thomas Elmore Lucy
Person interviewed: Sam Scott, Russellville, Arkansas
Age: 79

SAM SCOTT

"Hello dar, Mistah L----! Don' you dare pass by widout speakin' to dis old niggah friend of yo' chil'hood! No suh! Yuh can't git too big to speak to me!

"Reckon you've seen about all dar is to see in de worl' since I seen you, ain't you? Well, mos' all de old-time niggahs and whites is both gone now. I was born on de twentieth of July, 1879. Count up—dat makes me 79 (born 1859), don't it? My daddy's name was Sam, same as mine, and mammy's was Mollie. Dey was slaves on de plantation of Capt. Scott—yes suh, Capt. John R. Homer Scott—at Dover. My name is Sam, same as my father's, of course. Everybody in de old days knowed Sam Scott. My father died in slavery times, but mother lived several years after.

"No, I never did dance, but I sure could play baseball and make de home runs! My main hobby, as you calls it, was de show business. You remember de niggah minstrels we used to put on. I was always stage manager and could sing baritone a little. Ed Williamson and Tom Nick was de principal dancers, and Tom would make up all de plays. What? Stole a unifawm coat of yours? Why,

I never knowed Tom to do anything like that! Anyway, he was a good-hearted niggah—but you dunno what he might do. Yes, I still takes out a show occasionally to de towns around Pope and Yell and Johnson counties, and folks treat us mighty fine. Big crowds—played to $47.00 clear money at Clarksville. Usually take about eight and ten in our comp'ny, boys and gals—and we give em a real hot minstrel show.

"De old show days? Never kin forgit em! I was stage manager of de old opery house here, you remember, for ten years, and worked around de old printin' office downstairs for seven years. No, I don't mean stage manager—I mean property man—yes, had to rustle de props. And did we have road shows dem days! Richards & Pringle's Georgia minstrels, de Nashville students, Lyman Twins, Barlow Brothers Minstrels, and—oh, ever so many more—yes, Daisy, de Missouri Girl, wid Fred Raymond. Never kin forgit old black Billy Kersands, wid his mouf a mile wide!

"De songs we used to sing in old days when I was a kid after de War wasn't no purtier dan what we used to sing wid our own minstrel show when we was at our best twenty-five and thirty years ago; songs like 'Jungletown,' 'Red Wing,' and 'Mammy's Li'l Alabama Coon.' Our circuit used to be around Holla Bend, Dover, Danville, Ola, Charleston, Nigger Ridge, out from Pottsville, and we usually starred off at the old opery house in Russellville, of course.

"I been married, but ain't married now. We couldn't git along somehow. Yes suh, I been right here workin' stiddy for a long time. Been janitor at two or three places same time; was janitor of de senior high school here for twenty-two years, and at de Bank of Russellville twenty-nine years.

"Folks always been mighty nice to me—and no slave ever had a finer master dan old Captain Scott.

"In de old show days de manager of de opery always said. 'Let de niggers see de show,' and sometimes de house was half full of colored folks—white folks on one side de house and niggahs on de other—and dere never was any disturbance of any kind. Ain't no sich good times now as we had in de old road show days. No suh!"

NOTE: Sam Scott, who has been personally known to the interviewer for many years, is above the average of the race for integrity and truthfulness. His statement that he was born a few years after slavery and that his father died during slavery was not questioned the matter being a delicate personal affair and of no special moment.

Interviewer: Miss Irene Robertson
Person interviewed: Cora Scroggins, Clarendon, Arkansas
Age: 48 or 50

CORA SCROGGINS

"My mother was born in Spring Hill, Tennessee and brought to Arkansas by her master. Her name was Margaret. Dr. and Mrs. Porter brought my mother to Batesville, Arkansas when she was eight years old and raised her. She was very light. She had long straight hair but was mixed with white. She never knew much about her parents or people.

"Mr. William Brook (white) came to De Valls Bluff from Tennessee and brought her sister soon after the War. She was a very black woman.

"Dr. Porter had a family. One of their daughters was Mrs. Mattie Long, another Mrs. Willie Bowens. There were others. They were all fine to my mother. She married in Dr. Porter's home. Mrs. Porter had learnt her to sew. My father was a mechanic. My mother sewed for both black and white. She was a fine dressmaker. She had eight children and raised six of us up grown.

"My father was a tall rawbony brown man. His mother was an Indian squaw. She lived to be one hundred seven years old. She lived about with her children. The white folks all called her 'Aunt Matildy' Tucker. She was a small woman, long hair and high cheek bones. She wore a shawl big as a sheet purty nigh all time and smoked a pipe. I was born in Batesville.

"My mother spoke of her one long journey on the steamboat and stagecoach. That was when she was brought to Arkansas. It made a memorable picture in her mind.

"Dr. and Mrs. Porter told her she was free and she could go or stay. And she had nowheres to go and she had always lived with them white folks. She never did like black folks' ways and she raised us near like she was raised as she could.

"She used to tell us how funny they dressed and how they rode at night all through the country. She seen them and she could name men acted as Ku Kluxes but they never bothered her and she wasn't afraid of them.

"I cooked all my life till I got disabled. I never had a child. I wish I had a girl. I've been considered a fine cook all of my life."

STATE— Arkansas
NAME OF WORKER— Bernice Bowden
ADDRESS— 1006 Oak Street, Pine Bluff, Arkansas
DATE— November 4, 1938
SUBJECT— Ex-slaves
[TR: Repetitive information deleted from subsequent pages.]

SARAH SEXTON

- ## Circumstances of Interview

1. Name and address of informant—**Sarah Sexton**, Route 4, Box 685, Pine Bluff

2. Date and time of interview—November 3, 1958, 10:00 a.m.

3. Place of interview—Route 4, Box 685, Pine Bluff, Arkansas

4. Name and address of person, if any, who put you in touch with informant—Georgia Caldwell, Route 6, Box 128, Pine Bluff, Arkansas.

5. Name and address of person, if any, accompanying you—None.

6. Description of room, house, surroundings, etc.—Frame house, front porch with two swings. Fence around yard. Chinaberry tree and Tree of Paradise, Coxcomb in yard. Southeast of Norton-Wheeler Stave Mill just off Highway 65.

• Text of Interview

"Prewitt Tiller bought my mother and I belonged to young master. In slavery I was a good-sized-young girl, mama said. Big enough to put the table cloths on the best I could. After freedom I did all the cookin' and milkin' and washin'.

"Now listen, this young master was Prewitt's son.

"Grandpa's name was Ned Peeples and grandma was Sally Peeples. My mother was Dorcas. Well, my papa, I ain't never seed him but his name was Josh Allen. You see, they just sold 'em around. That's what I'm talkin' about—they went by the name of their owners.

"I'm seventy-eight or seventy-nine or eighty. That's what the insurance man got me up.

"I been in a car wreck and I had high blood pressure and a stroke all at once. And that wreck, the doctor said it cracked my skull. Till now, I ain't got no remembrance.

"You know how long I went to school? Three days. No ma'm I had to work, darlin'.

"I was born down here on Saline River at Selma. I done forgot what month."

"What kinda work have I done? Oh, honey, I done farmed myself to death, darlin'. You know Buck Couch down here at Noble Lake? Well, I hoped pick out eight bales of cotton for him.

"I wish I had the dollars I had workin' for R.A. Pickens down here at Walnut Lake. Yes, honey, I farmed for him bout fifteen or twenty years steady.

"And he sure was nice and he was mischievous. He called all of us his chillun. He use to say, 'Now you must mind your papa!' And we'd say 'Now Mr. Pickens, you know you ain't got no nigger chillun'. He use to say to me 'Sallie, you is a good woman but you ain't got no sense'. Them was fine white folks.

"Honey, these white folks round here what knows me, knows they ain't a lazy bone in my body.

"I'se cooked and washed and ironed and I'se house-cleaned. Yes'm, I certainly was a good cook.

"I belongs to the Palestine Baptist Church. Yes ma'm. I don't know what I'd do if twasn't for the good Master. I talks to Him all the time.

"I goes to this here government school. A man teaches it. I don't know what his name is, we just calls him Professor.

"Well, chile, I'll tell you the truf. These young folks is done gone. And some o' these white headed women goes up here truckin'. It's a sin and a shame. I don't know what's gwine come of 'em."

• Interviewer's Comment

This woman lives with her daughter Angelina Moore who owns her home.

Mother and daughter both attend government school. Both were neatly dressed. The day was warm so we sat on the front porch during the interview.

• Personal History of Informant

1. Ancestry—Grandfather, Ned Peeples; grandmother, Sally Peeples; Mother, Dorcas Peeples; Father, Josh Allen.

2. Place and date of birth—On Saline River, Selma, Arkansas. No date.

3. Family—Two daughters and granddaughter.

4. Places lived in, with dates—Desha County, Walnut Lake, Noble Lake, (Arkansas) Poplar Bluff, Missouri. No dates.

5. Education, with dates—Three days, "after freedom". Attends government school now.

6. Occupations and accomplishments, with dates—Farmwork, cooking, laundry work until 1936.

7. Special skills and interests—Cooking.

8. Community and religious activities—Member of Palestine Baptist Church.

9. Description of informant—Medium height, plump, light complexion and gray hair.

10. Other points gained in interview—Injured in auto wreck seven years ago.

Interviewer: Miss Irene Robertson
Person interviewed: Roberta Shaver, West Memphis, Arkansas
Age: 50

ROBERTA SHAVER

"I was born close to Natchez, Mississippi. Grandma was sold at Wickerson County, Mississippi. They took her in a wagon to Jackson, Tennessee. She was mother of two children. They took them. She was part Indian. She was a farm woman. Her name was Dicy Jackson. They sold her away from the Jacksons to Dobbins. She was a house woman in Jackson, Tennessee. She said they was good to her in Tennessee. Grandma never was hit a lick in slavery. Grandpa was whooped a time or two. He run off to the woods for weeks and come back starved. He tended to the stock and drove Master Clayton around. He was carriage driver when they wanted to go places.

"After freedom grandma set out to get back to grandpa. Walked and rode too I reckon. She brought her children back. After a absence of five years she and grandpa went back together. They met at Natchez, Mississippi. Mama was born after freedom.

"The way grandma said she was sold was, a strange man come there one day and the master had certain ones he would sell stand in a line and this strange man picked out the ones he wanted and had them get their belongings and put them in the wagon and took them on off. She never seen grandpa for five years."

Interviewer: Mrs. Bernice Bowden
Person interviewed: Mary Shaw
1118 Palm Street, Pine Bluff, Arkansas
Age: 77
Occupation: Laundry work

MARY SHAW

"I was born in Bolivar County, Mississippi. My mother didn't know how old I was but after freedom I went by Miss Ann Blanchet's—that was my mother's old missis—and she said I was born in 1861.

"But I don't know nothin' 'bout slavery or the War. I was born and bred in the desert and my mother said it was a long time after freedom 'fore she knowed anything about it. She said there was just lots of the folks said, to their knowin', they had been free three years 'fore they knowed anything about it.

"My husband brought me to Arkansas when I was 35 and I been workin' in the same family, Captain Jeter's family, ever since—forty odd years.

"I always have worked hard. I've had the flu only reason I'm sittin' here now. If I had to sit and hold my hands very long, they'd have to take me to Little Rock.

"I been married twice. My last husband was Sam Shaw. He was a great whiskey man and when whiskey went out, he went to bootleggin' and they got behind him and he left.

"He wrote me once and said if I'd borrow some money on my home and send it to him, he'd come back. I wrote and told him just like I'm tellin' you that after I had worked night and day to pay for this house while he was off tellin' some other woman lies just like he told me, I wasn't goin' to send him money. So I ain't seen him since.

"I ain't never been to school much. When schools got numerous in Mississippi they had me behind a plow handle.

"Mrs. Jeter made me mad once and I quit. My first husband was a porter on the railroad and I got on the train and went to Memphis with him.

"One time he come back from a trip to Pine Bluff and handed me a little package. I opened it and it was a note from Mrs. Jeter and a piece of corn bread. She said, 'Now, Mary, you see what I've had to eat. I want you to come back.' So I went back and stayed 'til she died. And now I'm workin' for her daughter, Mrs. McEwen. Mrs. Jeter used to say, 'Mary, I know you're not a Arkansas woman 'cause you ain't got a lazy bone in your body.'"

Interviewer: Miss Irene Robertson
Person interviewed: Violet Shaw, West Memphis, Arkansas
Age: 50

VIOLET SHAW

"I heard Grandma Katie Williams say she was put up on a high stump and auctioned off. She told how great-grandma cried and cried and never seen her no more. Grandma come from Oakland, Tennessee to Mississippi. Grandma took the two young children and left the other two with great-grandma. They took her from her husband. She never seen none of them again.

"After freedom she didn't know how to find them. She never could get trace of them. She tried. She never married no more. I was born at Clarksdale, Mississippi. I have seen Tom Pernell (white), the young master, come and spend the night with Henry Pernell. Henry had once been Tom's father's slave and carriage driver. I was too small to know the cause but I remember that several times mighty well. They fixed him up a clean bed by hisself. Henry lived in town. But he might have been drunk. I never seen no misbehavior out of him. It was strange to me to see that.

"Freedom—Aunt Mariah Jackson was freed at Dublin, Mississippi. She said she was out in the field working. A great big white man come, jumped up on a log and shouted, 'Freedom! Freedom!' They let the log they was toting down; six, three on a side, had holt of a hand stick toting a long heavy log. They was clearing up new ground. He told them they was free. They went to the house. They cooked and et and thanked God. Some got down and prayed, some sung. They had a time that day. They got the banjo and fiddle and set out playing. Some got in the big road just walking. She said they had a time that day."

Texarkana District
FOLKLORE SUBJECTS
Name of Interviewer: Cecil Copeland
Subject: Ex-Slave

This information given by: Frederick Shelton
Place of Residence: Dump Section, Texarkana, Arkansas
Occupation: None
Age: 81
[TR: Information moved from bottom of first page.]

FREDERICK SHELTON

In an humble cabin on the outskirts of the city lives a venerable old negro ex-slave. Although bent with rheumatism and age, he still retains his mental faculties to a remarkable degree.

An inquiry as to his health elicited the following reply: "I'se a willful mind but a weak body. Just like an old tree—de limbs are withered and almost dead. I'se been here a long tins, ovah 81 years, and am ready to go any time de good Lawd says de word. Dat's de trouble wid de people nowadays—dey ain't prepared. Back when I wuz a young man, dey wuzn't so much meaness, and such goings on as dey are nowadays. De young-peple know as much as de old folks. Yas, suh, de worl' am goin' to de dogs."

Asked about life in pioneer days, the old negro replied; "We had lots ob good times in dem days. Log rollings wuz lots ob fun to me as I wuz strong den, an' I could "show off" befo' de odder niggers. Dey wuzn't much rollin' to it, mostly carrying. I mind de time when I lifted de end ob a log, an' four men tried at different times to lift de odder, but dey couldn't do it. Three of dese men went to an early grave from trying to lift dis log—all tore up inside. Maybe dat's whut ails me.

"You had to be careful den, when traveling through de woods, or de varmints would git you, especially at night. I mind de time when a negro wuz comin' through de woods one nite, when he seed a panther about to spring on him.

"Dis nigger dropped in his tracks lack he wuz dead. De panther came up to him and smelled ob him, but de nigger held his breath, and de panther thought he wuz dead. De panther covered him wid leaves an' went about one hundred yards into de woods to call his friends to de feast. No sooner had he left when de nigger jumped up and climbed a tree, first rutting an old chunk of wood in de place where he wuz buried. De nigger could hear de panther out in de woods as he called for his friends, and pretty soon, here dey come, about five of 'em. Slowly circling aroun' de place where de nigger had been, all of a sudden dey all jumped. Findin' nothin' but de old chunk of wood, dem panthers got real mad. Wid angry growls, dey jumped on de one whut had called dem, and ate him up."

This old negro reserves all of the heroic roles for others. Asked if he had had any experience with the "varmints", as he termed them he said: "Yas, suh. De worst scared I ever got wuz frum a wolf. Walkin' down a trail one day, I spied a wolf not more than ten feet away. Man, I wuz so scared dat I seemed to freeze in my tracks, and couldn't move. I tried to holler but all I could do wuz croak. Den I tried to whistle but de only sound I could make wuz a hiss. After standing for whut seemed hours, wid his ears sticking straight up, de wolf finally turned around and trotted away."

The conversation drifted to other topics, and finally to ghosts and spirits. The old negro said he had never seen a ghost, and didn't believe in those things. No sooner had he said this when his wife, who had been listening in on the conversation from the inside of the door exclaimed: "I does! Seein' is believin' aint it? Well suh, about two years ago de negro dat lived next door died. A few weeks after he died I wuz settin' out on de porch when I see dis negro come out of de house, and walk slowly to de corner of mah yard where he vanished into de air. A few nights later de same thing happened again. No suh, dat nigger didn't go to Heaven and he didn't go to Hell. He's still around heah. He wuz a wicked negro and wuz scared to go."

United States. Work Projects Administration

STATE—Arkansas
NAME OF WORKER—Samuel S. Taylor
ADDRESS—Little Rock, Arkansas
DATE—December, 1938
SUBJECT—Ex-slave
[TR: Repetitive information deleted from subsequent pages.]

LAURA SHELTON

- **Circumstances of interview**

1. Name and address of informant—**Laura Shelton**, 1518 Pulaski Street, Little Rock, Arkansas.

2. Date and time of interview interview—

3. Place of interview—1518 Pulaski Street, Little Rock, Arkansas.

4. Name and address of person, if any who put you in touch with informant—

5. Name and address of person, if any, accompanying you—

Description of room, house, surroundings, etc.—

- **Personal History of Informant**

1. Ancestry—mother, Susan Barnett; father, Ben Bearden; grandfather, Harvey Barnett.

2. Place and date of birth—Arkansas, 1878

3. Family—Three children.

4. Education, with dates—

5. Places lived in with dates—Jerome, Arkansas and Little Rock. No dates.

6. Occupations and accomplishments, with dates—Farmed, wash and iron.

7. Special skills and interests—

8. Community and religious activities—Belongs to Baptist Church.

9. Description of informant—

10. Other points gained in interview—

• Text of Interview (Unedited)

"My mother used to sit down and talk to us and tell us about slavery. If she had died when I was young I wouldn't have known much. But by her living till I was old, I learned a lot.

"My mother's old master was Tom Barnett, so she said. No, not 'so she said' because I have seed him. He give her her age and all at that time. I have it in my Bible. He said that she was twelve years old the Christmas before the surrender. The surrender was in May, wasn't it?

"My mother's name was Susan Bearden. She married Ben Bearden. She worked in Tom Barnett's house. She milked and churned and 'tended to the children and all such as that. He never allowed her to go to the field.

Neither her mother, my grandmother. She was the cook. My mother's name before she married was Susan Barnett.

"An old colored lady that they had there seed after the colored children. She looked after my mother too. She was so old she couldn't do nothin' so they had her to look after the children. My grandmother was kept busy because she had the white folks to cook for and she had all the colored folks to cook for too.

"There is an old lady down on Spring Street that can give you a lot of information about slavery times.

"A boy was telling her that somebody was going 'round asking questions about slavery and she said she wished he would come and see her.

"My mother never had any chance to go to school before freedom and she never had any chance to go afterwards because she didn't have any money. When they turned them loose the white folks didn't give 'em anything, so they had to work. They didn't allow them to pick up a piece of paper in slave time for fear they would learn.

"My mother remembered the pateroles. She said they used to catch and whip the colored men and women when they would get out.

"My mother's old master was the one that told mama she was free. He told her she was free as he was. After they learned that they were free, they stayed on till Christmas.

"After Christmas, they went to another plantation. My gran'pa, he come and got them all to come. My gran'pa's name was Harvey Barnett. His old master's son had married and he had been staying with him. That made him be on another place. There was a good many of the children in my grandmother's family. Mama had a sister named Lucy, one named Lethe, one named Caroline, one named Annie, and one named Jane. She had two boys — one named Jack, and one named Barnett. She had another sister named — I don't remember her name.

"After freedom, we sharecropped for a number of years up until my father died. He died about twenty-four years ago.

"After that mama washed and ironed for about ten or twelve years. Then she got too old to work and we took care of her. My mother died last March on the ninth day. She always had good health for an old lady. Never got so she couldn't get up and do her light work such as dress herself, cooking, sweeping, and so on. She would even do her own washing and ironing if we would let her. She would hide from us and pick cotton till we stopped her.

"She was sick only one week and the doctor said she died of old age. He said it was just her time. She didn't have nothin' the matter with her but jus' old age he said so far as he could find. Dr. Fletcher was our doctor. She died in Jerome, Arkansas about sixteen miles from the Louisiana line. Leastwise, they tell me it's about sixteen miles from the line. She always told us that she had her business fixed with the Lord and that when she taken sick, It wouldn't be long. And sure 'nough, it wasn't.

"I farmed until my mother and brother died. Then I came up here with my sister as I had no children living. I jus' wash and iron now whenever I can get somethin' to do.

"I have been married once. I had three children. All of them are dead. My children are dead and my husband is dead.

"I belong to the Baptist church down on Spring Street. I always unite with the church whenever I go to a place. I don't care whether I stay there or not.

"My mama's master was good as far as white folks generally be in slavery times. He never whipped my grandmother nor my mother. He was good to the field hands too. He never whipped them. He would feed them too. He had right smart of field hands but I don't know just how many. I don't think he ever sold any of his slaves. I think he come by them from his father because I have heard them say that his father told him before he died never to 'part with Black Mammy. That was what he called her. And he kept them altogether jus' like his father told him to. His father said, 'I you to keep all my Negroes together and Black Mammy I don't want you let her be whipped because she nursed all of you.' She said she never was whipped 'cept once when she got a cockle berry up her nose and he got it out and gave her a little brushing—not as much as grandma would have given her.

"He kept them all in good shoes and warm clothes and give them plenty to eat. So many of the slaves on other plantations didn't have half enough to eat and were half naked and barefooted all the time."

Interviewer: Miss Irene Robertson
Person interviewed: Mahalia Shores, Marianna, Arkansas
Age: 77

MAHALIA SHORES

"I was born in Greene County, Georgia. My owner was Jim Jackson. He bought my mother's father. She was raised on Jim Jackson's place. I rec'collect a right smart about slavery times. He made us dress up and let the nigger traders see what little niggers I got. We thought it was nice. What fine limbs we had. Aunt Judy—some called her 'big mamma'—lived down under the hill. She was old and seen after the children. The biggest children took care and nursed the little ones. On Wednesday and Saturday the cook made ginger cakes for the little children. The house girl called us. She was Aunt Teena's girl. Aunt Teena was a housemaid. See little niggers coming from every direction to get our cakes.

"Jim Jackson's wife was named Mariah. They lived in a big fine white house. When it was freedom a soldier come, brought a paper and Massa Jim was settin' on the porch. Tom Chapman was his overseer. They rung the big farm bell and had the oldest niggers stand in a line and us little ones in front so we could all see. Tom Chapman read the paper and stood by the soldier. He had two big plantations. Massa Jim got sick that day and vomited and vomited. He lived a week or two weeks. They sent for Dr.

Ducham but he couldn't do him no good. He died. Massa Jim told them they could take the teams and go to town, all he ax of 'em was to feed and take care of 'em. Every one of the grown folks went and left us at home. Aunt Judy seen 'bout us like she been doing all the time. They went over to Greensboro to celebrate. They all come back. They was all ready fer their breakfastes. It was twelve miles from Greensboro. Then the next day Massa Jim or Tom Chapman, one called the grown folks to the house and told them, 'You can stay and I will pay you or you can go. I pay no more doctor bills. I don't feed you no more nor give you no more clothes.' Some moved and some hired to him. Some went to his father-in-law's place and some to his brothers' place and around. His wife was rich. She was Dave Butler's gal. No, I mean Massa Jim's wife—Miss Mariah. That big place was what her pa give her. Massa Jim had five hundred little niggers on that place and lots more on the big plantation. He had about two thousand little niggers. We went in droves is right.

"I never went to a table in slavery time. We had our plates and cup and took it to the pot and they put some victuals in 'em, then we went and et where we pleased. We had all the meat we could eat and all the milk we could drink all the time. Aunt Teena sewed and grandma would weave cloth. They made white aprons. My hair was nice and old mistress would tell Aunt Judy to curl my hair. They rolled it up on cloth and on little light cobs. If they wet it, it would stay curled.

"Massa Jim sold his niggers when he wanted to. He sold my grandpa and Uncle Steve. Grandma wanted him to sell her and he wouldn't do it. I don't know what become of grandpa. After freedom Uncle Steve come back to us all. Grandpa was crying. He come to our house and said he had to go. We never seen him no more.

"Some of the slaves wouldn't be whooped by Tom Chapman. I heard them say since I got grown he 'tacked 'em. It caused trouble. He couldn't whoop 'em then. Old master whooped some of 'em. Some would say, 'I take ten licks offen you and that is all.' Then he would sell them the first chance. They would go to the woods if he beat them too much. He didn't abuse his niggers. He said his niggers was his property. Aunt Sarah tended to the cows and Aunt Clarisa raised geese, turkeys, chickens, ducks, and churned.

"The Ku Klux come to our house, called Uncle Billy—that was my papa. They got him up out of bed. One man said, 'I ain't had no water since the battle of Shiloah.' He had pa draw water till daybreaking. He had a horn he poured the water in. We was all scared half to death. Next morning there was a branch from the well done run off. Something took place about a well. Uncle Neel Anderson and Uncle Cush dug wells for their living. They come after them. Aunt Mandy had a baby. They pitied her and Uncle Neel got so scared he run upstairs in his shirt tail and stuck his head in the cotton. They found him that way. Uncle Cush said, 'Come on, Neel, and go with me.' They whooped Uncle Cush in his shirt tail. If you didn't open the door they would break it in.

"I worked in the field in Georgia and Arkansas both. I cooked since I was twelve years old. I married when I was twenty years old. I cooked here in Marianna eighteen years and I have cooked three Sunday dinners on Saturday and Sunday together. I would make three dollars when I done that. I had five children and I raised one boy. I washed and ironed. I get some help from the Welfare but I saved and my good old man saved so we would have plenty when we got old. Folks burnt up two of my houses. I got three more not fitten to live in till they are covered. I got good property in Stuttgart but couldn't pay the tax on it and 'bout to loose it. I tried to get a loan and never could. We niggers have a hard time."

Interviewer: Mrs. Bernice Bowden
Person interviewed: Rosa Simmons
823 West 13th Street, Pine Bluff, Arkansas
Age: 85?

ROSA SIMMONS

"Yes mam, I was here during that Civil War. I was fifteen years old then. I was born In Tennessee.

"My boss man carried all the best hands to Texas and carried the scrub hands across Cypress Creek here in Arkansas, and that's where I come. I was fifteen when the Yankees come in on my boss man's place, so you know now I ain't no baby. I thank God that He left me here to get old.

"Before the war. I nussed two babies—my mistress' baby and her sister's baby. Yes'm we had a good master and mistress. We didn't suffer for nothin' and we didn't have no overseer over us. Colonel Maples was my master. No'm he wasn't no soldier—that was the name his mother give him.

"When my folks first come to Arkansas we lived in a cabin that just had a balin' sack hangin' in the door and one night a bear come in and my brother and I broke a board off the side and fell right out in the cane. We all hollered so some folks come down and shot the bear. I ain't never seed a bear before and I didn't know what it was.

"I 'member when the Yankees come to my boss man's place. They wanted to shake hands but he was scared to death and wouldn't do it. Another time the Yankees captured him and kept him three months. They took his horse and he finally come home on a mule that didn't have but three legs. I guess the Yankees give him the mule. He turned the old mule loose and said he never wanted to see another Yankee. If he saw any kind of a white man comin' down the road he run in the house and hid between the feather bed and the mattress.

"One time the Yankees come and drunk the sweet milk and took all the butter, turkeys and hogs and then broke the powder horn against the maple tree.

"The cook say 'I'm gwine tell Marse Joe you drink all this milk.' The Yankees say, 'Let the damn fool alone—here we are tryin' to free her and she ain't got no sense.' They said there wouldn't be any more hard times after the war.

"But I sure have seen some hard times. I have washed and cooked and done 'bout everything.

"When I get up in the morning I got the limburger (lumbago) in my back so I ain't able to do much. Sometimes I have something to eat and sometimes I don't."

Mrs. Carol Graham
Mrs. Mildred Thompson
El Dorado District

Fannie Sims.
Customs.

FANNIE SIMS

"How ole is ah? Ise about 78. Yes'm ah wuz live durin de wah. Mah ole moster wuz Mistuh Jake Dumas we lived near de Ouachita rivuh bout five miles fum El Dorado landin. Ah membush dat we washed at de spring way, way fum de house. What dat yo say? Does ah know Ca'line. Ca'line, lawsy, me yes. Ca'line Washington we use tuh call huh, she wuz one uv Mr. Dumas niggers. We washed fuh de soldiers. Had tuh carry day clo'es tuh dem aftuh dark. Me an Ca'line had tuh carry dem. We had tuh hide de horse tuh keep de soldiers fum gittin him. When we would take de horse tuh de plum orchard we would stay dah all day to dark wid "Blackie". Dat wuz de horse's name. Mah job mostly wuz tuh watch de chillun an feed mah mistress chickens.

"Ah kin recollect when dey took us an started tuh Texas an got as fur as El Dorado and found out dat us niggers wuz free. We went back an grandma's mistress's son took us home wid him fuh stretches and stretches. We lived on de ole Camden road.

"In mah days ah've done plenty uv work but ah don' do nothing now but piece quilts. Dat's whut ah've been doing fuh mah white fokes since ah been heah. Ah jes finished piecing and quiltin two uv em. De Glove[TR:?] and de Begger. Mah husban' been dead 31 years dis pas' August. No, ah counts is by dose twins ah raised. One uv em lives in dis heah place right heah. Ah aint much count now. Sometime mah laig gets so big ah jes had tuh sloop mah foot erlong."

Interviewer: Miss Irene Robertson
Person interviewed: Jerry Sims (Indian and Negro)
Brinkley, Arkansas
Age: Born 1859

JERRY SIMS

"I was born in 1859 close to Natchez, Mississippi. Chief Sims was my grandpa. He was Indian, full blood. His wife was a Choctaw Indian. Grandpa was a small red Indian. They kept my pa hid out with stock nearly all time of the Civil War. Both my mas' parents was nearly all Indian too but they was mixed. I'm more Indian than anything else. I heard pa talk about staying in the cane brakes. Mighty few cane brakes to be found now. I come with my grandpa and grandma to Arkansas when I was five years old.

"My ma belong to Quill and Sely Whitaker. I et and slept with Hattie and Bud and Rob Whitaker. Quill Whitaker was a Union surgeon in the Civil War.

"I don't think any of my folks was ever sold. They was of a porer class and had to have a living and sorter become slaves for a living. I never heard ma say how she got in bondage. Pa stayed with John Rob bout like a slave.

"I am a farmer. I am not on the PWA. Times for me is hard. You see some has so much and others hardly can live atall.

"It is not for me to say about the young generation. I have mighty little to do with any of them.

"I have voted but not lately. I never did understand voting."

Interviewer: Miss Irene Robertson
Person interviewed: Victoria Sims, Helena, Arkansas
Age: 76

VICTORIA SIMS

"I was born in Limestone County, Alabama. It was on a river. Where I was born they called it Elks Mouth. Our owners was Frank Martin and Liza Martin. They raised papa. Their daughter aired (heired) him. Her name was Miss (Mrs.) Betty Hansey. Papa's name was Ed Martin. I stood on a stool and churned for papa's young mistress. The churn was tall as I was. I loved milk so good and they had plenty of it—all kinds. Soon as ever I get through, they take up the butter. I'd set 'round till they got it worked up so I could get a piece of bread and fresh butter and a big cup of that fresh milk. They always fixed it for me.

"Mama was Minthy Martin. She cooked on another place. She was a nurse. Her papa belong to one person and her mother to somebody else. Mama was Minthy Bridgeforth but I don't have her owner's name. I guess she was sold. I heard her say the Bridgeforth's was good to her. Some white man whooped on her once. I never heard her say much about it. Papa's owners was good to him. They was crazy about him. I knowed papa's owners the best and I lived there heap the most. I was born a slave but I don't know who I belong to. I've studied that over myself. I used to go back to see papa's owners. They owned lots of slaves and lots of land. Papa done a lot of different things. He fed and farmed and cleaned off the yards and slopped the pigs. He done what they said do, well as I can recollect. I wasn't with mama till after freedom. Mama said her white folks was treated mighty mean during the War. Once the soldiers come and mama was so scared she took the baby and run got in the cellar. They throwed out everything they had to eat. They took off barrels of things to eat and left them on starvation. One soldier come one time and wanted mama to go to the camps. She was scared not to go, scared he'd shoot her down. She told him she'd go the next day soon as she could get up her things and tell her folks she had gone. He agreed to that. Soon as he left she and some other young women on the place put out to the cane brakes and caves. She said they nearly starved. The white folks sent them baskets of victuals several times. Mama said she had some pretty beads she wore. Somebody had made her a present of them. She loved 'em. I think she said they was red. Mama's mistress told her to hide her beads, the soldiers would take them. She hid them up in the loft of their house on a nail. One day a gang come scouting and they rummaged the whole house and place. When the soldiers left she thought about her beads and went to see and they was gone. She cried and cried about them. That was before she went to the canebrakes.

"When freedom come on, the owners told them they was free. They didn't leave and then they made a way for them to stay on. They stayed on.

"I was grown when we come to this state but we lived in Tennessee a few years. Mama had had nine children by that time. All was dead, but us two girls and my brother. We come to Arkansas with our parents. We heard the land was new and rich. I wasn't married then.

"I've worked hard in the field all my life till last year or so. I still do work.

"Times is tough here I tell you. I get a little help, six dollars.

"Some of the young folks won't work, some not able to work. If anybody saving a thing I don't hear about it."

United States. Work Projects Administration

Interviewer: Bernice Bowden
Person interviewed: Virginia Sims
1121 N. Magnolia
Pine Bluff, Ark.
Age: 93
Occupation: Retired Midwife

VIRGINIA SIMS

"I was born in 1844. I was twenty when peace was declared. I was born in Virginia. Yes ma'am, but I was sold, put up on a stump just like you sell hogs to the highest speculator. I was sold with my mother from a man named Joe Poindexter and bought by Tom Murphy and brought to Arkansas. My God, every Murphy round here knows me. Yes'm, my mother and me was sold. Papa wasn't sold, but he come here the second year after surrender.

"I was old enough to spin twelve cuts a day—had it to do. And I could weave cloth just like they do now.

"Had seven brothers and I'm the onliest girl.

"I can recollect when Miss Mary Poindexter died. They said I was two.

"My mistis in Arkansas was Mrs. Susan Murphy. That was out on the plantation, we didn't live in no city—my God, no!

"The way my people acts now, they looks foolish. I

never heard a person curse till I come up here. I was a grown young lady nineteen years old when our master lowed us to get out and cote. You better not. The first husband I married I was nineteen goin' on twenty. My husband fought on the Southern side. His master sent him as a substitute.

"My master put good clothes on me, I'd say. 'Master. I wants a dress like so and so, and I wants a pair of shoes.' Yes ma'am, and he got em for me. I was forty-three and married to a nigger fore I knowed what twas to cry for underwear.

"I member they was a white man called Dunk Hill and he said, 'Virginia, who freed the niggers?' I said, 'God freed the niggers.' He said, 'Now, Virginia, you goin' be just as free as I am some day!'

"General Shelby's troops was comin' on this side the ribber. That's one time I was scared. Never seed so many men in my life. They wanted something to eat. Mama cooked all night. They was nine hundred and somethin'. I toted canteens all night long.

"I member when they had that Marks Mill battle. My husband was there and he sent word for me to come cause he had the measles and they had went in on him. I had to put on boots and wade mud. Young folks now ain't got no sense. I see so many folks now with such dull understanding. Marks Mill was the onliest part of the war I was in.

"General Shelby and Captain Blank, they whetted their swords together when peace was declared. Captain said, 'General, I'm not crazy and neither am I a coward. I looked up and seem like a man was comin' out the clouds, and so I'm goin' to surrender.'

"Them cavalry men—they'd say, 'Ride!' and how they'd go.

"I seen em when they was enlistin'. Said they was goin' to whip the Yankees and be back for breakfast in the morning.

"Marse Ben was goin' and Miss Susan say, 'Virginia, if you think he ain't goin' come back you ought to kiss him goodbye.' I said, 'I ain't goin' to kiss no white man.'

"Miss Fanny went up the ladder and sot rite on the roof and watched the soldiers goin' by. Yes'm. Old master whipped me with a little peach stick cause I let Frankie—we called her Frankie—go up the ladder. I said I couldn't stop her cause she said if I told her papa, she and Becky goin' to whip me. He whipped Miss Fanny. Old miss come in and say, 'Ain't you goin' whip this nigger?' She was mean as the devil. Oh, God, yes. She so mean she didn't know what to do. But old master kep her down. You know some of these redheaded women, they just as devilish as they can be. We had some neighbors, Mrs. Davis and Mrs. Daniels and old miss would be out there on the lawn quarrelin' till it was just like a fog. Us niggers would be out there listenin'.

"But I was always treated good. You know if I had been beat over the head I couldn't recollect things now. My head ain't been cracked up. Nother thing. I always been easy controlled.

"I never went to school a day. After we was freed we stayed right on the Murphy place. They paid us and we worked on the shares. That's the reason I say I done better when I was a slave."

Interviewer: Mrs. Bernice Bowden
Person interviewed: Senya Singfield
1613 W. Second Avenue, Pine Bluff, Arkansas
Age: 74

SENYA SINGFIELD

"I was born in Washington, Virginia right at the foot of the Blue Ridge Mountains. My mother was sold when I was a babe in her arms. She was sold three times. I know one time when she had four children she was sold and one of my brothers was sold away unbeknownst to her. Her old master sold her away from her mistress. She was a cook and never was mistreated.

"I ain't never been to school. When I got big enough, my mother was a widow and I had to start out and make a living. I've always been a cook. Used to keep a boarding house, up until late years. I've washed and ironed, sewed a right smart and quilted quilts. I've done anything I could to turn an honest living. Oh I've been through it but I'm still here. I've been a widow over forty years.

"I think the folks nowdays are about run out. They are goin' too fast. When I was comin' up, I had to have some manners. My mother didn't low me to 'spute nobody."

Interviewer: Samuel S. Taylor
Person interviewed: Peggy Sloan
2450 Howard Street, Little Rock, Arkansas
Age: About 80, or more
Occupation: Farming

SENYA SINGFIELD

"I was born in Arkansas in Tulip, in Dallas County I think it is, isn't it?

"Charlotte Evans was mother's name and my father's name was Lige Evans. Gran'daddy David was my mother's father, and Cheyney was my mother's mother.

"Mr. Johnnie Sumner was the name of my young master, and the old man was Mr. Judge Sumner. The old people are all dead now. Mr. Judge Sumner was Johnnie Sumner's father. Me and Mr. Johnnie suckled together. Mr. Johnnie came to Fordyce they say looking for the old slaves. I didn't know about it then. I never would know him now. That is been so long ago. I sure would like to see 'im.

"My mother ain't told me much about herself in slave times. She was a nurse. She lived in a log cabin. You know they had cabins for all of them. The colored lived in log houses. The white people had good houses. Them houses was warmer than these what they got now.

"My grandma could cut a man's frock-tail coat. These

young people don't know nothin' 'bout that. Grandma was a milliner. She could make anything you used a needle to make.

"Lige Evans was the name my father took after the surrender. He wasn't named that before the surrender—in the olden times. My mother had fifteen children. She was the largest woman you ever seen. She weighed four hundred pound. She was young Master Johnnie's nurse. Mr. Johnnie said he wanted to come and see me. I heard he lives way on the other side of Argenta somewheres.

"I was my mama's seventh girl, and I got a seventh girl living. I had fifteen children. My mother's children were all born before the surrender.

"Mr. Judge Sumner and his son were both good men. They never whipped their slaves.

"They didn't feed like they do now. I et corn bread then, and I eat it now. Some people say they don't. They would give them biscuits on Sundays. They had a cook to cook for the hands. She got all their meals for them.

"They had a woman to look after the little colored children, and they had one to look after the white children. My mother was a nurse for the white children. My mother didn't have nothing to do with the colored children.

"I didn't never have no trouble with the pateroles. Sometimes they would come down the lane running the horses. When I would hear them, I would run and git under the bed. I was the scaredest soul you ever seen. I think that's about all I can remember.

"I was the mother of fifteen children. I had one set of twins, a boy and a girl. The doctor told me you never raise a boy and a girl twin. My boy is dead. All of my children are dead but two.

"I was raised on the farm. I want a few acres of ground now so bad.

"I never was married but once. My husband's name was David Sloan. I don't know exactly how long he and me were married. It was way over twenty years. My license got burnt up.

"You know I couldn't be nothin' but a Christian."

• Interviewer's Comment

Peggy Sloan's memory is going. She is not certain of the number of children her mother had although she knows there were more than seven because she was the seventh.

She remembers nothing about her age, but she knows definitely that all of her mother's children were born before the War—that is before the end of the War. Since the War ended seventy-three years ago and she was the seventh child with possibly seven behind her, I feel that she could not be younger than eighty. She remembers definitely running at the approach of men she calls pateroles during "slavery time."

Her mind may be fading, but it is a long way from gone. She questioned me closely about my reason for getting statements from her. She had to be definitely satisfied before the story could be gotten.

Interviewer: Miss Irene Robertson
Person interviewed: Arzella Smallwood
Hazen R.F.D., Green Grove, Arkansas
Age: 60 Doesn't know exact age

PEGGY SLOAN

"I was born about eight miles from Williston, South Carolina. After freedom my mother married Lee Ballinger and she had six children. He died when I was real small. My mother was named Hester McCrary. Old Master McCrary bought grandma and my mother in Virginia. One sister my mother never did run across after freedom. She was older and sold to other people. I think at freedom my mother left and I think grandma did too. My grandpa was half Indian, but I never did see him to remember what he looked like. Our young master is a doctor. He waited on my mother before she died. Grandma was blind and she lived with us. Our young master may still be living. Old mistress was named Sylvania and she sent for my mother to come wait on her when she got sick to die. I think they had pretty fair treatment there. My mother was to be a house girl and cook. I think grandma was a cook and field woman both.

"I heard them say the white folks took them to church to learn to pray, then they didn't allow them to pray for freedom. But I don't think they wanted freedom. After they was set free they died up so scand'lous. Grandma said they had to work harder. My mother brought a good price because she was real light color and sharp to learn. She had six children and we was all darker than she was a whole lots. She and grandma was both good on giving advice. Seem like they could see how things would turn out every time.

"I married a man with a roving nature. We come here. He left me, come back for me to look after before he died. I married again. I left him. He told me how I could do five washings a week and take care of us both. I didn't aim to do it. I mighter got some washings but I didn't aim to keep him.

"I get a little commodities along to help out. I'm picking berries now twenty-five cents a gallon for the first picking. Fifteen and twenty cents is the regular prices.

"I haven't got children and I don't know what they ought to do. I reckon they do the best they can.

"Times is hard on me. It takes me all the time to make a living."

Pine Bluff District
FOLKLORE SUBJECTS
Name of Interviewer: Martin & Barker
Subject: Negro Customs

This information given by: Sarah Smiley (Colored)
Place of Residence: Humphrey, Arkansas
Age: 76
[TR: Information moved from bottom of first page.]

ARZELLA SMALLWOOD

I was born the 10th of May, 1860. My home was in Charleston, S.C. I was not a slave, but my parents were.

My mother was a seamstress and my father, Edward Barnewill, was butler for their white folks.

I looks the door at sundown, and me and God are all by ourselves, and I am not afraid.

I came to Sherrill when I was a schoolgirl, and married when I was 14. Lived here after I was married. Taught school before I was married.

Had seven children by my first husband. My three husbands were Ike Williams, Eli Treadvan, and Calvin Smiley.

When asked about her books standing on her shelves—namely Golden Gems, arithmetic, and the Bible, also a blue back speller—said she just loved her books.

Young folks of today don't love like they did in the olden days. Now it is hot love, minute love, free love.

When my first child was born, I begged the midwife not to cut me open to get the baby out. The midwife told me the same place it went in the same place it will come out.

When my breasts began to grow (adolescence) I didn't want those bumps on me, and tied them down with wide rags.

Cures—I uses gasoline and cedar, soak it and rub on affected places for rheumatism.

I believe that you must not let your left hand know what your right hand is doing.

Heaven is a place of rest. If we are faithful to God, you can ride death home.

Hell is below—also here on earth.

Interviewer: Miss Irene Robertson
Person interviewed: Andrew Smith
R.F.D., Forrest City, Arkansas
Age: 73

SARAH SMILEY

"I was born after the surrender at Oxford, Mississippi. We belong to Master Jim Smith. Mother cooked and father worked in the field. He was on a average being good. They didn't trouble my mother as I recollect hearing 'em say but they whooped them in the field. Pattyrollers chased papa in sometimes. I heard him talk about it but I couldn't tell what he said now. Mama had two before freedom, then she married and had three children. He died. She married the second time and had two more children. That made seben in all.

"She said her first marriage was pronounced (announced). My mother said their master refugeed them to Texas till the year of the surrender. They didn't know nothing 'bout freedom till a while after they got back from Texas. They stayed on that year and longer too not knowing 'bout freedom. My rickerliction is short.

"Frank Houston was a neighbor of our'n. He lived on my folks' joining plantation close to Houston, Mississippi during slavery. During or before the War come on he put his money in a barrel—hogshead. They said it was gold and silver. I don't know. It might some been paper. He rolled the barrel down to the river. It was the Tallahassee (?) River eighteen miles northeast of Oxford, Mississippi. He hid his barrel of money in the river. They hunted and hunted it and never could find it. It might sunk in the mud and quick sand. Somebody might er hauled it out and stole it. The whole neighborhood hope him hunt it. They never did find it. I seen the old man and Jim Smith heaps of times.

"I voted in Mississippi. I couldn't read. They had a big fight in the country at Midway Church where we all voted. It was out a ways from Oxford, Mississippi. I never voted in Arkansas. I pay poll tax. Never 'lowed to vote.

"I never went to school a day in my life.

"I come to Forrest City fifty-four years ago. Married here. Never had a child. Now my wife dead. I farmed all my life. I bought a farm but they never let me have it. I never got it all paid out. They took it.

"I get Welfare help. I does some work. I'm nearly past hard work now."

Slave Narratives

STATE—Arkansas
NAME OF WORKER—Carol N. Graham
ADDRESS—Rear 456 West Main Street, El Dorado, Arkansas
DATE—November 1, 1938
SUBJECT—Ex-slaves
[TR: Repetitive information deleted from subsequent pages.]

CAROLINE SMITH

- **Circumstances of Interview**

1. Name and address of informant—**Caroline Smith**, Route 1, El Dorado. (Lives with Negroes by name of Green about 1 mile from Smith's Crossing)

2. Date and time of interview—November 1, 1938, Tuesday morning, 9:30-10:30

3. Place of interview—at the home of some Negroes named Green.

4. Name and address of person, if any, who put you in touch with informant—Had previously talked with Caroline.

5. Name and address of person, if any, accompanying you—Mrs. Ethel Depriest, 516 East Miles Street, El Dorado.

6. Description of room, house, surroundings, etc.—a typical Negro farm house.

- **Personal History of Informant**

    1. Ancestry—

    2. Place and date of birth—Camden, Arkansas? No date.

    3. Family—one child.

    4. Places lived in, with dates—Camden and El Dorado. No dates.

    5. Education, with dates—

    6. Occupations and accomplishments, with dates—None

    7. Special skills and interests—

    8. Community and religious activities—

    9. Description of informant—

    10. Other points gained in interview—This slave old enough to remember Civil War.

- **Text of Interview (Unedited)**

    "I first remembers living on the plantation of Mr. Jake Dumas near El Dorado Landing. You know it's Calion now. We lived up towards Camden and it was there that my ma and pa was married and buried. I was a big girl durin' the war. My job was to card and spin. And I use to carry the children to school. When I would get to the school I would put the children off, git straddle and ride that horse home. When I would get there old mos would say Ca'line did you run him? I'd say naw sir. Then he'd say, 'Oh, Carryline put the horse in the lot and come out here. I'd say, 'Master I didn't run that horse' but didn't do no good. He sure would whip me. I'd get down and roll. I would stomp and he would do the same. I wondered how he could tell I'd run that horse. But course he could cause that horse had the thumps (heart beating rapidly).

"I remember seeing the soldiers come through during the war. They come by droves stealing horses, setting the cotton on fire and taking sumpin to eat, too.

"Yes, I does still member the songs we sung durin' the war but I've got the asthmy and ain't got much wind fur singin'.

> "You want to know the reason,
> You want to know the reason,
> You want to know the reason, I'll tell you why,
> We'll whip them Yankees, whole hog or die."

> "Hooray, Hooray, Hooray for the Southern Girl.
> Hooray for the homespun dress the Southern ladies wear.
> My homespun dress is plain I know,
> I glory in its name;
> Hooray for the homespun dress the Southern ladies wear."

"I've got the asthmy honey and jest caint sing no more.

"You asked 'bout my husband and chillun. I been married fo' times. My first man's name was Dick Hagler, the next Frank Bibby, the next Henry Harris and the last one was Tom Smith. That's where I get my name Ca'line Smith. I never did have but one daughter but she had sixteen chillun. She's daid now and mah granchillun is scattered.

"I got the asthmy an jes don' feel like talkin' no more. Long time ago when I was sick master always had a doctor to me now I have to hire one. And they always fed me good and clothed me but after I was free I would go round and work around to git a little sumpin to eat."

Interviewer: Thomas Elmore Lucy
Person interviewed: Caroline Smith, Russellville, Arkansas
Age: 83

CAROLINE SMITH

"Ca'line Smith's my name and dey calls me 'Aunt Ca'line.' I was born about de year 1855 as I was about dis high (measuring) when de War broke out. I remembers de boys marching away in their grey uniforms just as plain. We chillen would watch dem as dey went away; we could see em as we peeped through de winders and de cracks in de walls.

"I was born in Mississippi close to Columbus on de plantation of my master, John Duncan. And he was a purty strict old master, sure, but sometimes he was kind to us. When we was set free he let us all go wherever we wanted to, but didn't pay us nothin'.

"All de slaves that I remembers stayed on around in different parts of Mississippi after de War and engaged in farmin', and workin' on roads and streets, and other public work. About forty years ago I come to Pope County, Arkansas wid my parents and has lived here ever' since.

"I don't remember nothin' about de Klu Klux Klan or if our folks was ever bothered wid em.

"Yes suh, I keeps workin' every day and likes to keep up my sewin'. Plenty of it to do all de time—jest like I'm doin' today. My health is purty good ceptin' I has a sort of misery in my side.

"I draws a pension of $7.50 a month, but I dunno who sends it.

"I belongs to de Adventist Church, and I sure believes in always tellin' de trufe and nofin' but de trufe; we better tell de trufe here, for some of dese days we all gwine where nofin' but de trufe will be accepted.

"No suh, I ain't never took any interest in politics and ain't never voted.

"Dese young'uns today is simply too much for me; I can't understand em, and I dunno which way dey headed. Some few of em seems to have sound common sense, but—well, I just refuse to talk about em."

Interviewer: Pernella Anderson
Person Interviewed: Edmond Smith
D Avenue
El Dorado, Ark.
Age: ?

EDMOND SMITH

"I was born in Arcadia, Louisiana a long, long time ago. Now my work when I was a child was farmin'. I did not stay a child long, I been grown ever since I was fourteen. My father lived till I was eleven, and I thought since I was the oldest boy I could take his place of bossin', but my mother would take me down a button hole lower whenever I got too high.

"Before my papa died we had a good livin'. We lived with his mistress's daughter, and we thought we lived in heaven. My papa made all of the shoes and raised all of the cattle from which he got the hide. We raised all the wool to make our wool clothes and made all of the clothes we wore. And food—we did not know what it was to go to a store to buy. Didn't have to do that. You see, people now living out of paper sacks. Every time they get ready to cook it's go to the store. We old timers lived out of our smokehouse.

"In there we had dried beef, cured pork, sugar from syrup, sweet potatoes, onions, Irish potatoes, plenty of dried fruit and canned fruit, peanuts, hickory nuts, walnuts; eggs in the henhouse and chickens on the yard, cows in the pen and milk and butter in the house.

"My mama even made our plow lines. She had a spinning wheel and you know how to spin?—you can make ropes for plow lines too. Just twist the cotton and have it about six inches long and put it in the loom and let it go around and around. You keep puttin' the twisted cotton in the loom and step on the peddle and no sooner than done, that was worked in a rope. Now, if you don't know what I am talking about it is useless for me to tell you.

"After papa died that left no one to work but mama and I tell you time brought about a change. A house full of little children—we lived from hand to mouth. Not enough corn to feed one mule. No syrup, no hogs, no cows. Oh! we had a hard time. I remember hearing my mama many a night ask God to help her through the struggle with her children. The more my mama prayed the harder times got with her. Wasn't no churches around so she had to sing and pray at home. The first Sunday School I remember going to was in 1892. I went to school and got as high as fifth grade, then I ran away from my mama.

"Just becaise I let old bad man overpower me I got grown and mannish. Couldn't nobody tell me a thing. I would steal, I would fight, I would lie. I remember in 1896 I went to church—that was about the fourth time I had been to church. The preacher began preachin' and I went outdoors and cut the harness off of his mule and broke one of his buggy wheels. I went down in the woods and cut a cow just for meanness. I stole a gun, and I would shoot anytime and anywhere, and nobody bothered me because they was scared to. I stole chickens, turkeys and anything.

"I got in trouble more times than a little, so the last time I got in trouble some white people got me out and I worked for them to pay my fine out. While working for them I made shoes. They taught me to do carpenter work. They taught me to paint; to paper; to cook; work in the field and do most anything. I came to my senses while working with those people and they made a man out of me. When I left there I was a first class carpenter. Those white people was the cause of me getting independent. I didn't get no book sense, but if you get with some good white people, that will be worth more than an education."

United States. Work Projects Administration

Interviewer: Miss Irene Robertson
Person interviewed: Emma Hulett Smith; Hazen, Arkansas
Age: 66

EMMA HULETT SMITH

"I was the first colored baby born here or very near here. There was only three houses in this town (Hazen). I think they muster been log houses.

"My folks belong to Dr. Hazen. He brought families from Tennessee. When the war broke out he took em to Texas. Then he brought em back here. When they was freed I heard my mother say they worked on for him and his boys (Alex and Jim Hazen) and they paid them. He was good to them. They had er plenty always. After the war they lived in good log houses and he give em land and lumber for the church. Same church we got cept a storm tore it down and this one built in place of it. He let em have a school. Same place it stands now. My mother (Mandy Hulett) got a Union pension till she died. She cooked at the first hotel in Hazen for John Lane. She washed and ironed till she died. We girls helped and we wash and iron all we can get now. None of us not on relief (Fannie nor Emma). I can't wash no more. My hands and arms swell up with rheumatism. I still iron all I can get.

"The present conditions seems awful unsettled; wages low, prices high and work scarce at times. Men can get work in the hay two months and bout two months work in the rice or pickin cotton, either one. Then the work has played clean out till hay time next year.

"How do they live? Some of their wifes cooks for white people and they eat all they make up soon as they get paid. Only way they live."

Interviewer: Samuel S. Taylor
Person interviewed: Ervin E. Smith
811 Ringo Street, Little Rock, Arkansas
Age: 84

ERVIN E. SMITH

"I have been in this state for forty-nine years. I will be here fifty years on the fifteenth of December.

"I was born in Ebenezer Township, York County, South Carolina, on the twenty-ninth day of April, in 1854. That makes me eighty-four years old on Friday. I was born on Good Friday—on Good Friday at six o'clock in the morning.

"I am telling you what I was instructed all of my life. My father, W.D. Smith, and my mother, Haria, told me these things. My mother carried a nickname, Salina, all her life, but her real name was Haria.

"I'll tell you how they happened to keep such good records. We had a little advantage over the other people of that day. My father never got any school education, but his brothers instructed him—his half-brothers. They were white. They was good, too. I mean them brothers thought just as much of me as they did of anybody else. So my father got pretty good training. He got it from his brothers and that's how he learned to keep such good records.

- **Relatives**

"I am told my mother cooked for one family for forty-two years. Her maiden name was Haria Harris. She was three-fourths white. She come from the Indian tribe—old Catawba Indians. Her own daddy was a white man, but her Grand daddy on her mother's side was an Indian.

"I am told that the old fellow bought my mother when she was fifteen years old. Finally he got hold of both my father and my mother. Both of them put together didn't have half colored blood. He must have loved them a lot to work so hard to get them together. My father was half white, but his mother was a mulatto woman (Interpreter's comment—This should make him a quadroon) [TR: sentence lined out.]; and my mother's great-grandmother was a colored woman.

"I never knew much about race troubles. The best friend I ever had was an old white grandmother. I was carefully shielded from all unpleasant things.

- **Fort Sumter**

"I was looking at the men when they were getting ready to get on the train to go to Fort Sumter. Mr. John White, Captain John White, I knew him personally. He was one of our neighbors. That was in Ebenezer that he was one of our neighbors. The soldiers going to capture Fort Sumter caught the Columbia and Augusta train going to Charleston. Looked like to me there was ten thousand of them. John White was the captain and Beauregard[HW: here Gustave Toutant Beauregard.] was the general.

"I didn't see the fighting because it was too far away. It was about eighty miles from us where they got on the train to Fort Sumter. They got on the train at Rock Hill. Rock Hill was a city—small city—real close to Ebenezer. We lived near Rock Hill. They was adjoining towns.

• Patrollers and Good Masters

"The only patrollers I knew of was some that come on the place once and got hurt. My mother had a brother Hobb and the patroller tried to whip him. Hobb knocked all his front teeth out with a stick. Ches[TR:?] Wood was the name of the patroller. It was like it is now. There were certain white people who didn't allow any of their niggers to be whipped. I never seen a patroller on my place. I have heard of them in other places, but the only one to come on our place was the one Uncle Hobb beat up. He had to take it, because you couldn't put anything over on Harris' plantation. My people was rich people. They didn't allow anybody to come on their places and interfere with then—their niggers.

"I have heard my mother say that no white man ever struck her in her life. I have had uncles that were struck. Two of them, and both of them killed the men that struck them. Uncle Saul killed Edmund Smith and Uncle George killed Ed McGehee. Uncle George's full white sister (his half-sister) sent him away and saved him. They electrocuted Uncle Saul—they executed him.

"White men struck them and they wouldn't take it. They didn't do nothin' at all to Hobb Baron. He got to his boss and the white folks was 'fraid to come there after him. All of this was in slavery. My people ain't never had no trouble with anybody since freedom; white people would get mad with my uncles and try to do something to them, and they wouldn't take it.

"There were three races in the neighborhood where I was raised—niggers, Indians, and white folks. They never sent the Indians out until 1876 when I was a grown man. They sent them over there to Utah when it became a state. I had a lot of Indian friends that went along at that time.

"Bad blood was mixed up there and you couldn't do nothing to anybody and get away with it.

- **First Pair of Shoes**

"I can remember the first pair of shoes my uncle gave me. They had a little brass on the top of the toes to keep you from kicking them out and skinning them up. That was way back yonder in the fifties.

- **Bible and Church in Slave Time**

"White people taught their niggers what Bible they wanted them to know.

"'Who made you?'

"'God.'

"'Why did He make you?'

"'For his own glory.'

"'Why ought you to love God?'

"'Because He made me and takes care of me.'

"That was all the Bible they wanted you to learn. That, and just a few more things. I could state them all.

• Education

"In 1866, everybody that was less than sixteen years old in South Carolina had to go to school. The little fellows that had been slaves had to go to school, and they got some education. You will hardly find an old man from South Carolina around my age who can't read and write. There was one hundred sixty pupils in my school. All boys. I never went to a mixed school—a school where they had boys and girls both.

"The first school I attended was in Ebenezer. I went to high school in Macklenburg. Miss Sallie Good and Miss Mattie Train, Elias Hill, and David G. Wallace—all of these were my teachers. They were all white except Elias Hill. He was the only colored teacher in that section of the country—at that time.

"When I finished high school, I went to Biddle University. Biddle was a boys' school. It was in Charlotte, North Carolina. They had a girls' school in Concord, North Carolina. Biddle is still running, but it has another name. Dr. Mattoon was president of Biddle then and Dr. Darling was president of the girls' school.

• Murders

"The first murder ever I saw was Violet Harris killed Warren Fewell. It come over a family quarrel some way. They fell out over something. She was not related to him. It was done right at the fence at her gate. She cut him with a butcher knife—stuck him just once right through the heart. That is the first murder I ever saw. They were both colored. The War was just winding up. It happened in Ebenezer. I don't recall that they punished her.

"I have seen a white man killed by a white man, and I have seen a colored man killed by a colored man; but I have never seen a colored man killed by a white man or a white man killed by a colored man. I have seen them after they were killed, but I never seen the killing. I have seen both races killing their own, but I have never seen them killing across the races.

"About fifty years ago, I saw a young man come in the church and kill another one. Just come in and shot him. That is been fifty years ago—back in 1881 in Ebenezer.

"Rock Hill, South Carolina, from 1876 to a while later, bore the name 'Bloody Town.' They killed a man there every Saturday night in the year—fifty-two times a year they killed a man. They had to send for the Federal troops to bring them down. They didn't just kill colored people. They killed anybody—about anything."

Interviewer: Mrs. Bernice Bowden
Person interviewed: Frances Smith
2224 Havis Street, Pine Bluff, Arkansas
Age: 77

FRANCES SMITH

"I specs I was born in slavery times. I remember seein' the Yankees. That was in Mississippi. I'm seventy-seven—that's my age.

"Spencer Bailey was old master. Just remember the name was 'bout the biggest thing I knowed about. I seen him all right but I didn't know much about him 'cept his name.

"Mother belonged to him, yes'm.

"I tell you the truf, what little I used to remember I done forgot it. I just didn't try to keep up with it. I wasn't concerned and just didn't try to keep up with it.

"I know our folks stayed there a while. First place we went to after the War was Tennessee.

"I don't know how long I been here—I been here a time though.

"Yes'm, I went to school several terms.

"I was married in Arkansas. My folks heard about

Arkansas bein' such a rich country, so they come to Arkansas.

"I farmed a long time and then I done housework.

"Deal a times I don't know what to think of this younger generation. I sits down sometimes and tries to study 'em out, but I fails.

"Well, what the old folks goin' to get out of this?"

Interviewer: Samuel S. Taylor
Person interviewed: Henrietta Evelina Smith
1714 Pine Street, Little Rock, Arkansas
Age:

HENRIETTA EVELINA SMITH

"I was born in Louisiana in East Felicie Parish near Baton Rouge on the twenty-eighth day of December. My mother's name was Delia White. Her maiden name was Delia Early. My father's name was Henry White. My mother's father was named Amos Early. My mother's mother's name was Julia. My father's father was named Tom White and his mother was named Susan.

"My father and mother both belonged to the Eason's. I don't know how they spelled it. Eason's daughter married Munday and my uncle bought this white man's place years after freedom. That is not far from Clinton—about four or five miles. It is three miles from Ethel, Louisiana.

"Amos, my grandfather, was the wagoneer on the old place. Father, he used to drive the wagon too. He'd haul cotton to Baton Rouge and things like that. He would run off and stay five or six months. I have heard them talk about how he used to come back and bring hogs and one thing and another that he had found out in the woods.

He would run off because the overseer would whip him. But he was such a good working man that once or twice, the boss man turned off his overseer on account of him. There wasn't nothing against his work. He just wouldn't take a blow. Most of the times after he had been out a while the boss man would tell the hands to tell Amos that if he would come on home they wouldn't whip him for running off.

"My grandmother's mother on my father's side was named Melissa. I think that was her name. My father's mother was named Susan like I told you.

She was part Indian—better work hand never was. But she wouldn't be conquered neither. When they got ready to whip her, it would be half a day before they could take her. When they did get her, they would whip her so they would have to raise her in a sheet. The last time they whipped her, it took her nearly a year to get over it. So the white man just turned her loose and told her she was free. She went on off and we never did know what became of her.

"The Easons were farmers and they had a large plantation. I don't know just how many slaves they owned.

"My father and mother were fed like pigs. They had an old woman that did the cooking. She was broke down from work. They would give the slaves greens and the children pot-liquor. My parents were field hands. My mother was too young to carry a row when she was freed, but she worked on an older person's row. They worked from can till can't. You know what I mean, from the time they could see till the time they couldn't. Reb time was something like the penitentiary now. It never got too cold nor too hot to work. And there wasn't any pay. My parents never were given any chance to earn any money. I heard that my grandpa used to make a little something. He was a wagoneer you know. He would carry a little extra on his load and sell it. His old master never did find it out. People knew he had stole it, but they would buy it just the same.

"The old boss man came down in the quarters and told them they were free when freedom came. Right after freedom they stayed there on the old place for a year or more. My mother wasn't grown and she and my father married after that. Afterwards they had kind of a fight to get away from the old man. He was carrying them the same way he was going before the War and they had a row (quarrel), and left him. I don't know just what terms they worked on. I don't think they did themselves. They took just what they could get and didn't know just how they was paid.

"If a man made a good crop, they would run him away and make him leave his crops behind.

"My folks continued to farm all their lives. They had trouble with the night riders. They had to vote like they were told. If you voted the wrong way they would get behind you and run you off. There were some folks who would take pay for voting and then vote different, and when the night riders found it out, there would be trouble. I don't believe in taking money for voting, and I don't believe in lying.

"My mother and father didn't get any schooling. That was allowed after slavery, but it wasn't allowed in slavery time. They learned a little from other people. They would slip and learn to read.

"My great-grandmother was considered pretty when she was young. She had glossy black hair and was a little short. She was brownskin and had big legs. Her master would take her out behind the field and do what he wanted. When she got free, she gave both of her children away. She had two children by him—a boy named Eli and a girl named Anna. She didn't want them 'round her because they reminded her of him."

• Interviewer's Comment

The subject did not wish to state her age. It is probably around sixty-five. Her mother was married shortly after freedom. And eight years is probably a liberal allowance for the distance of her birth from emancipation.

Interviewer: Mrs. Bernice Bowden
Person Interviewed: Henry Smith
702 Virginia, Pine Bluff, Arkansas
Age: 79
Occupation: Odd jobs

HENRY SMITH

"Yes mam, I was here in slavery times. I was born in Tennessee on a plantation near Jackson. I was eight years old when peace was declared. All I member is when they beat the folks pit near to death.

"My old master was Tom Smith. Mean? Cose he was mean. Old mistress was sorta good to us but old master was the devil. Used to make the men hold the women while they whipped em. Make em wear old brogan shoes with buckles across the instep. Had the men and women out fore day plowin'. I member they had my mother out many a day so dark they had to feel where the traces was to hitch up the mules.

"My mother worked in the field and I stayed in front and helped her up when she got behind.

"I member when the Yankees had thousands and thousands of bales of cotton in the streets right here in Pine Bluff and take a knife and cut it open and put a match to it, and burn peoples houses and the gin houses and everything. Take the hosses and mules and run em off.

"Old master and mistress carried us to Texas till peace was declared. I member one morning the mail come and old master had a long paper and he called all us colored folks up and told us we was free. He told us we could go or stay. They all wanted to stay so he brought em all back here to Arkansas. He give each one three acres of ground and all they could make on it. That's the nicest thing he ever done, but he didn't do that but one year. After that the land fell back to him. Then they worked on the halves.

"When the colored folks went to buy stock and rent land from the whites, it cost five and six dollars a acre. They sho could make some money that way, too.

"I was big enough to do right smart behind a plow. I could do a heap. We got along pretty well.

"I got married when I was bout eighteen and made a home for myself. Me and my wife had twenty-two children. White folks helped us a lot. My wife's dead and all my children dead 'cept four.

"I been here in Pine Bluff twenty-two years. I been here a good while—that ain't no joke. Used to make three dollars a day mowin' grass. Bought this place with the money. Can't make that now. They won't give you nothin' for your work.

"Oh yes'm, I voted and wouldn't know what I was votin' till 'twas too late.

"Never went to school much. Learned to read a little bit. They kep' me in the field. Yes ma'm, I've worked but I've never had a doctor to me in my life.

"Ain't much to this younger generation. The old race

can get along a lot better with the white folks than the young race can.

"I'm the head deacon of the Morning Star Church. Read the Bible right smart. I tell you one thing—I like all of it."

United States. Work Projects Administration

Interviewer: Samuel S. Taylor
Person interviewed: J.L. Smith
1215 Pulaski Street, Little Rock, Arkansas
Age: 76

J.L. SMITH

"I was born in 1862 in the month of September on the fifteenth. I was born at a place they call Indian Bay on White River down here in Arkansas. My mother was named Emmaline Smith and she was born in Tennessee. I don't know really now what county or what part of the state. My father's name was John Smith. He was born in North Carolina. I don't know nothing about what my grandfather's name and grandmother's names were. I never saw them. None of my folks are old aged as I am. My father was sixty years old when he died and my mother was only younger than that.

- **Experience of Father**

"I heard my father say that he helped get out juniper timber in North Carolina. The white man me and my sister worked with after my father died was the man my father worked with in the juniper swamp. His name was Alfred Perry White. As long as he lived, we could do work for him. We didn't live on his place but we worked for him by the day. He is dead now—died way back yonder in the seventies. There was the Brooks and Baxter trouble in 1874, and my father died in seventy-five. White lived a little while longer.

"My father was married twice before he married my mother. He had two sets of children. I don't know how many of them there were. He had four children by my mother. He had only four children as far as I can remember.

"I don't know how my father and my mother met up. They lived in the same plantation and in the same house. They were owned by the same man when freedom came. I don't know how they got together. I have often wondered about that. One from Tennessee and the other from North Carolina, but they got together. I guess that they must have been born in different places and brought together through being bought and sold.

"My mother was a Murrill. My father was a Cartwright. My father's brother Lewis was a man who didn't take nothing much from anybody, and he 'specially didn't like to take a whipping. When Lewis' master wanted to whip him, he would call his mother—the master's mother—and have her whip him, because he figured Uncle Lewis wouldn't hit a woman.

"I have six children altogether. Two of them are dead. There are three girls and one boy living. The oldest is fifty-seven; the next, fifty; and the youngest, forty-eight. The youngest is in the hospital for nervous and mental diseases. She has been there ever since 1927. The oldest had an arm and four ribs broken in an auto accident last January on the sixteenth of the month. She didn't get a penny to pay for her trouble. I remember the man did give her fifteen cents once. The truck struck her at the alley there and knocked her clean across the street. She is fifty-seven years old and bones don't knit fast on people that old. She ain't able to do no work yet. All of my daughters are out of work. I don't know where the boy is. He is somewheres up North.

• Slave Houses

"I have seen some old log houses that they said the slaves used to live in. I was too young to notice before freedom. I have seen different specimens of houses that they lived in. One log house had a plank house builded on to the end of it. The log end was the one lived in during slavery times and the plank end was built since. That gal there of mine was born in the log end. There were round log houses and sawed log houses. The sawed log houses was built out of logs that had been squared after the tree had been cut down, and the round log houses was built out of logs left just like they was when they was trees. There's been quite an improvement in the houses since I was a kid.

• Food

"I have heard my father and mother talking among themselves and their friends, but they never did tell me nothing about slave times. They never did sit down and talk to me about it. When they'd sit down and start talkin', it would always be, 'Now you children run on out and play while we old folks sit here and talk.' But from time to time, I would be sitting on the floor playing by myself and they would be talking 'mongst themselves and I would hear them say this or that. But I never heered them say what they et in slave times.

- **Work**

"My father worked in the juniper swamp in North Carolina, like I told you. I think I heard my mother say she cooked. Most I ever heard them say was when they would get with some one else and each would talk about his master.

- **Cruelties**

"I heard my mother say that her mistress used to take a fork and stick it in her head—jog it up and down against her head. I don't know how hard she punched her. My mother was very gray—all her hair was gray and she wasn't old enough for that. I reckon that was why.

- **How Freedom Came**

"I don't remember how freedom came. They were refugeed—I call it that—my father and mother were. My sister was born in Texas, and they were back in Arkansas again when I was born. I was born and raised right here in Arkansas. They were running from one place to the other to keep the Yankees from freeing the slaves. I never even heard them say where they were freed. I don't know whether it was here or in Texas.

- **Right After the War**

"I have no knowledge of what they did right after the War. The first thing I remember was that they were picking cotton in Pine Bluff or near there. It was a smoky log house I had to stay in while they were out in the field and the smoke used to hurt my eyes awful.

• Ku Klux and Patrollers

"I don't remember nothing about the Ku Klux. I heard old folks say they used to have passes to keep the pateroles from bothering them. I remember that they said the pateroles would whip them if they would catch them out without a pass. When I first heard of the Ku Klux Klan, I thought that it was some kind of beast the folks was talking about. I didn't hear nothing special they did.

• Occupational Experiences

"When I got old enough, I worked a farm—picked cotton, hoed, plowed, pulled corn—all such things. That is about all I ever did—farming. Farming was always my regular occupation. I never did anything else—not for no regular thing.

• Marriage

"I married in 1879. My father and mother married each other too after freedom. I remember that. It was when the government was making all those that had been slaves marry. I have been married just the one time. My wife died in April 1927.

• Present Condition

"I am not able to do anything now. I don't even tote a chair across the room, or spade up the ground for a garden, or hoe up the weeds in it. I am ruptured and the doctor says it is the funniest rupture he ever seen. He says that there's a rupture and fat hanging down in the rupture. They have to keep me packed with ice all the time. The least little thing brings it down. I can't hold myself nor nothing. Have to wear something under my clothes.

"I don't get a pension."

• Interviewer's Comment

Smith is sensitive about his first name—doesn't like to give it—and about his condition. He doesn't like to mention it or to have it referred to.

He has an excellent memory for some things and a rather poor one for some others. He got angry when his granddaughter supplied data about his wife which he apparently could not recall.

His physical condition is deplorable and his circumstances extremely straitened.

Interviewer: Mrs. Bernice Bowden
Person interviewed: John H. Smith
2602 W. Twelfth Street, Pine Bluff, Arkansas
Age: 81

JOHN H. SMITH

"I reckon I was here, I member seein' the smoke from the guns look like a cloud.

"I was born in Missouri in 1856. I member way back. Yes'm. I'm old—I'm old.

"I member seein' the soldiers—Yankees—eight or ten in a squad and they asked me did I want to ride with em? Old mistress say, 'That's my boy!' I member way back when they used to put the folks upon a block and sell em. I member one night we was in the cabin and the Ku Klux come up on horses. And I member when they was hollerin' peace was declared.

"Mama told me I was born in 1856. Mama had all our ages in that big Bible.

"We stayed in St. Louis six years then we went to Chrystal City. Missouri and I went to the glass factory and went to work.

"Did I vote? Me? Yes'm, I voted many a time—Republican. I'm still a Republican—always will be I reckon. I haven't voted for a long time but I think everybody ought to have the liberty to vote.

"I like to live in the North better cause the white folks treats you better. They treats me all right here cause I don't do nothin'.

"I member my white folks was good to me.

"I went to school after the war whar I was born. C.N. Douglas, the son of Napoleon Douglas, was my teacher. First teacher we had was Miss Mary Strotter. I know she couldn't learn us anything so they got C.N. Douglas. He brought that paddle with the little holes and he learned us something. I know my sister was next to me and she couldn't get her spelling and I'd work my mouf so she could see. C.N. Douglas caught me at it and he whipped me that day. I never worked my mouf again.

"I was the best speller in the school. I won a gold pen and ink stand and George Washington picture.

"Before the war I member the overseer would say, 'If you don't have that done tonight, I'll whip you tomorrow.' They had one man was pretty bad and I know they give him a thimble and a barrel and told him he had to fill up that barrel, but he couldn't do it you know and so they whipped him.

"Mama used to whip me. She called me the 'Devil's Egg Bag' for a long time. I used to take a darning needle and punch the eyes out of guineas or chickens just to see em run around. She broke me of that. I know now she never whip me enough, but she made a man of me. I got a good name now. Always been a good worker. Done my work good and that's what they want to know. Yes ma'm, I'm old."

Interviewer: Miss Irene Robertson
Persons interviewed: Maggie Snow and Charlie Snow
R.F.D., Brinkley, Arkansas
Ages: 69 and 75

MAGGIE SNOW AND CHARLIE SNOW

"My parents' names was Mary and Henderson Kurkendall. They had seven children. Mama died when I was three years old. Papa was a Yankee soldier.

"They belong to the same white folks, Moster Jake and Peggy Kurkendall. They had a big farm.

"My papa told me that one morning they woke up and looked out over the field. The Yankees had pitched their camps far as you could see on Moster Jake's farm. They come up to his house. Moster Jake had a big house and a big family. The Yankees come up there and throwed out all they had and told the slaves to take it. No, they didn't; they was scared to take it and it belong to them. They didn't want it all wasted like they was doing. Papa said they rode their horses up to the house. They took all the soldiers on the place to the camp. They was scared not to go.

"Papa left mama at the old home place and Moster

Jake let them work all they could. Papa stayed in the war till after the battle at Vicksburg. Then he come home. They stayed awhile at Moster Jake's and worked. He got his knee hurt and his health ruined. He never was no count after he got back home. Mama could pick six hundred pounds of cotton a day he said. They worked from daybreak till pitch dark in them days.

"Little Jake Kurkendall is living now Enoch or Harrison Station, Mississippi. He is older than I am. He got a family. But he is all the son old Moster Jake had that I know living now.

"Papa said the Yankees made all the slaves fight they could run across. Some kept hid in the woods. Seem like from way he told bout it they wanted freedom but they didn't want to go to war.

"When we heard bout Arkansas being so rich and a new country, we wanted to come. Some white and some colored come. We come to Aubrey, Arkansas. We got six living, five dead children. I been here fourteen years (at Brinkley). I hired out to cook in Mississippi but I wash and iron and work in the field till I bout wore out. My husband in a terrible condition. He picked some cotton. He got rheumatism in his legs.

"We own a little home bout a mile from town and a pig. I wish I could get a cow. I ain't got the money to buy one. Jess can't get one no way. We had a fine garden. Two of us get $10 and commodities. Times so far this year been good. When it gets cold times may be hard. Times better this year than last or it been for a long time.

"I didn't know I could vote. Guess my husband done my part of the voting."

"I am seventy-three years old. There was two boys and two girls of us. My aunts and uncles raised me. My mother died when I was little and fore that my papa went to the army and never come home. They said he got killed or died—they didn't know. My parents belong to Berry Bruce. He had a family I heard em say. He lived at Louisville, Mississippi.

"I recollect the Ku Klux. I heard em talk a whole lot about em. One time they rode round our house and through the hall of our house. Yes ma'am, it scared us so bad it most paralyzed us all. They went on. We didn't know what they wanted. We never did find out.

"I don't vote. I never voted in my life. I don't recken I ever will. I have been a hard worker all my life. I farmed. I loaded and unloaded on a steamboat with my family farmin' in the country. The boat I run on went from Memphis to New Orleans.

"My family farmed at Batesville in the country out from there. For a long time I made staves with the Sweeds. They was good workers. We would make 1,000, then load the barge and send or take them to Vicksburg. I got my board and $1 a day.

"The present conditions for the cotton farmer has been better this year than last. When it gets cold and no work, makes it hard on old men. I got no job in view for the winter.

"I would like to have a cow if I could raise the money

to get one. I been tryin' to figure out how to get us a cow to help out. I can't make it.

"I suffer all the time. I can't sit still, I can't sleep I suffer so wid rheumatism. Nobody knows how I do suffer. My general health is fine.

"This President has sure been merciful to the poor and aged. Surely he will be greatly rewarded hereafter."

Interviewer: Miss Irene Robertson
Person interviewed: Robert Solomon, Des Arc, Arkansas
Age: 73

ROBERT SOLOMON

My father was African. He was born in Atlanta. My mother was a Cherokee Indian. Her name was Alice Gamage. I was born in 1864. I don't know where I was born—think it was in the Territory—my father stole my mother one night. He couldn't understand them and he was afraid of her people. He went back to Savannah after so long a time and they was in Florida when I first seen any of her people. When I got up any size I asked my father all about him and my mother marrying. He said he knowed her 'bout two year 'fore they married. They sorter courted by signs—my mother learned me her language and it was natural fur me to speak my father's tongue. I talked for them. She was bout fifteen when she run away. I don't know if a preacher ever did marry em or not. My father said she was just so pretty he couldn't help lovin' her. He kept makin' signs and she made signs. I liked my Gramma Gamage. She couldn't understand much. We all went to the Indian Territory from Florida and Georgia. That's how I come out here.

I don't remember the Ku Klux. I remember hearing ma and gramma talk 'bout the way they tried to get way from 'em. My father was a farmer till freedom. He farmed around here and at Pine Bluff. He died at West Point. My mother and step-mother both died at Pine Bluff. They took my mother to her nation in Oklahoma. She was sick a good while and they took her to wait on her. Then come and took her after she died. There show is a fambly. My father had twenty-two in his fambly. My mother had five boys and three girls and me. My stepmother had fourteen more children. That's some fambly aint it? All my brothers and sisters died when I was little and they was little. My father's other children jess somewhar down round Pine Bluff. I guess I'd know em but I aint seed none of them in I don't know how long.

The first work I ever done was sawmilling at Pine Bluff. Then I went down in Louziana, still sawmilling—I followed dat trade five or six years. Den I got to railroading. I was puttin down cross ties and layin' steel. I got to be straw boss at dat. I worked at dat fifteen years. I worked doing that in six different states. That was show fine livin'—we carried our train right along to live in. I married and went to farming. Then I come to work at this oil mill here (in Des Arc). The reason I quit. I didn't quit till it went down and moved off. I aint had nothin' much to do since. I been carryin' water and wood fur Mrs. Norfleet twenty years and they cooks fur me now. My wife died 'bout a year ago. She been dead a year last January. She was sick a long time 'fore she died. Well the relief gives me a little to eat, some clothes and I gets $5.00 a month and I takes it and buys my groceries and I takes it up to Mrs. Norfleet's. They says come there and eat. They show is good to me 'cept I aint able to carry the wood up the steps much no more. It hurt me when I worked at the oil mill. I helped them 'bout the house all the time.

What I do wid my money I made? I educated my girls. Yes maam I show is got children. One my girls teaches school in St. Louis and de other at Hot Springs. They both went to college at Pine Bluff. I sent em. No'm dey don't help me. They is by my second wife and my first wife live with my son, down close to Star City. Dey farm. It's down in Lincoln County. They let me live in this house. It belongs to him. I went to the bank fo' it closed and got my money whut I had left. I been livin' on it but it give out.

The conditions are all right. They kin make a right smart but everything is so high it don't buy much. Some of 'em say they ain't goiner do the hardest work, hot or cold and liftin' for no dollar a day. Don't nobody work hard as I used to. There's goiner be another war and a lot of them killed—'cause people ain't doin right. Some don't treat the others right. No'm they never did. They used to threaten em and take 'em out in cars and beat 'em up, just for disputin' their word or not paying 'em and de lack. The white man has cheated a heap because we was ignorant and black. They gamble on the cotton and take might' near all of it for the cheap grub they let out to make de crop on. Conditions are better but a heap of the young black and white too deblish lazy to work. Some of dem get killed out goin' on at their meanness.

I heard of uprisings since the war but I never was 'bout none of them.

I votes the Republican ticket. The last I voted was for Hoover. Sure they have tried to change my way of voting but I ain't goiner change. I ain't heard nothin' 'bout no restrictions 'bout votin'. If a woman wanter vote it's all right. My girs and my boy votes right along. They are all Republicans.

The most money I ever has at one time was $600.00. I did save it. I spent it on my girls' clothes and education. They did go to college at Pine Bluff but they went to the Catholic High School first down at Pine Bluff. No'm they don't help me. They say it's all dey can do to get along. They never have told me how much they make.

Interviewer: Mrs. Bernice Bowden
Person interviewed: James Spikes
2101 Bell Street, Pine Bluff, Arkansas
Age: 91

JAMES SPIKES

"Good morning. Yes'm I remember the Civil War. I was a soldier. I was between sixteen and seventeen when I enlisted in the war.

"'Why did you enlist?'

"I didn't know no better. I thought I would be took care of. They told us the war was sposed to set the darkies free. My old master didn't want me to go—cose not. But they was very good to me. I regard them just the same as myself.

"I enlisted in the 55th regiment of colored soldiers. Then I went off with the Yankees. I was with them when they had the battle at Corinth, Mississippi.

"I was with them when the Yankees taken Corinth and whupped. The rebels tried to take it back and the Yankees whupped 'em again. The regiment I was with whupped 'em away from several places and kept 'em runnin'.

"When we was in Fort Pickens I 'member they had a poll parrot—some of the officers had trained it to say 'Corporal of the guard, Jim Spikes, post No. 1." Sometimes

I would draw my gun like I was going to shoot and the poll parrot would say, 'Jim, don't you shoot me!' They got plenty a sense.

"The war was funny and it wasn't funny. Well, it was funny for the side that won when we had scrummishes (skirmish). I never was captured but I hoped capture a lot.

"I stayed in the war till I was mustered out in Baton Rouge, Louisiana. I was a good big fellow then. Oh Lord yes, I knowed most anything.

"After that I went to Memphis and then I come to Arkansas and went to farming with some white fellows named French. The river overflowed and we lost 'bout all the cotton.

"The government gives me a pension now cause I was a soldier. Yes'm it comes in right nice—it does that."

Interviewer: Mrs. Bernice Bowden
Person interviewed: Kittie Stanford
309 Missouri Street; Pine Bluff, Arkansas
Age: 104

KITTIE STANFORD

"Yes'm, I used to be a slave. My mother belonged to Mrs. Lindsey. One day when I was ten years old, my old mistress take me over to her daughter and say 'I brought you a little nigger gal to rock de cradle.' I'se one hundred and four years old now. Miss Etta done writ it down in the book for me.

"One time a lady from up North ask me did I ever get whipped. Honey, I ain't goin' tell you no lie. The overseer whipped us. Old mistress used to send me to her mother to keep the Judge from whippin' me. Old Judge say 'Nigger need whippin' whether he do anything or not.'

"Some of the hands run away. Old Henry run away and hide in the swamp and say he goin' stay till he bones turn white. But he come back when he get hongry and then he run away again.

"When the war come some of the slaves steal the Judge's hosses and run away to Pine Bluff and he didn't never find 'em. The Judge think the Yankees goin' get everything he got so we all left Arkansas and went to Texas. We in Texas when freedom come. We come back to Arkansas and I stay with my white folks awhile but I didn't get no pay so I got a job cookin' for a colored woman.

"I been married fo' times. I left my las' husband. I didn't leave him cause he beat me. I lef' him cause he want too many.

"No'm I never seen no Ku Klux. I heard 'bout 'em but I never seen none that I knows of. When I used to get a pass to go to 'nother plantation I always come back fo' dark.

"This younger generation is beyond my onderstanding. They is gettin' weaker and wiser.

"I been ready to die for the last thirty years. 'Mary (her granddaughter with whom she lives), show the lady my shroud.' I keeps it wropped up in blue cloth. They tells me at the store to do that to keep it from turning yellow. 'Show her that las' quilt I made.' Yes'm I made this all by myself. I threads my own needle, too, and cuts out the pieces. I has worked hard all my life.

"Now the Welfare gives me my check. My granddaughter good to me. I goes to church on the first and third Sundays.

"Lady, I glad you come to see me and God bless you. Goo' bye!"

Interviewer: Miss Irene Robertson
Person Interviewed: Tom Stanhouse
R.F.D.
Brinkley, Ark.
Age: 74

TOM STANHOUSE

"I was born close to Greenville, South Carolina. I lived down close to Spartanburg. My mother was named Luvenia Stanhouse and Henry Stanhouse. They had nine children. Grandma belong to Hopkins but married into the Stanhouse family. Grandpa's name was Tom. They set him free. I guess because he was old. He lived about mong his children.

"When they was set free old man Adam Stanhouse was good to em. He treated em nice but they never got nothing but their clothes. They moved on another place and started working sharecropper.

"Before freedom old man Adam Stanhouse would give my pa a pass or his pocket knife to show to go to see my ma. She lived at Dr. Harrison's farm five miles apart. They all knowed Adam Stanhouse's knife. I don't know how they would know it. He never let his Negroes be whooped unless he said so. Owners didn't 'low the Ku Klux whoop hands on their place.

"Adam Stanhouse brought my pa from Virginia with him. Some of them men thought might near much of his slaves as they did their children. Or I heard em say they seem to. My pa married my ma when she was thirteen years old. They had nine children.

"I heard ma say Dr. Harrison practiced medicine. His wife was named Miss Lizzie. They had two boys and three girls.

"Ma was a house girl. Pa was a field hand. One time traders come round and ma's owner wanted to sell her and his wife objected. She wasn't sold that time. I don't know if she was sold or not.

"I don't know no more about that war than I do about the German war (World War). I was a little boy when it was all over. I left South Carolina in 1888. Ma was a part Red Indian and pa was a half Black Creek Indian. I had two children before I left South Carolina. I was married back there. I paid my own way and come to Fargo. I was trying to better my condition. In 1896 I come to Brinkley. Before that I lived at Dark Corner eight years. In 1920 ma and pa come to me and died with me. I paid $25.00 for my second class ticket to Fargo—in 1888.

"Since 1864 to 1937 I farmed, sawmilled, threshed, run a grist mill, run a cotton gin and worked about em. I farmed eight or nine years across the bayou here.

"I own a home. My wife is living. I get 'demodities', no money. I got two girls living. One girl is in New Jersey and one in Michigan. They make their living.

"I think the world is going on worse than ever I seen it. Folks can't live without money. They don't try to raise their living no more. I ain't no prophet. The world going to nothing way I see it."

Interviewer: Miss Irene Robertson
Person interviewed: Isom Starnes, Marianna, Arkansas
Age: 78

ISOM STARNES

"I was born in Marshall County, Alabama near Guntersville. Father belong to the Starnes. They bought him in Alabama. My parents' name was Jane and Burrel Starnes. They had two children I knew of. When they was set free they left and started renting. I don't remember much that happened before freedom. I picked up chips and put them in a split basket I just could chin. I'd fill all the baskets and they would haul them up to put under the iron skillet. Other chaps was picking up chips too. They used some kinds to smoke the meat. I could tote water on my head and a bucket in each hand. They was small buckets. We had to come up a path up the hill. I stumped my toe on the rocks till they would bleed; sometimes it looked like the nail would come off. My mother was a good cook. I don't know what she was doing in slavery.

"I been farming all my life. Yes, I owned ninety-eight acres in Alabama. I had a home on it. I lost it. We brought a suit for water damage. We lost it, I reckon. They fixed a dam that ruined my place. I left and went to the North—to Springfield, Ohio. I started public work and worked three or four months in a piano factory. I liked farming the best and come back to it. My boys hope me down hill.

I got two boys. My girl left me all I got now. She is dead. I got a home and twenty-five acres of ground. She made the money washing, ironing and farming. I 'plied for the old folks' pension but didn't get it and give it up. I made four bales cotton, one hundred pounds seed cotton. My place is half mile from town. I have to get somebody to do all the work.

"My father did vote. He voted a Republican ticket. I have voted but I don't vote now. I voted a few days ago for a little cotton this year. It was the cotton control election. I voted a Republican ticket. I found out Democrat times is about the best time for us in the South. I quit voting because I'm too old to keep up with it. If a woman owns anything—land or house—she ought to be allowed to vote.

"The times is mighty hard. I need a little money now and I can't get it nowhere. It looks like bad times for me. The young folks don't work hard as I did. I kept study (steady) at farming. I liked it. My race is the best fitted for farming and that is where we belong. I never been in jail. I never been arrested in my whole life."

- **Interviewer's comment**

I stopped this clean, feeble, old Negro—humble as could be—on the edge of town. He had a basket of groceries taking to his old wife. It was a small split basket. His taxes worried him. He couldn't get a holt on any money, so I told him about the Farmers' Loan. He was so scared looking I felt he didn't tell me all he knew. He looked tired. I gave it up and jokingly asked him if he had ever been in jail. He said, "I never been in jail. I never been arrested in my whole life." I laughed good and thanked him. I told a young woman who had curiously been trying to catch the conversation from her yard that I feared I frightened the old man till he couldn't think to tell me all he knew. She said, "Maybe so but he has a reputation of being good as gold and his word his bond."

United States. Work Projects Administration

Interviewer: Mrs. Bernice Bowden
Person interviewed: Ky (Hezekiah) Steel
West Fifth Avenue (rear), Pine Bluff, Arkansas
Age: 85
Occupation: Yard man

KY HEZEKIAH STEEL

"What is it you want to know? Well, I was born in North Carolina. I know they brought me here from North Carolina in slavery times. I couldn't keep no count of it, lady, 'cause I didn't know. I know I was big enough to walk behind the wagon pickin' up corn. I know that. That was in slavery times.

"Mr. June Ingraham's father brought me here.

"Oh, that's a long time ago. Mr. June and I was boys together. I was born in the Ingraham family.

"They carried me from here to Texas. I stayed there till I was grown and married. Then I come back to Arkansas I got with Mr. June's son and I been here since.

"Never have gone to school a day. Can't read but I can spell a little.

"I've done most all kinds of work—split rails, cut wood, farm work, and railroad work on the section.

"Ku Klux come out there where I was in Texas. Didn't

bother me—they was just around first one place, then another.

"I voted once. I guess it was Republican. I don't remember now who I voted for. I didn't take much interest in politics—only just what I'd hear somebody say.

"Yankees was camped near us in Texas to keep the wild Indians back. That was after the War. Yes'm, sure was.

"I know the very night old missis told us we was free. Called all us slaves up there together. Told us we was just as free as she was. I always will remember that.

"I stayed there till we got through the crop. Then I went to Paris, Texas and portered in a little hotel there. Then I went wagonin'—haulin' stuff.

"They used to whip me in slavery times when they got ready. Need it? well, they said I did. Hurt my feelin's and hurt my hide too, but they raised me to do whatever they said.

"This younger generation ain't no good—they ain't raised up like I was. Things is a whole lot different than they used to be. The folks ain't prayin' to God like they used to. Ain't livin' right.

"I had two brothers killed in time of the War. That's what the old people told me after I come back from Texas.

"Yes'm, I've had plenty to eat all my life—up until now; I ain't got so much now.

"I keep the rheumatism pretty much all the time but I ain't never been down sick so I couldn't help myself.

"I'm telling you just what I know and what I don't know I couldn't tell you. Good-bye."

United States. Work Projects Administration

Interviewer: Miss Irene Robertson
Person Interviewed: Maggie Stenhouse,
(a mile down the railway track),
Brinkley, Arkansas
Age: 72?

MAGGIE STENHOUSE

"Mama was owned by Master Barton. She lived on the line of North Carolina and South Carolina. Her husband was sold away from her and two children. She never seen him no more. Rangments was made with Master Barton to let Master Liege Alexander have her for a cook. Then she went to Old Pickens, South Carolina. Liege Alexander had a white wife and by her he had two girls and a boy. He had a black cook and by her he had two boys and a girl. One of these boys was my papa and I told you the old man bought my mama from Master Barton for his colored son. My papa never was sold you see cause he was the old white man's boy. After his white wife died his two girls married and the boy left Old Pickens, and they told his colored wife and her two boys and girl if they would stay and take care of him as long as he lived they could have the property. My papa went off five or six miles and built him a log house.

"The old man—Master Liege Alexander—was blind when his wife died and he had to be tended to like a child. He would knock his stick on the wall and some of the small children would lead him about where he wanted to go. His white children didn't like the way he had lived so they didn't want to be bothered with him.

"My parents' names was Cheney Barton and Jim Alexander. Papa was medium dark and so was his own brother but their sister was as white as the woman's two girls and boy.

"After the railroads sprung up the town moved to New Pickens.

"Master Liege Alexander had lots of slaves and land. I reckon the white wife's children fell heir to the farm land.

"My aunt and grandma cooked for him till he died. They kept him clean and took care of him like as if his white wife was living. The colored wife and her girl waited on the white wife and her children like queens. That is what papa said.

"Durin' slavery there was stockmen. They was weighed and tested. A man would rent the stockman and put him in a room with some young women he wanted to raise children from. Next morning when they come to let him out the man ask him what he done and he was so glad to get out. Them women nearly kill him. If he said nothin' they wouldn't have to pay for him. Them women nearly kill him. Some of the slave owners rented these stockmen. They didn't let them work in the field and they kept them fed up good.

"Fore the Civil War broke out mama said Master Barton hid a half bushel solid gold and silver coins over the mountains. He had it close to the spring awhile. Mama had to go by it to tote water to the house. She said she never bothered it. He said he could trust her and she wouldn't tell a lie. He took another sack of money over the mountains and the silverware. His wife died during the war. A lot of people died from hearing of the war—heart failure. I don't know what become of his money. He lost it. He may forgot where he hid it. It was after his wife died that he sold mama to Jim Alexander's papa.

"The Yankees rode three years over the country in squads and colored folks didn't know they was free. I have seen them in their old uniforms riding around when I was a child. White folks started talking about freedom fore the darkies and turning them loose with the clothes they had on and what they could tote away. No land, no home, no place; they roamed around.

"When it was freedom the thing papa done was go to a place and start out share croppin'. Folks had no horses or mules. They had to plough new ground with oxen. I ploughed when I was a girl, ploughed oxen. If you had horses or mules and the Yankees come along three or four years after the war, they would swap horses, ride a piece, and if they had a chance swap horses again. Stealing went on during and long after the war.

"The Ku Klux was awful in South Carolina. The colored folks had no church to go to. They gather around at folks' houses to have preaching and prayers. One night we was having it at our house, only I was the oldest and was in another room sound asleep on the bed. There was a crowd at our house. The Ku Klux come, pulled off his robe and door face, hung it up on a nail in the room, and said, 'Where's that Jim Jesus?' He pulled him out the room. The crowd run off. Mama took the three little children but forgot me and run off too. They beat papa till they thought he was dead and throwed him in a fence corner. He was beat nearly to death, just cut all to pieces. He crawled to my bed and woke me up and back to the steps. I thought he was dead—bled to death—on the steps. Mama come back to leave and found he was alive. She doctored him up and he lived thirty years after that. We left that morning.

"The old white woman that owned the place was rich—big rich. She been complaining about the noise—singing and preaching. She called him Praying Jim Jesus till he got to be called that around. He prayed in the field. She said he disturbed her. Mama said one of the Ku Klux she knowed been raised up there close to Master Barton's but papa said he didn't know one of them that beat on him.

"Papa never did vote. I don't vote. I think women should vote much as men. They live under the same law.

"I come to Arkansas about forty-five years ago. Papa brought us to a new country, thought we could do better. I been farming, cooking, washing. I can't do my own cooking and washing now. I got rheumatism in my joints, feet, knees, and hands. We don't get no help of no kind.

"My daughter is in Caldwell, New Jersey at work. She went there to get work. She heard about it and went and haven't come home. I jes' got one child."

Interviewer: Beulah Sherwood Hagg
Person interviewed: Mrs. Charlotte E. Stephens
1420 West 15th Street, Little Rock, Arkansas
Age: 83

CHARLOTTE E. STEPHENS

I was born right here in Little Rock. My father was owned by a splendid family—the Ashleys. The family of Noah Badgett owned my mother and the children. Pardon me, madam, and I shall explain how that was. In many cases the father of children born in slavery could not be definitely determined. There was never a question about the mother. From this you will understand that the children belonged to the master who owned the mother. This was according to law.

My father's family name was Andrews. How did it happen that it was not Ashley?... Oh, my dear, you have been misinformed about all slaves taking the name of the master who owned them when peace came.... No, madam. My father was named William Wallace Andrews after his father, who was an English gentleman. He had come to Missouri in early days and owned slaves.... Yes, my grandfather was white. The Ashleys brought my father to Arkansas Territory when they came. They always permitted him to keep his family name. Many other masters did the same.

From the standpoint of understanding between the white and colored races, Little Rock has always been a good place to live. The better class families did not speak of their retainers as slaves; they were called servants. Both my parents were educated by their masters. Besides being a teacher and minister my father was a carpenter and expert cabinet worker.

The first school for Negroes in Little Rock was opened in 1863 and was taught by my father. I went to school to him. A few months later there came from the north a company of missionary teachers and opened a school which I attended until 1867. My father was a minister of the Methodist Episcopal church for colored people on what is now Eighth and Broadway. He also had a chapel on the property of Mr. Ashley. You probably know that during slavery days the slaves belonged to and attended the same church as their white folks. They sat in the back, or in a balcony built for them. My father was considered the founder of Wesley Chapel, which was Methodist Episcopal. From that time until this day I have been a member of that church. Seventy-three years, I think it is. Before the break came in the Methodist church, you know, it was all the same, north and south. After the division on account of slavery the Methodist church in the south had the word "south" attached. For a long time my father did not realize that. In 1863 he and his church went back into the original Methodist church.

In 1867 the Society of Friends—we called them Quakers—came and erected a large two-story schoolhouse at Sixth and State streets. It was called Union school. When it was built it was said by the Quakers that it was to be for the use of colored children forever, but within a year or two the city bought the property and took charge of the school. As far as I can now recall, white and colored children never did attend the same school in Little Rock. There have always been separate schools for the races. I am able to remember the names of the first teachers in the Quaker school; J.H. Binford was the principal and his sister taught the primary department. Other teachers were Miss Anna Wiles (or Ware), Miss Louise Coffin, Miss Lizzie Garrison, and Sarah Henley.

I was about 11 years old when peace came and was living with my mother and the other children on the Badgett plantation about 7 miles east of Little Rock. Mother did laundry and general house work. Being a small child, all that was asked of me was to run errands and amuse the little white children. Madam, if I could tell you the great difference between slave owners it would help you in understanding conditions of today among the colored people. Both my father and my mother had peculiar privileges. The Ashley family were exceptional slave owners; they permitted their servants to hire their time. There was class distinction, perhaps to greater extent than among the white people. Yes, madam, the slaves who lived in the family with master and mistress were taught just about the same as their own children. At any rate, they imitated them in all matters; to speak with a low voice, use good English, the niceties of manners, good form and courtesy in receiving and attending guests.

I began teaching in Little Rock schools when I was 15 years old and am still teaching. In all, it is 69 years, and my contract is still good. My first experience as a teacher, (as

I told you I was fifteen) was by substituting for a teacher in that first Missionary school, in 1869. For some reason, she did not return, and the School Board appointed me in her place. After one year I was given leave of absence to attend Oberlin College in Ohio. I spent three years there, but not in succession. When my money would give out I would come home and the School Board would provide work for me until I could earn enough to carry me through another term. I finished at Oberlin in 1873. I extended my work through courses at Normal schools and Teacher's Institutes. I have taken lecture courses in many colleges, notably the University of California in 1922. I have taught all grades from the first to the twelfth. My principal work, for the last 35 years, however, has been high school Latin and English and Science.

At present I am serving as librarian at the Senior high school and Junior College. I have twice served as principal of city schools in Little Rock. First at Capitol Hill. The Charlotte E. Stephens school at 18th and Maple was named in my honor. I have a book I have kept for 68 years regarding those first schools, and I'm told it is the only one in existence. I also have the first monthly report card ever issued in Little Rock. Mr. Hall (Superintendent of Little Rock City Schools) has asked me to will it to the School Board.

I could recall many interesting events of those early schools for the colored race. Old, old slaves came, desiring to learn to read and spell. They brought the only books they could find, many of which proved to be almanacs, paper bound novels discarded by their mistress and ancient dictionaries, about half of which might be missing.

Yes, madam, I do remember that the emancipated slaves were led to believe they would be given property and have just what their masters had been accustomed to enjoy. I remember hearing my mother tell, in later years, that she really had expected to live as her mistress had; having some one to wait upon her, plenty of money to spend, ride in a carriage with a coachman. But she always added that the emancipated ones soon found out that freedom meant more work and harder than they had ever done before.

What did they work at? Pardon me please for so often reminding you of conditions of that time. Few of the trades workers were white. Brick makers and brick layers, stone masons, lathers, plasters,—all types of builders were of the freed men. You must remember that slaves were the only ones who did this work. Their masters had used their labor as their means of income. Not all slaves were in the cotton fields, as some suppose. The slave owners of towns and villages had their slaves learn skilled trade occupations and made a great deal of money by their earnings. The Yankee soldiers and the many Northern people who lived here hired the freed men and paid them. Quite soon the colored people were buying homes. Many were even hired by their former masters and paid for the work they formerly did without pay under slavery.

I remember Bill Read and Dave Lowe. They had been coachmen before freedom. By combining their first savings, they bought a hack, as it was called. It was more of a cab. For all those who did not have private conveyances, this was the only way of getting about town. It was Little Rock's first taxi-cab business, I should say. Bill and Dave made a fortune; they had a monopoly of business for years and eventually had enough cabs to take the entire population to big evening parties, theater, and all places where crowds would gather.

No, madam, I do not recall that we had any inconvenience from the Ku Klux Klan. If they made trouble in Little Rock I do not now remember it. I did hear that out in the country they drove people from their homes. Yes, madam, I do remember, quite distinctly, the times when colored men were voted into public offices. John C. Corbin was State Superintendent of Public Instruction. Phillips county sent two colored men to the legislature; they were W.H. Gray and H.H. White, both from Helena. J.E. Bush of this city followed M.W. Gibbs as Police Judge. After reconstruction when all colored people were eliminated from public life all these people returned to their trade.

I was 22 when I married. My husband was a teacher but knew the carpenter trade. During the time that Negroes served in public office he served as deputy sheriff and deputy constable. He was with me for 41 years before his death; we raised a family of six children and gave each one a college education.

Now, you have asked my opinion of present conditions of the younger generation. It seems to me they are living in an age of confusion; they seem to be all at sea as to what they should get for themselves. I do know this. In some respects the modern frankness is an improvement over the old suppression and repression in the presence of their elders. At the same time, I think the young people of today lack the proper reverence and respect for age and the experience it brings as a guide for them. During my long years of teaching I have had opportunity to study this question. I am still making a study of the many phases of modern life as it affects the young people. I do not like the trend of amusements of today; I would like for our young people to become interested in things more worth while; in a higher type of amusement. Conditions of morality and a lack of regard for conventions is deplorable. Smoking among the girls has increased the common use of liquor between the sexes.

Did you ask me about the voting restrictions for the colored race in this State? I will tell you frankly that I think the primary law here is unjust; most unjust. We are citizens in every other respect; the primary voting privilege should be ours also. This restriction has been explained as coming down from "the grandfather clause" inserted in early legislation. I cannot give you the exact wording of the clause but the substance was that no person whose ancestor—grandfather—was not entitled to vote before 1863 should have the right to the ballot. Of course it is readily seen that this clause was written purely for the purpose of denying the vote to the colored people.

Perhaps, madam, my talk has been too much along educational lines. You asked me about my life since freedom came and how I have lived to the present time. I have had the blessed privilege of being a teacher—of doing the work I love best of all in the world to do. I have written the story of my life work; it is all ready to be published. I have written "The Story of Negro Schools in Little Rock" and "Memoirs of Little Rock." Madam, I have written, I suppose, what would amount to volumes for our church papers and local Negro newspaper. My daughter was, at one time, editor of the Womens' Page.

No, I'm indeed sorry that I have not kept a scrapbook of such writings. In these latter years my friends scold me for having destroyed all the papers as fast as they were read. The most of the news in the articles, however, I have used in the manuscripts of the books I hope to have published.

Interviewer: Miss Irene Robertson
Person interviewed: William J. Stevens, Brinkley, Arkansas
Age: Up in 70's

WILLIAM J. STEVENS

"I was born in Pleasant Hill, Alabama. My owners were Haley and Missouri Stevens. They owned Grandma Mary. Pa was born on the place. Mother was sold from the Combesses to Stevens. Mother's mother was a Turk Dark Creek Indian. She was a free woman. Her name was Judy. I called her Grandma Judy. She was old but not gray. She had long black hair as I remember her. Mother was named Millie. Haley bought her for my pa. My pa's father was Haley Stevens' own son. He was his coachman. Pa never worked a great deal. Mother never cooked till after emancipation. She was the house girl and nurse. Life moved along smoothly as much as I ever heard till freedom come on. The Indians was independent folks. My mother was like that. Haley Stevens took his family to Texas soon as freedom come on. Mother went with them. They treated her so nicely. Pa wouldn't follow. He said she thought more of them than she did him. He kept me with him. He married again. He was a barber at Selma, Alabama. He died a barber at Anniston, Alabama. While my mother was in Texas she went to see her mother in Hickory, Alabama. She was talking with a tramp. He had helped my pa in the shop at Selma. Mother took the train and come to pa's and my stepmother's house. I was fourteen years old then and still wore a long shirt-like dress. They treated her the nicest kind. She told them she was married to a man named Sims down in Mississippi. She went back. I don't know where. The barber business was a colored man's trade in the early days.

"Soon after freedom I made two trips a day and carried my young mistress' books to school. It was a mile for us to go 'round the road to Pleasant Hill. She married C.C. Williams. I cooked for her. I cooked her daughter's weddin' supper. She had two girls, Maude and Pearl. I worked there fourteen years for my clothes and something to eat. Then I went to myself. When I wasn't cooking I worked in Mr. C.C. Williams' sash and blind factory. They was big rich folks. Mrs. Williams had a hundred rent houses. She went about in her carriage and collected rent. That was at Meridian, Mississippi. They learned me more than an education—to work. She learned me to cook. I cooked all my life. I cooked here at the Rusher Hotel till I got so old I was not able to do the work.

"I do little odd jobs of work where I can find them. I 'plied for the Old Age Pension but they give me commodities and that's all. I supports my own self such as it be.

"I find the young generation don't stick to jobs like I had to do. Seems like they want an education to keep them out of work. Education does some good and some more harm than good. Oh, times! Times is going fast. Well with some I reckon. Some like me is done left. I mean I got slower. Time getting faster. I'm done left outen the game. Time wait for no man."

Interviewer: Samuel S. Taylor
Person interviewed: Minnie Johnson Stewart
3210 W. Sixteenth Street, Little Rock, Arkansas
Age: Between 50 and 60?

MINNIE JOHNSON STEWART

"My mother's name was Mahala McElroy. Her master's name was Wiley McElroy. She was living in Howard County, Arkansas near Nashville. She worked in the field, and sewed in the house for her mistress. One time she said she never would forget about slavery was a time when she was thirteen years old, and the overseer beat her.

"My mother was a real bright woman with great long black hair. Her master was her father. She told me that the overseer grabbed her by her hair and wound it 'round his arm and then grabbed her by the roots of it and jerked her down to the ground and beat her till the blood ran out of her nose and mouth. She was 'fraid to holler.

"Mother married when she was fourteen. I can't remember the name of her husband. The preacher was an old man, a faith doctor, who read the ceremony. His name was Lewis Hill.

"I heard mother say they beat my brother-in-law

(his name was Dave Denver) till he was bloody as a hog. Then they washed him down in salt and water. Then they beat him again because he hollered.

"She told us how the slaves used to try to pray. They were so scared that the overseer would see them that early in the morning while they were going to their work in the field at daybreak that they would fall down on one knee and pray. They were so 'fraid that the overseer would catch them that they would be watching for him with one eye and looking for God with the other. But the Lord understood.

"My mother was seventy years old when she died. She has been dead thirty years."

Interviewer: Miss Irene Robertson
Person interviewed: Liza Stiggers, Forrest City, Arkansas
Age: 70 plusv

LIZA STIGGERS

"I was born in Poplar Grove, Arkansas on Col. Bibbs' place. Mama was sold twice. Once she was sold in Georgia, once in Alabama, and brought to Tennessee, later to Arkansas. Master Ben Hode brought her to Arkansas. She had ten children and I'm the only one living. Mama was a dancing woman. She could dance any figure. They danced in the cabins and out in the yards.

"The Yankees come one day to our house and I crawled under the house. I was scared to death. They called me out. I was scared not to obey and scared to come on out. I come out. They didn't hurt me. Mr. Ben Hode hid a small trunk of money away. He got it after the War. The slaves never did know where it was hid. They said the hair was on the trunk he hid his money in. It was made out of green hide for that purpose.

"Mama had a slave husband. He was a field hand and all kind of a hand when he was needed. Mama done the sewing for white and black on the place. She was a maid. She could cook some in case they needed her. She died first. Papa's foot got hurt some way and it et off. He was so old they couldn't cure it. He was named Alfred Hode. Mama was Viney Hode. She said they had good white folks. They lived on Ben Hode's place two or three years after freedom.

"I farmed, cooked, and ironed all my life. I don't know how to do nothing else.

"I live with my daughter. I got a son."

Interviewer: Samuel S. Taylor
Person interviewed: James Henry Stith
2223 W. Nineteenth Street
Little Rock, Arkansas
Age: 72

JAMES HENRY STITH

"I was born la Sparta in Hancock County, Georgia, in January 26, 1866. My father was named William Henry Stith, and I was a little tot less than two years old when my mother died. My father has called her name often but I forget it. I forget the names of my father's father, too, and of mother's people. That is too far back.

"My father was born in 1818. He was born in Georgia. His master was named W.W. Simpson. He had a master before Simpson. Simpson bought him from somebody else. I never can remember the man's name.

• **Houses**

"The first houses I saw in Georgia were frame or brick houses. There weren't any log houses 'round where I was brought up. Georgia wasn't a log house state—leastwise, not the part I lived in. In another part there were plenty of sawmills. That made lumber common. You could get longleaf pine eighty to ninety feet long if you wanted it. Some little towns didn't have no planing mills and you would have to send to Augusta or to Atlanta for the planing work or else they would make planed lumber by hand. I have worked for four and five weeks at a time dressing lumber—flooring, ceiling, siding, moldings, and so on.

"My father was still with Simpson when I remembered anything. At that time the house we lived in was a weatherboarded house just like the ones we live in now. It was a house that had been built since freedom. Old man Simpson sent for my father and told him to build a house for himself on the grounds. My father had been with Simpson for so long and had done so much work for him during slave time that Simpson didn't want to do without him. He supplied all the lumber and materials for my father. During slave time, Simpson had hired my father out to the other planters when he had nothing for him to do in the line of building on his own plantation. He had had him to superintend his grist mill. All that was in slavery time. My father was a highly skilled laborer. He could do a lot of other things besides building. So when freedom came, he wanted my father 'round him still. They both fished and hunted. He wanted my father to go fishing with him and keep him company. My father was a carpenter of the first class, you see, even in slave time. That was all he done. He was brought up to be a carpenter and did nothing but that all his time. My daddy was a mighty good mechanic.

• Good Master

"My daddy's master was a very good and kind one. My father was not under any overseer. He worked directly under his master.

"I remember one incident he told me. His master

hired a new overseer who hung around for a bit watching my father. Finally, my father asked him, 'Now, what are you able to do?' The overseer answered. 'Why, I can see all over and whip all over, and that's as much as any damn man can do.'

"Nobody was allowed to touch my father. He never had no trouble with the pateroles either. Old man Simpson didn't allow that. He was a free agent. When he wasn't working for Simpson, he was working for the next big farmer, and then the next one, and then the next one, and old man Simpson got wages for his work. Sometimes he worked a contract. Old man Simpson couldn't afford to have him handicapped in his going and coming. He could go whenever he wanted to go, and come back whenever he got ready, with a pass or without one. His time was valuable.

"The reason why so many slaves suffered as much as they did as a rule was not because of the masters but because of the poor white trash overseers. I know of several rich white women that had slaves that wouldn't allow them to be mistreated. They would fire four and five overseers to keep their slaves from being mistreated.

- **Mean Masters**

"But there were some mean masters. I have heard that right there in Georgia there was one white planter—I think it was Brantley---who put one of his slaves that had been unruly in a packing screw and ran it down on him till he mashed him to death. The cotton screw was the thing they pressed cotton bales in. They run it down by steam now, but then, they used to run it down with two mules. They tell a lot of things like that on Brantley.

Of course, I couldn't personally know it, but I know he was mighty mean and I know the way he died.

• Bushwhacking the Ku Klux

"He belonged to the paterole gang and they went out after the Negroes one night after freedom. The Negroes bushwhacked them and killed four or five of them. They give it out that the men that was killed had gone to Texas. Brantley was one of the killed ones. The pateroles was awful bad at that time. Ku Klux they called them after the War, but they was the same people. I never heard of the Klan part till this thing come up that they have now. They called them Ku Klux back when I was a boy. My stepmother carried me over to Brantley's house the night he got killed. So I know the Texas he went to. That was in '69 or '70. He lived about a mile from us and when he got killed, she carried me over to see him just like we would have gone to see any other neighbor.

"The Negroes were naturally afraid of the Ku Klux but they finally got to the place where they were determined to break it up. They didn't have no ropes, but they would take grapevines and tie them across the road about breast high when a man would be on horseback. The Ku Klux would run against these vines and be knocked off their horses into the road and then the bushwhackers would shoot them. When Ku Klux was killed in this manner, it was never admitted; but it was said that they had gone to Texas. There was several of them went to Texas one night.

• Amusements

"There weren't many amusements in slave times.

They had dances with fiddle music. There was mighty few darkies could get out to go to dances because the pateroles was so bad after them. I don't know of any other amusements the slaves had. They were playing baseball when I was born. There were boys much older than I was already playing when I was old enough to notice, so I think they must have known about it in slave time. They didn't play much in that way because they didn't have time.

- **Slaves who Bought Themselves**

"I have heard tell of some Negroes that was thrifty and got money enough from side work to buy themselves. They had to go North then because they couldn't live in the South free. I don't remember their names just now.

- **Church**

"The slaves had church. Sometimes they had church at one another's house. I don't think they ever built them a church house. But they could go to the white folks' church if they wanted to.

- **How Freedom Came**

"My daddy's master told my father he was free. He told him that in 1865. He told him that he was free to do as he pleased, that he could come when he pleased and go when he pleased. 'Course, he told him he wanted him to stay around him—not to go off.

- **Soldiers**

"I have heard my father speak of soldiers, but they were too busy 'round Atlanta and up that way to git down where my father was. They don't seem to have bothered his town. They never made my father do any labor in the army neither. My father was mixed Indian, white, and Negro.

• Marriage

"Slaves had to get the consent of their masters to marry. Sometimes masters would want them to go and would even buy the woman they wanted to keep them contented on the plantation. Sometimes the masters wouldn't do anything but let them visit. They would marry—what they called marriage in those days—and the husband would have to git permission from his master to go visit his wife and git permission from her master to come there. He would go on Saturday night and get back in time for his work on Monday morning. It was just like raising stock and mating it.

"I have been married fifty-one years. I have been married twice though. My first wife died in 1900. I have been married to my second wife thirty-four years last April. Those were real marriages.

• Opinions

"I can't say much along these lines. The chance to make a living looks so dark I can't see much of a future. Things seem to be getting worse. Nearly everybody I talk with, white or colored, seems to think the same. It is like Senator Glass said. 'If Congress would close up and go home at once, times would get better.' People don't know what kind of fool law Congress is going to make and they are not going to spend much money. I don't think Mr.

Roosevelt's pump priming will do much good because you must keep adding to it or it will go away.

"I don't think much of the young people. These nineteenth or twentieth century Negroes is something fierce I'm telling you.

• Vocational Experiences

"I am a carpenter. I wish I wasn't. The depression has made it so that the Negroes get very little to do. What they have they give to their own people. They don't have much for nobody. Even if the nigger gets something, he gets very little out of it. But the main trouble is there isn't anything to do.

"I have been a carpenter for fifty-four years. I have been here fifty-one years. I have never had no trouble earning a living till now. I can't do it now. The biggest obstacle of the success of the Negro carpenter is that Negroes don't have the money to build with. They must get the money from the white man. The white man, on the other hand, if he lets out the money for the building, has the say-so on who will do it, and he naturally picks out another white man. That keeps the majority of Negroes out of work as far as carpentry is concerned. It does in a time like this. When times is better, the white man does not need to be so tight, and he can divide up."

Interviewer: Pernella Anderson, colored
Caroline Stout

CAROLINE STOUT

I was born in Alabama in slavery time. I was sold from my mother after I was five years old and never did see her again. Was sold to a family by the name of Mr. Games. There were six of them in family and I was the seventh. They were very nice to me until I was about 10 years of age. I would attend to the little kids. They were all boys. Had to sleep on straw beds and been cooking for myself ever since I was 8 years old. When about ten they started putting hard work on me and had to pick cotton and do the work around the house. Was a slave for about 15 years. After I was freed I moved to Union County and been here ever since.

United States. Work Projects Administration

Interviewer: Samuel S. Taylor
Person interviewed: Felix Street
822 Schiller Street, Little Rock, Arkansas
Age: 74

FELIX STREET

I was born in Dickson County, Tennessee, fifty miles north of Nashville, in 1864. It was on December twenty-eighth. My father told me when he was living how old I was. He told me all the way along, and I remember it.

"Nannie, Jeff, Hardy, John Mack, and Felix (that's me) are my father's children by his first wife. Lena, Martha, Esther are his children by his second wife. He had five children by my mother, and four of them lived to be grown, and one died in infancy. My mother was his first wife. Her name was Mary Street. Her name before she married—hold a minute, lemme see—seems like it was Mary—Mary—Street.

"My father and my mother couldn't have lived on the same plantation because she was a May and he was a Street. I don't know how they met.

"My father's master's name was Jick Street. He owned, to my knowing, my father, Bill Street; Henry Street, and Ed Street. He might have owned more but I heard my father say he owned those.

"My father said his white people weren't very wealthy. He and his brother had to go and cut cordwood, both summer and winter. And they was allowed so much work for a task. Their task was nine cords a week for each man. That was equal to a cord and a half a day for each man each day. My father would cut his wood like a man ought to cut it. But he said my uncle wouldn't git at his task. He would drink whiskey all the week. They'd get after him about bein' behind with his work, but he would say, 'Never mind that; I won't be behind Monday morning.' On Sunday morning at nine o'clock, he would get up and begin to cut on that wood. And on Monday morning at nine o'clock, he would have nine cords cut for his white folks and four or five for himself. It would all be done before nine o'clock Monday morning.

• Living Brother

"I recently seen my brother Jeff Davis Street. I haven't seen him before for sixty-one years. He blew in here from Texas with a man named Professor Smuggers. He lives in Malakoff, Texas. It's been sixty-one years since he was where I could see him, but he says he saw me fifty-nine years ago. He came back home and I was 'sleep, he says, and he didn't wake me up. He rambled around a little and stood and looked at me awhile, he says. He was seventeen years old and I was twelve.

"My brother had a lot of children. He had four girls with him. He had a boy somewheres. He is older than I am.

"I heard my father say that in time of war, they were taking up folks that wouldn't join them and putting them in prison. They picked a white fellow up and had him tied with a rope and carried him down to a creek and were tying him up by his thumbs. He saw my father coming and said: 'There's a colored man I know.' My father said he knew him. They let him go when my father said he knew him and that he didn't harbor bushwhackers. Every time he saw my father after that he would say, 'Bill, you sure did save my life.'

"My father and mother lived in a log cabin. They had homemade furniture. They had a bunk up side the wall and a trundle bed. That was the cabin they lived in in slavery time.

• Soldiers

"My father said once that when the men were gone, the soldiers came in and asked the women to cook for them. They wouldn't do it; so the soldiers made them bring them a chunk of fire. They throwed the fire on the bed and when it got to burning good, the officer wouldn't let them put it out. But he told them that they could get some of the boys to help them carry out their things if the boys were willing to do it. It was the officers who wanted the women to cook for them. It wasn't the slaves they asked; it was the white folks.

• Sold His Master

"I heard my stepmother—I call her my mother—say some thing once. She belonged to a white family named Bell. They had a lot of slaves. My stepmother was the house girl; so she could get on to a lot of things the others couldn't. She stayed in the house. That was in slavery times. The speculators who were buying colored folks would put up at that place. Looked like a town but it all belonged to one person. The name of the place was Cloverdale, Tennessee. My stepmother said that a gang of these folks put up at Cloverdale once and then went on to Nashville, Tennessee. On the next day a nigger sold the speculator. He was educated and a mulatto, and he sold his master in with a bunch of other niggers. He was just fixin' to take the money, when his master got aware of it, and come on up just in time. I don't know what happened to the nigger. It was just an accident he got caught. My stepmother said it was true.

- **Good Masters**

"My mother had a good master. At least, she said he was good. Slaves from other plantations would run away and come to her master's place to stay. They would stay a good while.

"My father said his master was good to him too. My father's young master has come to see us since the War. He got down low and used to come 'round. My father would give him turns of corn. You know when you used to go to the mill, you would carry about two bushels of corn and call it a milling or a turn. My father would let his young master shell a bushel or two of corn and carry it to the mill. He got poor and sure 'nough you see. We had moved away from them then, and he got in real hard luck. He used to come and sit a half day at a time at our house. And father would give him the corn for his family. We were living in Dickson County, Tennessee then. Seems like we was on Frank Hudson's place. We hadn't bought a place for ourselves then.

- **Ku Klux Klan**

"You know they used to ku klux the niggers. They went to the house after the War of an old man named Hall. They demanded for him to let them in but he wouldn't. They said that they would break open the door if he didn't let them in. He didn't let them in, and they broke it down. When they started in, his wife threw fire brands in amongst 'em and he knicked one down with an ax. Them that wasn't hurt carried the wounded man away and it was reported the next day that he was sick. They never did bother the nigger no more and he never had no charges made against him.

- **Runaway Negroes—After Freedom**

"It was over forty years ago. Me and my wife lived at a big sawmill near Elliott, Arkansas, just ten miles outside of Camden. White folks used to come up there and catch niggers and carry them back to Louisiana with them, claiming that they owed debts. One time two white men came to Elliott looking for a nigger. They came through the Negro quarters and all the men were off that day because it was a holiday. The nigger saw them first and ran to the woods. They ran after him and caught him. They came back through the quarters and tied him to one of the horses and then went on to Louisiana—them ridin' and him walkin' tied up with his arms behind him and roped to the horse like he was some kind of cattle or something. The niggers followed them with guns a little distance, but one nigger telephoned to El Dorado and the officers there were on the lookout for them. At night, the officers in plain clothes went over and chatted with them white men. When they saw the nigger, they asked what it was they had there. They told the one that asked that it was a damn nigger that owed money back in Louisiana and got smart and run away without paying up. The officers drew their guns and put handcuffs on them and carried them and the nigger away to Jail.

"They put everybody in jail that night. But the next morning they brought them to trial and fined the white men a hundred and fifty dollars apiece and after the trial they turned the nigger loose. That broke up the stealing of niggers. Before that they would come and take a Negro whenever they wanted to.

"Niggers were just beginning to wake up then, and know how to slip away and run off. We had whole families there that had run off one by one. The man would run away and leave his children, and as they got old enough, they would follow him one by one.

- **Right After the War**

"Right after the War, my people farmed on shares. We had a place we leased on the Hudson place that we stayed on. We leased it for five years but we stayed there seven or maybe eleven years. When we left there we bought a place of our own. On the Hudson place we cleared up about thirty acres of land and 'tended it as long as we stayed there. We put out a lot of fruit trees on it. Had lots of peaches, and plums, and quinces—do you know what quinces are?—and danvils (these danvil plums you know). They are kinda purple looking fruit made in the shape of a prune. They are about two inches through—jus' about half as big as your fist.

"When we moved to our own place, we stayed in the

same county. It was just about three-fourths of a mile from the Hudson place—west of it.

• Moving to Arkansas

"I came to Arkansas with the intention of going to school. But I jus' messed myself up. Instead of goin' to school, I went and got married. I was out here just one year before I got married. I married the first time in 1887—February fourteenth, I think. My first wife taken sick with rheumatism and she died in 1908. We were married thirty-one years. I married again about 1913.

• Vocational Experiences

"When I was able to work, I worked in the railroad shops—boiler maker's helper. Before that I farmed and did other things. Went from trackman to machinist's helper and boilermaker's helper.

• Opinions

"Young folks Just need the right handlin'.

"I don't mix in politics."

Interviewer: Miss Irene Robertson
Person interviewed: Mary Tabon, Forrest City, Arkansas
Age: 67

MARY TABON

"Pa was sold twice to my knowing. He was sold to McCoy, then to Alexander. He was Virginian. Then he was carried to Alabama and brought to Holly Grove by the Mayos. I have wore four names, Alexander, Adams, Morgan, and Tabon.

"My mother's owners was Ellis from Alabama. She said she was sold from the Scales to Ellis. Her father, sister, and two brothers was sold from Ellis. She never seen them no more. They found Uncle Charles Ellis dead in the field. They never knowed how it come.

"My parents had hard times during slavery. Ma had a big scar on her shoulder where the overseer struck her with a whoop. She was chopping cotton. She either wasn't doing to suit him or wasn't getting along fast enough to suit him.

"Ma had so many little ones to raise she give me to Nancy Bennett. I love her soul in her grave. I helped her to do all her work she taught me. She'd leave me with her little boy and go to church and I'd make cakes and corn bread. She brag on me. We'd have biscuits on Sunday morning. They was a rarity.

"One day she had company. She told me to bake some potatoes with the jackets on. I washed the potatoes and wrapped them up in rags and boiled them. It made her so mad she wet the towel and whooped me with it. I unwrapped the potatoes and we had them that way for dinner. That was the maddest she ever got at me. She learned me to cook and keep a nice house and to sew good as anybody. I rather know how to work than be educated.

"Mr. Ash give me a lot of scraps from his garment factory. I made them up in quilts. He give me enough to make three dresses. I needed dresses so bad." (One dress has sixty-six pieces in it but it didn't look like that. They sent it to Little Tock and St. Louis for the county fairs. Her dresses looked fairly well.)

"I was born at Holly Grove, Arkansas. Alexander was the name my pa went by and that was my maiden name."

Interviewer: Miss Irene Robertson
Person interviewed: Liza Moore Tanner, Helena, Arkansas
Age: 79

LIZA MOORE TANNER

"I was born in north Georgia. It was not fer from Rome. We belong to Master Belton Moore and Miss Jane Moore. They had a big family, some grandchildren old as their own. That was my job playing wid the children. My parents' name Rob Moore and Pilfy Calley. She lived five miles from Belton Moore's house. She was hired out over at Moore's the way she and papa met up. I know now I was hired out too. I run after them children a long time it seemed like to me. I loved them and they cried after me. I get so tired I'd slip off and go up in the loft and soon be asleep. I learned to climb a ladder that very way. It was nailed up straight against the side of the wall. They'd ask me where I been. They never did whoop me fer that. I tell 'em I been asleep. I drapped off 'sleep. I was so tired. Papa helped with the young calves and the feeding and in the field too. Mama was a fast hand in the field. They called her a little guinea woman. She could outdo me when I was grown and she was getting old. She washed fer the Calley's. All I remember they was a old man and woman. Mama lived in the office at their house. He let her ride a horse to Moore's to work. I rode home wid her many a time. She rode a side saddle. I rode sideways too. She used a battling stick long as she lived when she washed.

"Papa died two years after the surrender in Atlanta, Georgia. The Moore's moved there and he went along. He left mama at Master Calley's and I was still kept at the old home place. Aunt Jilly kept me and my two oldest sisters. Her name was Jilly Calley. I seen mama right often. They fetched papa back to see us a few times and then he died. We all went to Atlanta where he was buried. Mama lived to be purty nigh a hundred years old. She had fourteen children. I had two sisters and eight half-brothers and three half-sisters. Some died so young they never was named. My stepfather was mean to her and beat her, caused some of their deaths. She was a midwife in her later years. She made us a living till I married. She was gone with Dr. Harrison a lot. He'd come take her off and bring her home in the buggy. I married and immigrated to Dell, Arkansas. We lived there a year and went to Memphis. Mama come there and died at my house. She got blind. Had to lead her about. My steppapa went off and never come back. He got drunk whenever he could get to it. We hunted him and asked about him. I think he went off with other women. We heard he did.

"Freedom—I heard Miss Jane say when she was packing up to go to Atlanta, 'I will get a nurse there. They will make her go to school.' I thought she was talking about me. I wanted to go. I loved the children. I got to go to school in the country a right smart. I can read and write. Me and my two sisters all was in the same class. It seemed strange then. We had a colored man teacher, Mr. Jacobin. It was easier for me to learn than my sisters. They are both dead now.

"I got three living children—one here and two in

Memphis. After I got my hip broke I live about with them so they can wait on me.

"I don't know about this new way of living. My daughter in Memphis raising her little girl by a book. She don't learn her as much manners as children used to know. She got it from the white lady she works for. It tells how to do your child. Times done changed too much to suit my way of knowing. 'The Old Time Religion' is the only good pattern fer raising a family. Mighty little of that now."

United States. Work Projects Administration

Interviewer: Pernella M. Anderson
Person interviewed: Fannie Tatum, Junction City, Arkansas
Age: Born 1862

FANNIE TATUM

"I was born on Wilmington landing in 1862 on the Ouachita River and was carried away when I was two years old. My mother ran away and left my sister and me when we was three and five years old. I never saw her any more till I was eight and after I was eight years old I never saw her again in forty years. After my mama left me old Master Neal come here to El Dorado and had me bound to him until I was twenty-one. I stayed there till I was twenty-one. I slept by the jamb of the fireplace on a sack of straw and covered with saddle blankets. That was in the winter when snow was waist high. In summer I slept on naked floor and anywhere I laid down was my bed just like a dog.

"I wasn't allowed to eat at the table. I et on the edge of the porch with the dogs with my fingers. I worked around the house and washed until I was nine and then I started to plowing. At ten I started splitting rails. My task was two hundred rails a day. If I didn't cut them I got a beating. I did not know what a coat was. I wore two pieces, a lowel[HW:?] underskirt and a lowel[HW:?] dress, bachelor brogans and sacks and rags wrapped around my legs for stockings. That was in winter. Summer I went barefooted and wore one piece. My sun hat was a rag tied on my head.

"I did not know anything about Sunday School nor church. The children would try to teach me my ABC's but master would not let them. Never visited any colored people. If I see a colored person coming I run from them. They said they might steal me. After I got grown they let me go to a colored party and they whipped me for going. Tried to make me tell whether or not a boy come home with me but I did not tell it; one come with me though. That was the first time I got out. Of course they sent one of the boys along with me but he would not tell on me.

"I never slept in a bed until I was twenty-two years old. Never was with any colored people until I was grown. My play was with white children. My father was a white man. He was my ma's old master and they was Neals. They kept my hair cut off like a boy's all the time. I never wore a stocking until I was twenty-two and my hair did not grow out and get combed until I was twenty-two. My old master and mistress would have been mean to me but I was so smart they did not get a chance. The only thing I was treated like a dog.

"I live in Junction City but am here visiting my daughter."

Interviewer: Samuel S. Taylor
Person interviewed: Anthony Taylor
2424 W. Ninth Street, Little Rock, Arkansas
Age: 68, or 78?

ANTHONY TAYLOR

"I was born in Clark County adjoining Hot Spring County, between Malvern and Arkadelphia. Clark County was named after old man General Clark. He was worth four or five thousand acres of land.

"My father's name was Anthony McClellan. Why they called me Anthony Taylor was my stepfather was named Taylor. My mother's name was Lettie Sunnaville. My mother has been dead thirty or forty years and my father died six months before I was born. He died a natural death. Sickness. He was exposed and died of pneumonia.

"Fayette Sunnaville was my grandfather on my mother's side. That was my mother's father. Rachel Sunnaville was my mother's mother's name. I don't know the names of my father's people. They was sole[HW:?] in slavery. But it is been so far back; I don't remember nothing, and I don't know whether they would or not if they was living.

"We stayed on the old plantation for seven or eight years before we had sense enough or knowed enough to get away from there and git something for ourselves.

That is how I come to raise such big potatoes. I been raising them fifty years. These are hill potatoes. You have to know how to raise potatoes to grow 'em this big. (He showed me some potatoes, sweet, weighing about seven pounds—ed.)

"I have heard my mother and my grandfather tell lots of stories about slavery. I can't remember them.

"Old man Bullocks had about eight or ten families that I knew about. Those were the families that lived right near us in the quarters. I didn't say eight or ten hands—I said eight or ten families. Them was the ones that was right near us. We was awful small after freedom but them what was with him stayed with him quite a while—stayed with the old master. He would pay them so much after freedom come.

"Lawd. I could tell you things about slavery. But I'm forgitful and I can't do it all at once. He had the whole county from Arkadelphia clean down to Princeton and Tulip—our old mars did. Lonoke was between Princeton and Tulip. Princeton was the county-seat. He must have had a large number of slaves. Those ten families I knew was just those close 'round us. Most of the farm was fur pine country land. There would be thirty or forty acres over here of cultivation and then thirty or forty acres over there of woods and so on. He had more land than anybody else but it wasn't all under cultivation.

"He's been dead now twenty or thirty years. I don't know that he was mean to his slaves. If he had been, they wouldn't have gone on after freedom. They would have moved out. You see, they didn't care for nothing but a little something to eat and a fine dress and they would have gone on to somebody else and got that.

"Wasn't no law then. He was the law. I worked all day long for ten cents a day. They would allowance you so many pounds of meat, so much meal, so much molasses. I have worked all day for ten cents and then gone out at night to get a few potatoes. I have pulled potatoes all day for a peck of meal and I was happy at that. I never did know what the price of cotton was.

"Where we was, the Ku Klux never did bother anybody. All there was, every time we went out we had to have a pass.

"My grandfather and grandmother were both whipped sometimes. I don't know the man that whipped them. I don't know whether it was the agent or the owner or who, but they were whipped. Lots of times they had work to do and didn't do it. Naturally they whipped them for it. That was what they whipped my grandparents for. Sometimes too, they would go off and wouldn't let the white folks know where they was going. Sometimes they would neglect to feed the horses or to milk the cows— something like that. That was the only reason I ever heard of for punishing them.

"I heard that if the boss man wanted to be with women that they had, the women would be scared not to be with him for fear he would whip them. And when they started whipping them for that they kept on till they got what they wanted. They would take them 'way off and have dealings with them. That is where so much of that yellow and half-white comes from.

"There was some one going through telling the people that they was free and that they was their own boss. But yet and still, there's lots of them never did leave the man they was with and lots of them left. There was lots of white people that wouldn't let a nigger tell their niggers that they was free, because they wanted to keep them blind to that for years. Kept them for three or four years anyway. Them that Bullocks liked was crazy about him. He would give them a show—so much a month and their keeps. I don't remember exactly how much it was but it was neighborhood price. He was a pretty good man. Of course, you never seen a white man that wouldn't cheat a little.

"He'd cheat you out of a little cotton. He would have the cotton carried to the gin. He would take half the corn and give us five or six shoats. After he got the cotton all picked and sold, the cotton it would all go to him for what you owed him for furnishing you. You never saw how much cotton was ginned, nor how much he got for it, nor how much it was worth nor nothing. They would just tell you you wasn't due nothing. They did that to hold you for another year. You got nothing to move on so you stay there and take what he gives you.

"Of all the crying you ever heard, one morning we'd got up and the pigs and hogs in the lot that we had fattened to go on that winter, he was catching them. After we'd done fattened them with the corn that was our share, he took 'em and sold 'em. We didn't even know we owed him anything. We thought the crops had done settled things. Nobody told us nothin'. All we children cried. The old man and the old woman didn't say nothing, because they was scared. My mother would get up and go down and milk the cows and what she'd get for the milking would maybe be a bucket of buttermilk.

"We'd have a spoonful of black molasses and corn bread and buttermilk for breakfast. We got flour bread once a week. We would work hard all the week talkin' 'bout what good biscuits we'd have Sunday morning. Sack of flour would last two or three months because we wouldn't cook flour bread only once a week—Saturday night or Sunday morning.

"We had no skillet at that time. We would rake the fireplace and push the ashes back and then you would put the cake down on the hearth or on a piece of paper or a leaf and then pull the ashes over the cake to cook it. Just like you roast a sweet potato. Then when it got done, you would rake the ashes back and wash the cake and you would eat it. Sometimes you would strike a little grit or gravel in it and break your teeth. But then I'm tellin' you the truth about it.

"When our hogs was taken that time, we didn't have nothing to go on that winter. They would compel us to stay. They would allowance us some meat and make us split rails and clear up land for it. It was a cinch if he didn't give it to you you couldn't get nothin'. Wasn't no way to get nothing. Then when crop time rolled 'round again they would take it all out of your crops. Make you split rails and wood to earn your meat and then charge it up to your crop anyhow. But you couldn't do nothin' 'bout it.

"Sometimes a barrel of molasses would set up in the smokehouse and turn to sugar. You goin' hungry and molasses wastin'. They was determined not to give you too much of it.

"I made my way by farming. After I got to be some size, I started at it. I farmed all my life. While I could work, things was pretty good. Wisht I was on a farm now. Even when I'm 'round here sick, I can git these potatoes raised with a little help from the neighbors.

"I don't belong to church. I oughter, but I don't. Then again, I figure that a man can be just as good out of it as he can in it. I've got good desires, but I never confessed to the public.

"I have had three hundred dollars worth of stuff stolen from me. Everything I produced is stolen from me because I have no way to protect myself. What I raise if I don't get shet of it right away, the people get shet of it for me. I had eighty head of chickens in the barn out there runnin' 'round. When I got sick and was in the bed and couldn't help myself, the chickens went. In the daytime, they would fix traps and jerk a string and pull a board down on them and then go out in the weeds and get them. I never reported nothin' to the police. I wasn't able to report nothing. I was just batching, and now and then people would come in and report them to me. They would wait till they saw somebody come in and when they saw that I was talking and wouldn't notice them, they would steal anything they wanted. The police came by here and ran them once. But that didn't do no good.

"Once somebody stole an automatic shotgun. They stole a colt one time. They stole all my clothes and pawned them to a whiskey dealer. He got sent to the pen for selling whiskey, but I didn't get my clothes. They come in the yard and steal my potatoes, collards, turnips, ochre (okra?), and so on. I lay there in the bed and see them, but I can't stop them. All I can do is to holler, 'You better go on and let them things alone.' Ever since the last war, I haven't been able to work. I am bare-feeted and naked now on account of not bein' able to support myself.

"I just come out of the hospital. I been too sick even to work in my garden. After I come home I taken a backset[TR: ?] but I am still staying here. I am just here on the mercies of the people. I don't get nothing but what the people give me. I don't get no moddities nor nothin' from the Government.

"I ain't never been able to get no help from the Government. Long time ago, I went down to the place and asked for help and they told me that since I was alone, I oughta be able to help myself. They gimme a ticket for twenty meals and told me by the time I ate them up, they might have something else they could do for me. I told them I couldn't go back and forth to git the meals. I have the ticket now. I couldn't git to the place to use it none, so I keep it for a keepsake. It is 'round here somewheres or other. I was past the pension age. I ain't been able to do no steady work since the war. I was too old for the war—the World War."

• Interviewer's Comment [HW: omit]

The spelling of the name Sunnaville is phonetic. I don't recognize the name and he couldn't spell it of course.

When I called, he had potatoes that weighed at least seven pounds. They were laid out on the porch for sale.

He had a small patch in his yard which he cultivated, and had gotten about ten bushels from it.

His account of slavery times is so vivid that you would consider his age nearer eighty than sixty-eight. A little questioning reveals that he has no idea of his age although he readily gives it as sixty-eight—a memorized figure.

Interviewer: Miss Irene Robertson
Person Interviewed: Lula Taylor, R.F.D., east of town, Brinkley, Arkansas
Age: 71

LULA TAYLOR

"My mother was sold five times. She was sold when she was too little to remember her mother. Her mother was Charity Linnerman. They favored. She was dark and granny was light colored. My mother didn't love her mother like I loved her.

"Granny lived in a house behind the white church (?) in Helena. After freedom we kept writing till we got in tetch with her. We finally got granny with us on the Jefferies place at Clarendon.

"A man (Negro) come by and conjured my mother. She was with Miss Betty Reed (or Reid) up north of Lonoke. They was my mother's last owners. That old man made out like she stole things when he stole them his own black self. He'd make her hide out like she stole things. She had a sweetheart and him and his wife. She had to live with them. They stole her off from her last owner, Miss Betty Reed. They didn't like her sweetheart. They was going to marry. He bought all her wedding clothes. When she didn't marry him she let him have back all the weddin' clothes and he buried his sister in them. This old man was a conjurer. He give my mother a cup of some kind of herbs and made her drink it. He tole her all her love would go to Henry Deal. He liked him. He was my papa. Her love sure did leave her sweetheart and go to my papa. He bought her some nice clothes. She married in the clothes he got her. She was so glad to let go that old man and woman what conjured her 'way from her white folks to wait on them.

"Granny's head was all split open. I lived to see all that. White folks said her husband done it but she said one of her old master's struck her on the head with a shoe last.

"My papa said he'd hit boards and stood on them all day one after another working cold days.

"Master Wade Deal at freedom give papa a pair of chickens, goats, sheep, turkeys, a cow; and papa cleared ten acres of ground to pay for his first mule. He bought the mule from Master Wade Deal.

"Old Master Deal used to run us from behind him plowing. We tease him, say what he'd say to the horse or mule. He'd lock us up in the smokehouse. We'd eat dried beef and go to sleep. He was a good old man.

"Grandpa Henry Pool went to war. Papa was sold from the Pools to the Deals. Grandpa played with us. He'd put us all up on a horse we called Old Bill. He said he got so used to sleeping on his blanket on the ground in war times till he couldn't sleep on a bed. He couldn't get off asleep.

"Grandpa found a pitcher of gold money been buried in old Master Pool's stable. He give it to them. They knowed it was out there.

"Mother was with Miss Betty Reed in most of war times. Miss Betty hid their jewelry and money. She spoke of the Yankees coming and kill pretty chickens and drink up a churn of fresh milk turned ready for churning. It be in the chimney corner to keep warm. They'd take fat horses and turn their poor ones in the lot. They never could pass up a fat hog. They cleaned out the corn crib.

"All my kin folks was field hands. I ploughed all day long.

"Papa said his ole mistress Deal was out under an apple tree peeling apples to dry. A white crane flew over the tree and fluttered about over her. Next day she died. Then the old man married a younger woman.

"It is so about the pigeons at Pigeon Roost (Wattensaw, Arkansas). They weighted trees down till they actually broke limbs and swayed plenty of them. That was the richest land you ever seen in your life when it was cleared off. Folks couldn't rest for killing pigeons and wasted them all up. I was born at Pigeon Roost on Jim High's place. I seen a whole washpot full of stewed pigeon. It was fine eating. It was a shame to waste up all the pigeons and clear out the place."

United States. Work Projects Administration

Interviewer: Mrs. Bernice Bowden
Person interviewed: Millie Taylor
1418 Texas Street, Pine Bluff, Arkansas
Age: 78

MILLIE TAYLOR

"Yes'm, I was born in slavery times in Calhoun County, Mississippi.

"Bill Armstrong was my owner. He's been dead a long time.

"My folks stayed on there a good while.

"Pa said they was good to him but they wasn't good to my ma. I heered pa say they beat her till she died. I don't remember a thing 'bout my ma.

"I heered 'em talk 'bout the Ku Klux. They kep' that in my hearin' so much that I kep' that in my remembrance.

"I know when we stayed on the place pa said was old master's. Yes'm, I sure 'members dat. I know we stayed there till pa married again.

"Bill Armstrong's wife made our clothes. I know we stayed right in the yard with some more colored folks.

"Pa worked on the shares and rented too.

"I was twenty-four when I come from Mississippi

here. I was married then and had three chillun. But they all dead now. I stays here with my grandson. I don't know what I'd do if it wasn't for him. I reckon I'd just be knockin' around—no tellin'.

"I got another grandson lives in Marvell. I went there to visit and I got so I couldn't walk, so my grandson carried me to the doctor. And he just looked at me—he had been knowin' me so long. I said, 'Don't you know me?' And he said, 'If you'd take off your hat I think I'd know you.' And he said, 'Well, for the Lawd, if it ain't Millie Taylor!'

"I've always done farmin'. That's the way I was raised—farmin'. I just looks at these folks in town and it seems funny to me to buy ever'thing you need. Looks to me like they would rather raise it.

"Oh, Lawd, don't talk about this young race. It looks to me like they is more heathe'nish. The Bible say they would be weaker and wiser but they is just too wise for their own good. I just looks at 'em and I don't know what to think about this young race. They is a few respects you and theirselves.

"I seen things here in town I didn't think I'd ever see. Seems like the people in the country act like they recognize you more.

"I has a good remembrance. Seems like I gets to studyin' 'bout it and it just comes to me like ABC. I know pa used to talk and tell us things and if I didn't believe it, I didn't give him no cross talk. But nowadays if chillun don't believe what you say, they goin' try to show you a point.

"Yes ma'am, folks is livin' a fast life—white and colored.

"Looks like the old folks has worked long enough for the white folks till they ought to have enough to live on."

United States. Work Projects Administration

Interviewer: Miss Irene Robertson
Person interviewed: Sarah Taylor, R.F.D., Madison, Arkansas
Age: 70

SARAH TAYLOR

"I was born in Releford County, Tennessee, ten miles from Murfreesboro. My parents belonged to Dr. Jimmy Manson. He was off and gone from home nearly all the time. He didn't have a Negro driver. Because he didn't they called us all Manson's free niggers. Folks didn't like it because we had so much freedom. One day a terrible thing happened broke up our happy way of living on Dr. Manson's place.

"Grandpa was part Indian. Dr. Jimmy didn't whoop. He visited and he'd get a jug of whiskey, call his niggers and give them a little, make them feel good and get them in a humor for working. Dr. Jimmy had a nigger overseer. They was digging a ditch and making a turnpike from Dr. Manson's place to Murfreesboro. They told grandpa to drive down in the ditch with his load of rock and let the white folks drive up on the dump. They was hauling and placing rock on the dump to make a turnpike. In Tennessee it was a law if a man owned a nigger he had to whoop him or have him whooped. If he didn't he had to sell him. They told grandpa if he didn't do as they said they would whoop him, then they said they would break his back. They took the fussing to Dr. Jimmy for him to whoop grandpa. He sold him to nigger traders and they drove him to Mississippi. Mother never seen him no more. Grandma died of grief. She had nine girls and no boys. After freedom seven went North and mama, was Jane, and Aunt Betty lived on in Tennessee, and I lived some in Mississippi. That's the reason I hate Mississippi to this very day.

"The day they fit on Stone River in Tennessee, brother Hood was born. He was born during the battle. I guess they moved off of Dr. Jimmy's place at freedom, for I was born on Jack Little's place.

"The times is passing faster than I want it to and I'm doing very well. I don't never meddle in young folks' business and I don't 'low them meddling in mine. Folks is the ones making times so hard. Some making times hard for all rest of us can't help ourselves. It is sin and selfishness makes times so hard. Young folks no worse than some not so very old. It ain't young folks making times hard. It's older ones so greedy. They don't have no happiness and don't want to see old ones live nor the young ones neither."

Interviewer: Samuel S. Taylor
Person interviewed: Warren Taylor
3200 W. Seventeenth Street, Little Rock, Arkansas
Age: 74

WARREN TAYLOR

My people are all from Richmond, Virginia. I was just four years old when they come here. My father was in charge of all the machinery. He ran the gin. Didn't do anything else. My mother was a house girl. The kids learned her everything they learned in school. She knew everything. My father died when I was young. My mother lived till she was eighty. But the time she was fifty, I bought her a home and sat her down on Pulaski Street in that home. And that is why I have so little trouble.

"My ma belonged to Hoffman. He sold her to Wiley Adams. He carried her to Mississippi. She stayed there for a short time and then came to Arkansas. He settled in a little place called Tulip, Arkansas. Then freedom came and we came to Little Rock and settled at what is now Seventh and Ringo Streets; but then it was just a stage road leading to Benton, Arkadelphia, and other places. Stages passed twice a day with passengers and freight. No railroads at all then. The government kept the roads up. They had the arsenal hall where the city park is and had a regiment of soldiers there. The work on that road was kept up by the soldiers. That was under Grant's administration. I never saw but three presidents—three Democratic presidents—Cleveland, Wilson, and Roosevelt.

"My father's master was named Lee. He married my mother back in Virginia. My daddy's people when he was freed was named Taylor. He died when I was young and he never gave me any details about them.

• Good Masters

"The Adamses were good to my mother. And they help her even after freedom. Charlie Adams and Mack Adams of Malvern, Arkansas. John was the sheriff and ran a store. Mack was a drummer for the Penzl Grocery. When my mother was ill, he used to bring her thirty dollars at a time. Every two months she had to go down to Malvern when she was well and carry an empty trunk and when she would come back it would be full. My mother was wet-nurse to the Adamses and they thought the world and all of her.

• Marriage

"They had a good opinion of their house servants. That is how she and my father came to belong to different families. One white man would say to the other, 'I got a good boy. I'm going to let him come over to see your girl.' He would be talking about a Negro man that worked around his house and a Negro girl that worked for the other man. That would be all right. So that's the way my father went to see my mother. He was married in the way they always married in those days. You know how it was. There was no marriage at all. They just went on out and got the woman and the white man said, 'There she is. You are man and wife.'

• Right After the War

"My father died before freedom. My mother lived with him until her folks moved away from his folks. Then she was separated from him and left him in Mississippi. She belonged to one white man and he to another, and that could happen any time.

"Right after freedom, she stayed with these white people, doing the house work. She had the privilege of raising things for herself. She made a garden, and raised vegetables and such like.

"My brother who had run off during slavery time and who later became a preacher in the North invited us to live in the city with him.

• Vocational Experiences

"I wasn't fourteen years old when I was tending to flowers for the Cairo and Fulton Railroad. That was a railroad which later became Missouri Pacific. They beautified everything. There wasn't any bridge. They had a boat to take you into the town of Argenta then, and when the trains came through, the same boat would carry the cars across. An engine would be on the other side to finish the journey with them.

"There is one engineer living now who was active in that time, Charlie Seymour, retired, of Little Rock. He used to run the first train over the Baring Cross Bridge, and then he ran the first engine over the new bridge here.

He had already been retired when they finished the new bridge, but they had him pull the first train over the new bridge because he had pulled the first one over the old bridge. They wanted to give him that honor.

"My manager in that time was Superintendent A.E. Buchanan.

"From this work, I was advanced to the office and stayed there twenty years. I served under Commissioner Thomas Essex and later under Commissioner J.A. Dean. This service included twenty years in various departments.

"After that I billed freight for the Missouri Pacific at the Baring Cross Storerooms under Mr. H.S. Turner for eight months or more. Then I was transferred, because the location was not good for my health, to De Soto, Missouri, forty-five miles this side of St. Louis. Sedentary work had proved bad for me and I needed more active work. I waited on the master mechanic there. After that I came back to Little Rock and worked for the Pacific Express Company under Mr. G.F. Johnson, superintendent. After that, I worked for the Quapaw Club[HW?] during its heyday when Johnie Boyle, Hollenberg, Acie Bragg, Will Mitchell, Mr. Cottman, Captain Shaw, and oodles of others were members. Mr. Moorehead White was secretary. After that I went to doing my own work.

"Now I am past my prime and I do the best I can with what little help I get from the government. I get eight dollars a month and commodities. Mr. Roosevelt has got guts. Mighty few men would attempt to do what he has done. He is the greatest humanitarian president the country has ever had.

"But I've got a pile of recommendations. I've got recommendations from

>Thomas Essex, Land Commissioner, St. Louis, Iron Mountain,
>and Southern Railway

>W.S. Thomas, Geologist, St. Louis, Iron Mountain, Southern

>J.H. Harvey, General Foreman of Bridges and Building

>G.A.A. Deane, Land Commissioner succeeding Essex, St. Louis,
>Iron Mountain, and Southern

>S.W. Moore, General Secretary, Railway Y.M.C.A.

>Arthur B. Washburn, Superintendent, Arkansas Deaf Mute Institute

>A.C. St. Clair, Manager of the College of Physicians and Surgeons

>(Note comment) [TR: No additional comment found.]

You can read these for yourself, and you see what they say. They can't get me work now, but it's great to know you did good work and be able to prove it.

"The same commodities they give now were given in 1870. They had what they called the Freedman's Bureau. They used to have what they called the LICK SKILLET on Spring Street from Fifth to Seventh. Leastwise, the colored people called it that. Bush and a lots of other big niggers used to go there and get free lodgings until they were able to get along alone without help. The niggers they call BIG NIGGERS now stayed in wagon yards when they first come here.

- **Former Morals**

"There was a time when a low-down person, colored or white, couldn't stay in the community. They would give him a ticket and send him to Memphis or somewhere else.

"Reuben White built the First Baptist Church. In those days, people were Christian. White baptized one hundred fifty people twice a month. You didn't have to put a lock on your door then.

- **Bachelor**

"I haven't been married; marriage holds a man back. A woman won't do as she is told.

- **Successful Negroes in Little Rock**

"They had three Negro aldermen in this city: one of them was Green Thompson; but the Negroes butchered him. He was murdered as he came in from a festival. M.W. Gibbs, Land Office Man for the Government, was the only nigger here who wasn't bothered by no one—by no colored person. Dr. Smith was the leading colored dentist once, and the leading dentist of the city in his day. Almost all the white people went to him. Colored people had the barber shops. McNair had a barber shop on Main between Second and Third. His boy killed him—no good reason. His boy went to school with us; he was always stubborn and mean.

"Henry Powell was jailer here once. Sam Wilkins, a man that weighed about three hundred pounds, was the turnkey at the penitentiary. He lived in one of the finest houses in the town at that time. Nigger bands had all the music then. I have seen white organizations like the Odd Fellows and Masons follow Negro bands. Nigger orchestras played here all the big to-dos among white people. White people used to get nigger dancers to come here to dance and show them so that they could learn the late steps.

"Colored caterers had the big jobs. Henry Miller was one of them. He's going pretty strong still. You get some smart niggers 'round the Marion Hotel right now. We used to have some smart cooks. But they did too much peddling out of the back door. Dishonesty put them back. White people have taken all that work now. The nigger ruined himself in this town. They are paying white men now for what they know. They used to pay niggers for what they knowed.

• **Opinions**

"If the government would give you a job today, niggers would be up to take you out of it tomorrow. Niggers are dirty, and these 'round here are ignorant.

"The parents don't teach the children, and the children can't amount too anything. If children are not taught to work, they will never have nothing. A bunch of these young people don't mean to work. They just lay 'round waiting for the old people to die so they can get what little the old folks accumulated and run through it. But a man never keeps what he himself doesn't earn. He can't.

"The children are raised now without manners. When I have to go past Capitol Hill School, I have to get off the sidewalk. Ain't nothin' but these graduates teachin' now, young graduates that don't know nothin' but runnin' about. When I come along, the carpetbaggers were teaching and they knew their business. Mrs. Stephens went to Fisk and finished there. Mrs. Spight graduated from Union High School. We had all white teachers at first. Miss Sarah Henley used to teach with old ex-slaves where the Bethel A.M.E. Church is now. There wasn't no church there then—just a little shanty. I was just five years old. My mother used to take me there and leave me, but she taught me herself at home. She taught me just like I see you teach your kids.

"Boys don't do nothing but play now. They had to hustle then. They can't do nothing now. They have this departmental system now. They didn't have it then. The different temperaments ruin children. They used to review, now they don't. They change text-books so fast the old ones can't be sold."

- **Interviewer's Comment**

Warren Taylor holds recommendations from a number of prominent people referring to his excellent character, high morals, unusual intelligence, wide information, industry, thrift, honesty, and trustworthiness. Some of the names occur in the interview. The letters and documents proving his long service and good record were brought out during the interview and given to me to read.

He has an unusual memory and penetrating insight into conditions.

United States. Work Projects Administration

Interviewer: Miss Irene Robertson
Person interviewed: Sneed Teague
Brinkley, Arkansas
Age: 68
Occupation: Works on railroad

SNEED TEAGUE

"My owners was Miss Betsy and Master Teague. Miss Betsy had a sister lived with them. Her name was Miss Polly. They was French folks from the old country.

"My ma had belong to the Cox before the Teagues owned her. The Teagues had three families of servants.

"I remember them—yes mam—they was very saving people. They made everything that they used. The shettle, the carding machine, the spinning wheel and all, they made em. They had a carding machine different to anybodys in the country. It worked by a foot treadle. Another thing wasn't like nobody elses in the whole country was the bed. It had four tall post. The head board a little higher than the one at the foot but instead of using slats across from the railings it was mortised together and hemp ropes wove bout a inch apart. It was strong and didn't seem to give (stretch) much.

"They raised sheep and they wove and spun wool altogether. They didn't fool with cotton. Never did, not even down to my time. That carding machine I'm telling bout turned out rolls of wool. It was right pretty. They made all kinds of wool things and sold them. The old man had three or four boys. Mr. Jim Teague run a wood and blacksmith shop. He sold plows, wagons, hoes. They made spoons, knives, and forks out of sheets of some kind of metal. Everything they used they made it and they sold mighty near every thing folks wanted. The servants stayed on after the war. My ma stayed till she died. My family had a little dispute when I was twelve years old and I left. Ma died and I never went back. I come to Forrest City and got work. I been farmin' and working on the railroad. I have done track work. I got 10 acres land and a house. I don't need on the relief. If I need it I would want it. The reason I ain't got a garden and cow is I work out and not there to see after it.

"Some times I vote. You make enemies cause they all want you to vote for them and I can't do that. I don't care nothin' bout votin'. I don't enquire no more bout politics.

"The fellow what raises things to sell is better off with prices high but if he is working for money, times is hard for him. Cause the money is hard to get and hard to keep now. The young folks morals ain't like young folks used to have. Seemed like young folks too smart to be trained in morals like they was when I was comin' up."

Interviewer: Miss Irene Robertson
Person interviewed: Mary Teel
Holly Grove, Ark.
Age: 74

MARY TEEL

"Our Masters was Wade and Curls. Miss Fannie was Master Wade's wife. They was kin somehow. I heard Ma say they wouldn't let their boys work. We girls growd up together. They called Ma 'Cousin'.

"Ma say she come from Marshal County Tennessee to Holly Springs Mississippi. She never did see her pa. My papa's papa was a white man. My pa was Lewis Brittman. He was a carriage driver. He made and mended shoes. My Ma was a fine cook. She had nine children but jes three living now. One of the girls—Miss Fannie's girls—married bout when I did. We jes growd up lack that. I left the girls at Mt. Pleasant, Mississippi. I stayed on their place a while. I wish I had money to go back to my old home and see all 'em livin'. I never heard 'em say if they give 'em somepin. Pa lernt us to do all kinds of work. He knowd how to do nearly everything cause he was brought up by white folks. Measles broke out, then small pox and the white folks put us in a room all together at the white house so we could be seen after. We lay on the same beds. My brother would whistle. I was real little but I member it well as yesterday. Ma say stop whistlin' in that bed and

Miss Fannie say let him whistle I want to hear him cause I know he better. They say it bad luck to sing in bed or look in the lookin'-glass (mirror) if you in the bed. We all got over it.

"Pa made us go clean. He made me comb and wrop my hair every night. I had prutty hair then. I had tetter and it all come out. I has to wear this old wig now. When I was young my eye-sight got bad, they said measles settled in em and to help em Ma had these holes put in em (in her ears). I been wearin' earbobs purt nigh all my life.

"The Ku Klux never bothered us. They never come nigh our house no time. Pa died and Ma married a old man. They stayed in the same place a while. When Pa died he had cattle and stock that why I don't know if he got somepin at Freedom. He had plenty.

"We lived at Holly Springs (Miss.) when they started the first colored schools. There was three lady teachers. I think a man. One of the white teachers boarded at my Ma's. On Saturday the other two eat there. I recollect Ma cooking and fixing a big dinner Saturday. No white folks let em stay with em or speak to em. They was sent from up north to teach the darky chaps. I was one went to school. They wasn't nice like my white folks then neither. They paid high board and white folks sent em to Ma so she get the money. I was 14 years old when I married. I lived wid my husband more an 50 years. We got long what I'ze tellin' you. This young set ain't got no raisin' reason they cain't stand one nother. I don't let em come in my yard. I cain't raise no children, I'm too old and they ain't got no manners and the big ones got no sense. Jes wild. They way they do. They live together a while and quit. Both them soon livin' wid somebody else. That what churches fer, to marry in. Heap of em ain't doin' it. No children don't come here tearin' up what I work and have. I don't let em come in that gate, I have to work so hard in my old days. I picked cotton. I can, by pickin' hard, make a dollar a day. I cooked ten years fore I stopped, I cain't hold up at it. I washed and ironed till the washing machines ruined that work fer all of us black folks. Silk finery and washin' machines ruint the black folks.

"Ma named Elsie Langston and Lewis Langston. They took that name somehow after the old war (Civil War), I recken it was her old master's name.

"After I was married and had children I was hard up. I went to a widow woman had a farm but no men folks. She say, 'If you live here and leave your little children in my yard and take my big boys and learn em to work, I will cook. On Saturday you wash and iron.' She took me in that way when my color wouldn't help me. I stayed there—between Memphis and Holly Springs.

"I live hard the way I live. I pick cotton when I can't go hardly. They did give me a little commodity but I lose half day work if I go up there and wait round. Don't know what they give me. I don't get a cent of the penshun."

Interviewer: Miss Irene Robertson
Person interviewed: Wade Thermon,
R.F.D. (PWA Reservation), Des Arc, Arkansas
Age: 67

WADE THERMON

"I was born in Boswell, Oklahoma. My mother and father was both slaves some wha in the eastern states. Soon as freedom was declared they kept going till I was born. They finally come back and farmed round Pine Bluff. My folks last time I heard from them was at Garland City. There's wha my mother died. I had three brothers and one sister, but one brother died long time ago. Oklahoma was pore farmin'. The family could do pretty good farmin' in Arkansas. I come here from Pine Bluff. I got a wife, two girls and a little grandchild. When I first come to dis county I done public work—piece work. I handled cotton and cross ties. I used to help load and unload the boats and I worked helpin' build railroads. Then I had to farm about a little fur a living. I worked on Victor Gates place six years. Then I worked on the widow Thomas place till the Government bought it. Then the last eighteen months I got work wid the PWA on the rezer/va/tion. They turned me off now and I ain't got no place to work.

"I voted the Republican ticket the last time. I don't know nothing 'bout stricted sufage. I voted in Oklahoma some and here some. No I sho don't think the women needs to vote. They won't let us vote in the Primary. No I wouldn't know who would suit in dem high offices. I reckon it is all right. We is in you might say a foreign country. What I blames 'em fur is not puttin' us in a country all to our selves and den let us run it all to our selves. It is gettin' us all mixed up here every year worse and worse.

"I don't know nuthin' 'bout the Civil War. That was before I was born. I heard my folks talk some 'bout it, been so long I forgot what they did say. My folks owned a place in Oklahoma, at least I recken they did. I never did own no home nor no land. Well, missus, cause I never could get but berry little ahead ever and it takes all I makes to live on and I ain't got nuthin' to go on now.

"Times is changin' so much I don't know whut goin' to happen to the next generation. Prices is mighty high now the reason you have to spend every cent you makes fore you get paid off. Dats the reason I don't like the PWA work I done. It cuts you off without a thing to go on. I likes farm work whole heap the best."

Interviewer: Samuel S. Taylor
Person interviewed: Mrs. Dicey Thomas
2500 Center Street, Little Rock, Arkansas
Age: About 82

DICEY THOMAS

"I was born in Barbour County, Alabama. When I was born, the white folks kept the children's age, not that of their parents. When the Yankees came through our white folks' plantation, the white folks was hiding away things.

• **Father**

"My father was named Ben See. See was my maiden name. Thomas comes from my marriage.

• **Yankees**

"It was about twelve o'clock when the Yankees came through, because we had just gone to bring the bowls. They used to serve us out of these gourds and wooden spoons. Me and another little girl had gone to get some bowls and spoons and when we got back the Yankees were swarming over the place. They said, 'You are free. Go where you please.'

"My mother had a little baby. The old women would tend to this baby and we would sit and rock the cradle till mother would come. I know I wasn't very old, because I didn't do anything but sit and rock the baby. I had just gotten big enough to carry the bowls.

"When the Yankees came through they stole Ben See's horse and brought him out here in Arkansas. In those days, they used to brand horses.

Some woman out here in Arkansas recognized the horse by his brand and wrote to him about it. He came out and got the horse. We had gone by that time.

• Visiting the Graves

"Ben See used to take the little darkies to the cemetery and show them where their master and missis was laying. He never would sell none of his father's slaves.

• The Slave Block

"He would buy other slaves and sell them though. He used to buy little kids that couldn't walk. Maybe some big white man would come that would want to buy a nigger. He used to have servants in the yard and he would have the slaves he'd bought saved up. One of the yard servants would catch a little nigger with his head all knotty and filled with twigs. He would swing the hair and the little nigger would yell, but he wouldn't be hurt.

"He had a block built up high just like a meat block out in the yard. He would have the yard man bring the little niggers out and put them on this block. I don't know nothing about their parents, who they were nor where they were. All I know he would have this child there what he'd done bought.

"If there would be about five or six come in, here's this nigger sitting up here. Here's a lot of folks waitin' to buy him. One would say, 'I bid so much.' Another would say, 'I bid so much.' That would go on till the biddin' got as high as it would go. Then the little nigger would go to the highest bidder if the bid suited master.

"My mother and father didn't know their age. The white folks kept the ages, and that was something they didn't allow the slaves to handle. I must have been four or five years old when my mother was in the field, because I wasn't allowed to take the baby out of the cradle but just to sit and rock it.

• Arkansas

"When I come to Arkansas, stages was running from Little Rock down toward Pine Bluff. Jesse James robbed the Pine Bluff train. That about the first train came in. They cut down the trees across the train track. They had a wooden gun and they went in there and robbed that train with it. They sent him to the pen and he learned a trade making cigars.

"The Union Station was just like that hillside. It was just one street in the town. I don't know what year nor nothing about it because when I came here it was just like somebody didn't have any sense.

• Plantation

"The slave quarter was a row of houses. The plantation was high land. The houses were little log houses with one room. They had fire arches. They would hang pots over the fire. They would have spiders that you call ovens. You would put coals on top of the spider and you would put them under it and you could smell that stuff cooking! The door was in the top of the spider and the coals would be on top of the door.

"You couldn't cook nothin' then without somebody knowin' it. Couldn't cook and eat in the back while folk sit in the front without them knowin' it. They used to steal from the old master and cook it and they would be burning rags or something to keep the white folks from smelling it.

The riding boss would come round about nine o'clock to see if you had gone to bed or not. If they could steal a chicken or pig and kill and cut it up, this one would take a piece and that one would take a piece and they would burn the cotton to keep down the scent. The rider would come round in June and July too when they thought the people would be hunting the watermelons.

"When the soldiers came, the niggers run and hid under the beds and the soldiers came and poked their bayonets under the bed and shouted, 'Come on out from under there. You're free!'

- **Destructiveness of Soldiers**

"The soldiers would tear down the beehives and break up the smoke houses. They wasn't tryin' to git nothin' to eat. They was just destroying things for devilment. They pulled all the stoppers out of the molasses. They cut the smoked meat down and let it fall in the molasses.

- **Rations**

"Every Saturday, they would give my father and his wife half a gallon of molasses, so much side meat. And then they would give half a bushel of meal I reckon. Whatever they would give they would give 'em right out of the smoke house. Sweet potatoes they would give. Sugar and coffee they'd make. There wasn't nothing 'bout buying no sugar then.

- **How the Day Went**

"The riding boss would come round before the day broke and wake you up. You had to be in the field before sun-up—that is the man would. The woman who had a little child had a little more play than the man, because she had to care for the child before she left. She had to carry the child over to the old lady that took care of the babies. The cook that cooked up to the big house, she cooked bread and milk and sent it to the larger children for their dinner. They didn't feed the little children because their mothers had to nurse them. The mother went to the field as soon as she cared for her child. She would come back and nurse the child around about twice. She would come once in the morning about ten o'clock and once again at twelve o'clock before she ate her own lunch. She and her husband ate their dinner in the field. She would come back again about three p.m. Then you wouldn't see her any more till dark that night. Long as you could see you had to stay in the field. They didn't come home till sundown.

"Then the mother would go and get the children and bring them home. She would cook for supper and feed them. She'd have to go somewheres and get them. Maybe the children would be asleep before she would get all that done. Then she would have to wake them up and feed them.

"I remember one time my sister and me were laying near the fire asleep and my sister kicked the pot over and burned me from my knee to my foot. My old master didn't have no wife, so he had me carried up to the house and treated by the old woman who kept the house for him. She was a slave. When I got so I could hobble around a little, he would sometimes let the little niggers come up to the house and I would get these big peanuts and break them up and throw them out to them so he could have fun seeing them scramble for them.

"After the children had been fed, the mother would cook the next day's breakfast and she would cook the next day's dinner and put it in the pail so that everything would be ready when the riding boss would come around. Cause when he came, it meant move.

- **The Old Lady at the Big House**

"The old lady at the big house took care of the gourds and bowls. The parents didn't have nothing to do with them. She fed the children that was weaned. Mother and daddy didn't have nothing to do with that at noontime because they was in the field. White folks fed them corn bread and milk. Up to the big house besides that, she didn't have anything to do except take care of things around the house, keep the white man's things clean and do his cooking.

"She never carried the gourds and bowls herself. She just fixed them. The yard man brought them down to the quarters and we would take them back. She wash them and scrape them till they was white and thin as paper. They was always clean.

"She wasn't related to me. I couldn't call her name to save my life.

- **Relatives**

"We come from Barbour, Alabama with a trainful of people that were immigrating. We just chartered a train and came, we had so many. Of all the old people that came here in that time, my aunt is the oldest. You will find her out on Twenty-fourth Street and Pulaski. She has been my aunt ever since I can remember. She must be nearly a hundred or more.

- **Patrollers**

"When we had the patrollers it was just like the white man would have another white man working for him. It was to see that the Negroes went to bed on time and didn't steal nothing. But my master and missis never allowed anybody to whip their slaves.

- **What the Slaves Expected and Got**

"I don't know what the slaves was expecting to get, but my parents when they left Ben See's place had nothing but the few clothes in the house. They didn't give em nothing. They had some clothes all right, enough to cover themselves. I don't know what kind or how much because I wasn't old enough to know all into such details.

"When we left Ben See's plantation and went down

into Alabama, we left there on a wagon. Daddy was driving four big steers hitched to it. There was just three of us children. The little boy my mother was schooling then, it died. It died when we went down betwixt New Falls and Montgomery, Alabama. I don't know when we left Alabama nor how long we stayed there. After he was told he was free, I know he didn't make nare another crop on Ben See's plantation.

• 1865-1938

"My father, when he left from where we was freed, he went to hauling logs for a sawmill, and then he farmed. He done that for years, driving these old oxen. He mostly did this logging and my mother did the farming.

"I can't tell you what kind of time it was right after the Civil War because I was too young to notice. All our lives I had plenty to eat. When we first came to Arkansas we stopped at old Mary Jones down in Riceville, and then we went down on the Gates Farm at Biscoe. Then we went from there to Atkins up in Pope County. No, he went up in the sand hills and bought him a home and then he went up into Atkins. Of course, I was a married woman by that time.

"I married the second year I came to Arkansas, about sixty-two or sixty-three years ago. I have lived in Little Rock about thirty-two or thirty-three years. When I first came here, I came right up here on Seventeenth and State streets.

• Voting

"I never voted. For twenty years the old white lady I

stayed with looked after my taxes. None of my friends ever voted. I ain't got nothing but some children and they ain't never been crazy enough to go to anybody's polls.

• Family

"I have two brothers dead and a sister. My mother is dead. I am not sure whether or not my father is dead. The Ku Klux scared him out of Atkins, and he went up in Tulsa, Oklahoma, and I ain't never heard of him since. I don't know whether he is dead or not.

"I have raised five children of my own.

• Ku Klux Klan

"These Ku Klux, they had not long ago used to go and whip folks that wasn't doing right. That was mongst the white people and the colored. Comer that used to have this furniture store on Main Street, he used to be the head of it, they say.

"I used to work for an old white man who told me how they done. They would walk along the street with their disguises hidden under their arms. Then when they got to the meeting place, they would put their disguises on and go out and do their devilment. Then when they were through, they would take the disguise off again and go on back about their business, Old man Wolf, he used to tell me about it.

• Occupation

"I nursed for every prominent doctor in Little Rock,—

Dr. Judd, Dr. Flynch, Dr. Flynn, Dr. Fly, Dr. Morgan Smith, and a number of others."

Interviewer: Mrs. Bernice Bowden
Person interviewed: Mandy Thomas, 13th and Pearl Streets, Pine Bluff, Arkansas
Age: 78
Occupation: Laundress

MANDY THOMAS

"I know my sister told me I was five when my mama was freed. I was born down below El Dorado. Andrew Jaggers was my mother's old master.

"I just remember the soldiers goin' past. I think they was Yankees. They never stopped as I knows of.

"I've seed my young missis whip my mother.

"My papa belonged to the Agees. After I got up good sized, they told me 'bout my papa. He went with his white folks to Texas and we never did see him after we got up good size. So mama took a drove of us and went to work for some more white folks.

"I was good and grown when I married and I been workin' hard ever since. I was out pickin' huckleberries tryin' to get some money to buy baby clothes when my first girl was born. Yes ma'am."

United States. Work Projects Administration

Interviewer: Samuel S. Taylor
Person interviewed: Omelia Thomas
519 W. Ninth Street, Little Rock, Arkansas
Age: About 70
Occupation: Making cotton and corn

OMELIA THOMAS

"I was born in Louisiana—in Vidalia. My mother's name was Emma Grant. My father's name was George Grant. My mother's name before she married was Emma Woodbridge. I don't know the names of my grand folks. I heard my mother say that my grandmother was named Matilda Woodbridge. I never got to see her. That is what I heard my mother say.

"I don't know the names of my mother's master, and I don't know the names of my father's white folks.

"My father was George Grant. He served in the War. I think they said that he was with them when Vicksburg surrendered. My father has said that he was really named George LaGrande. But after he enlisted in the War, he went by the name of George Grant. There was one of the officers by that name, and he took it too. He was shot in the hip during the War. When he died, he still was having trouble with that wound. He was on the Union side. He was fighting for our freedom. He wasn't no Reb. He'd tell us a many a day, 'I am part of the cause that you are free.'

I don't know where he was when he enlisted. He said he was sold out from Louisville—him and his brother.

"I never did hear him say that he was whipped or treated bad when he was a slave. I've heard him tell how he had to stand up on dead people to shoot when he was in the War.

"My brother started twice to get my father's pension, but he never was able to do anything about it. They made away with the papers somehow and we never did get nothin'. My father married a second time before he died. When he died, my stepmother tried to get the pension. They writ back and asked her if he had any kin, and she answered them and said no. She hid the papers and wouldn't let us have 'em—took and locked 'em up somewheres where we couldn't find 'em. She was so mean that if she couldn't get no pension, she didn't want nobody else to get none.

"I don't know just when I was born, nor how old I am. When I come to remember anything, I was free. But I don't know how old I am, nor when it was.

"I heard my father speak of pateroles. Just said that they'd ketch you. He used to scare us by telling us that the pateroles would ketch us. We thought that was something dreadful.

"I never heard nothin' about jayhawkers. I heard something about Ku Klux but I don't know what it was.

"My father married my mother just after the War.

"I been married twice. My first husband got killed

on the levee. And the second is down in the country somewheres. We are separated.

"I don't get no help from the Welfare, wish I did. I ain't had no money to get to the doctor with my eyes."

- **Interviewer's Comments**

The old lady sat with her eyes nearly closed while I questioned her and listened to her story. Those eyes ran and looked as though they needed attention badly. The interview was conducted entirely on the porch as that of Annie Parks. Traffic interrupted; friends interrupted; and a daughter interrupted from time to time. But this daughter, while a little suspicious, was in no degree hostile. The two of them referred me to J.T. Tims, who, they said, knew a lot about slavery. His story is given along with this one.

I got the impression that the old lady was born before the War, but I accepted her statement and put her down as born since the War and guessed her age as near seventy. She was evidently quite reserved about some details. Her father's marriage to her mother after the War would not necessarily mean that he was not married to her slave fashion before the War. She didn't care so much about giving any story, but she was polite and obliging after she had satisfied herself as to my identity and work.

Interviewer: Samuel S. Taylor
Person interviewed: Omelia Thomas
1014 W. Fifth Street, Little Rock, Arkansas
Age: 63

OMELIA THOMAS

"I was born in Marianna, Lee County, in Arkansas. I wasn't born right in the town but out a piece from the town in the old Bouden place, in 1875. My father kept a record of all births and deaths in his Bible. He never forgot whenever a new baby would come to get down his glasses and pen and ink and Bible. My daddy learned to read and write after the emancipation.

"My father's name was Frank Johnson and my mother's name was Henrietta Johnson. I don't know the given names of my father's and mother's parents. I do know my mother's mother's name. Lucinda, and my father's mother was named Stephens. I don't know their given names. My mother's master was a Trotter.

"My father was a free man. He hired his own time. He told me that his father hired his own time and he would go off and work. He made washpots. He would go off and work and bring back money and things. His mother was free too. When war was declared, he volunteered to go. He was with the Yankees. My father worked just like my grandfather did. Whenever he had a job to do. He never had a lick from anybody, carried his gun strapped down on his side all the time and never went without it.

"After the War, he worked on a steamboat. They used to kick the roustabouts about and run them around but they never laid the weight of their hands on him.

"They wouldn't allow him to go to school in slavery time. After the War, he got a Blue Back Speller and would make a bowl of fire and at night he would study—sometimes until daybreak. Then he found an old man that would help him and he studied under him for a while. He never went to any regular school, but he went to night school a little. Most of what he got, he got himself.

"He was born in Louisville, Kentucky. I don't know how he happened to meet my mother. During the time after the War, he went to running on the boat from New Orleans to Friar Point, Mississippi. Then he would come over to Helena. In going 'round, he met my mother near Marianna and married her.

"Mother never had much to say, and the other girls would have a big time talking. He noticed that she was sewing with ravelings and he said, 'Lady, next time I come I'll bring you a spool of thread if you don't mind.' He brought the thread and she didn't mind, and from then on, they went to courting. Finally they married. They married very shortly after the War.

"My mother was a motherless girl. My daddy said he looked at her struggling along. All the other girls were trying to have a good time. But she would be settin' down trying to make a quilt or something else useful, and he said to a friend of his, 'That woman would make a good wife; I am going to marry her.' And he did.

"She used to spin her fine and coarse sewing thread and yarn to make socks and stockings with. Her stockings and socks for the babies and papa would always be yarn. She could do pretty work. She had a large family. She had seventeen children and she kept them all in things she made herself. She raised ten of them. She would make the thread and yarn and the socks and stockings for all of these. I have known the time when she used to make coats and pants for my father and brothers. She would make them by hand because they didn't have any machines then. Of course, she made all the underwear. She put up preserves and jellies for us to eat in the winter. She used to put up kraut and stuff by the barrel. I have seen some happy days when I was with my daddy and mother. He raised pigs and hogs and chickens and cows. He raised all kinds of peas and vegetables. He raised those things chiefly for the home, and he made cotton for money. He would save about eight or ten bales and put them under his shed for stockings and clothes and everything. He would have another cotton selling in March.

"When my father was in the army, he would sometimes be out in the weather, he told us, and he and the other soldiers would wrap up in their blankets and sleep right in the snow itself.

"I farmed all my life until 1897. I farmed all my life till then. I was at home. I married in 1895. My first husband and I made three crops and then he stopped and went to public work. After that I never farmed any more but went to cooking and doing laundry work. I came from Clarendon here in 1901.

"I never had any experiences with the Yankees. My mother used to tell how they took all the old master's stuff—mules and sugar—and then throwed it out and rode their horses through it when they didn't want it for theirselves.

"I married a second time. I have been single now for the last three years. My husband died on the twentieth of August three years ago. I ain't got no business here at all. I ought to be at my home living well. But I work for what I get and I'm proud of it.

"A working woman has many things to contend with. That girl downstairs keeps a gang of men coming and going, and sometimes some of them sometimes try to come up here. Sunday night when I come home from church, one was standing in the dark by my door waiting for me. I had this stick in my hand and I ordered him down. He saw I meant business; so he went on down. Some of them are determined.

"There's no hope for tomorrow so far as these young folks are concerned. And the majority of the old people are almost worse than the young ones. Used to be that all the old people were mothers and fathers but now they are all going together. Everything is in a critical condition. There is not much truth in the land. All human affection is gone. There is mighty little respect. The way some people carry on is pitiful."

- **Interviewer's Comment**

The men who bother Omelia Thomas probably take her for a young woman. She hasn't a gray hair in her head, and her skin is smooth and must be well kept. She looks at least twenty-five years younger than she is, and but for the accident of her presence at another interview, I would never have dreamed that she had a story to tell.

I went to see her in the quarters where she lives—over the garage in the back yard of the white people she works for. When I got halfway up the stairs, she shouted, "You can't come up here." I paused in perplexity for a moment, and she stuck her head out the door and looked. Then she said, "Oh, I beg pardon; I thought you were one of those men that visit downstairs." I had noticed the young lady below as I entered. She is evidently a hot number, and as troublesome as a sore thumb to the good old lady above her.

United States. Work Projects Administration

Interviewer: Mrs. Bernice Bowden
Person interviewed: Tanner Thomas
1213 Louisiana, Pine Bluff, Arkansas
Age: 78

TANNER THOMAS

"I was born down here at Rob Roy on the river on the Emory place. My mother's name was Dinah Thomas and my father's name was Greene Thomas. He taken sick and died in the War on the North side. That's what my mother told me. I was born under Mars Jordan Emory's administration.

"I 'member somebody brought me here to Pine Bluff to Lawyer Bell's house. I stayed two or three months, then Mars Jordan sent for me and carried me back out to Rob Roy and I stayed with my mother. She had done married again but I stayed with her all the time till I got grown and I married.

"I come here in 1892 and I been here ever since—forty-six years. Oh, whole lots of these white folks know me.

"I worked at the Standard Lumber Company and Bluff City Lumber Company and Dilley's Foundry. Then I went to the oil mill. I was the order man. I was the best lumber grader on the place.

"Course I knows lots of white folks and they knows

me too, I done a heap of work 'round here in different places in forty-six years.

"I went to school a little but I didn't learn nothin'.

"My mother said they come and pressed my daddy in the War. 'Course I don't know nothin' 'bout that but my mother told me.

"Now, what is this you're gettin' up? Well, I was born in slavery times. You know I was when my daddy was in the War.

"Oh Lord yes, I voted. I voted Republican. I didn't know whether it would do any good or not but I just voted 'cause I had a chance. My name's been in Washington for years 'cause I voted, you know.

"My way is dark to the younger generation now. I don't have much dealin' with them. They are more wiser. Education has done spread all over the country.

"God intended for every man in the world to have a living and to live for each other but too many of 'em livin' for themselves. But everything goin' to work out right after awhile. God's goin' to change this thing up after awhile. You can't rush him. He can handle these people. After he gets through, with this generation, I think he's goin' to make a generation that will serve him."

Interviewer: Miss Irene Robertson
Person interviewed: Wester Thomas, Marianna, Arkansas
Age: 79

WESTER THOMAS

"I was born in Sumpter County (Mississippi?). My mother was sold to Dr. and Miss Kate Hadley. My mother's name was Lettie Williams and she married Wesley Thomas. My name is Wester Thomas. I'm seventy-nine years old. Mistress Kate raised me. Dr. Hadley had more than a hundred slaves.

"I can tell you about freedom. Two men in uniforms come and told master. He had the farm bell rung. They told them the Civil War was over. They was free. The niggers went back to their quarters. Some moved later. My folks never left. Dr. Hadley died. Mistress Kate took all that wanted to go to Louisiana then. We cleared up land down there. Later I farmed."

United States. Work Projects Administration

Interviewer: Miss Irene Robertson
Person interviewed: Annie Thompson, Biscoe, Arkansas
Age: 55?

ANNIE THOMPSON

"I was raised by my father's sister and my grandmother. Later on I come to my daddy here and my stepmother had other children. I soon married. I've had a hard time.

"My grandparents was Harriett Edwards and William Snow. Grandmother said they were nice to her. She was Master Edwards' house girl. She cooked and was a spinner. When I was a girl she had her spinning-wheel and she taught me to spin and knit. She spun thread for caps, mittens, stockings, socks, suspenders, and coats. We knit all those things when I was a girl. Grandmother said the white folks never whooped her. Grandmother was her old master's own girl and she nursed with one of his white wife's children. She was real light.

"My father's mother was a squaw. I don't know her name. She was sold from grandpa and he went to Master Snow. He never seen her any more. He took another wife and jumped over the broom on the Snow place. He thought some of his owners was terrible. He had been whooped till he couldn't wear clothes. He said they stuck so bad.

"My own father whipped me once till my clothes stuck to my back. I told you I had seen a pretty hard time in my own life. I was born in Starkville, Mississippi.

"Since I was a girl there has been many changes. I was married by Rev. Bell December 14, 1902. My husband is living and still my husband. I can see big changes taking place all the time. I was married at De Valls Bluff."

• **Interviewer's Comment**

This woman could give me some comparative views on the present generation but she didn't. It is one of the Saturday gathering halls. She depends on it somewhat for a living and didn't say a word either pro or con for the present generation.

Interviewer: Samuel S. Taylor
Person interviewed: Ellen Briggs Thompson
3704 W. Twelfth Street, Little Rock, Arkansas
Age: 83

ELLEN BRIGGS THOMPSON

- **Birth and Relatives**

"I was born in October 1844, in Nashville, Arkansas. I don't remember the exact day. I have went through thick and thin. I was a small girl when my mother died. I got the rheumatism so bad I can't hardly walk. It hurts me now. My oldest brother, Henry Briggs, was five years older than me, and my youngest brother, Isaac Briggs, was five years younger than me. I was born October, but he was born at Christmas Eve just after surrender. My oldest brother died last year. My youngest brother is in Galveston, Texas. If he is living, he is there. My name was Briggs before I married. I was just studying about my sister-in-law when you come up. If I could get the money, I would go to see her. She was my oldest brother's wife. Her name was Frances Briggs after she married. She lives in Emmet, Arkansas, where he married her. I just had two brothers, no sisters.

"My husband's name was Henry Thompson. He has

been dead about twelve or thirteen years. I have had so much sickness I can't remember exactly. I married him a long time ago. I got it put down in the Bible. I married yonder in Emmet, Arkansas. I ain't got the Bible nor nothing. My brother had it and he is dead.

"My father's name was Daniel Briggs. He died in Hot Springs. We were small children when he and my mother was separated. He was in one place and we were in another. He tried to get us children when he died, but we was little and couldn't get to him. My mother was dead then.

"My mother's name was Susanna Briggs. Her father's name was Isaac Metz. The children left him in South Carolina. The white folks sold them away from him. My mother just had three children: me, and my two brothers. I don't know how many my grandfather had. There were four sisters that I know besides my mother and two boys: Aunt Melissa, and Aunt Jane, and Aunt Annie, and Aunt Sarah, and Uncle Albert Mitchell, and Uncle Ben. My grandmother's name was Betsy. I never got to see her but they told me about her.

- **Good Masters**

"I have heard them say that their white folks didn't whip them. My master was a good man. My young master, when it come to the surrender, slipped back home and told them they was going to be free as ever he was. His name was Joe Mitchell. I never seed my white folks whip anybody in my life. They just never whipped anybody. They never whipped me. I have seen the white folks next to us whip their Negroes and I asked grandma about it. She said that those were their Negroes and she would explain what they was being whipped for. They was on another farm. I don't remember what they was being whipped for.

"My young master told the slaves when he notified them they was free that if they didn't want to stay with him, he would give them enough to go on till they could make it, you know, to keep them from starving. He was a good man.

"The old man, Joe's father, was named Thomas Mitchell. He died before I was born. I never seed him, just knowed his name. Joe's mother was named Isabel Mitchell. I came to be named Briggs because her husband's name was Briggs. He belonged to a Briggs. I don't know what his name was else. They didn't belong to the same master. They used to let them marry. They would fix great big tables. Sometimes they would marry in the house; that was in the winter. Then sometimes they would marry outdoors. Then they would set a long table for all their associates to eat just like you would fix a table for your friends. Looked like they would be so glad to see their boys and girls marry. They would have regular preacher and marry just like they do now.

"There wasn't no breeders on our place. But I have heard of people who did keep a woman just for that purpose. They never whipped her nor nothing. They just let her have children. As soon as she had one, they would take it away from her so that she could have another one right away.

- **Jayhawkers**

"When my young master was gone to the War and

the jayhawkers would come around, my young master's mother would take all the colored women and children and lock them up and she would take a big heavy gun and go out to meet them. The Jayhawkers were white people who would steal corn and horses and even slaves if they could get them. But colored folks was sharp. They would do things to break their horses' legs and they would run and hide. My uncle was a young boy. He saw the Jayhawkers coming once. And he ran and pressed himself under the crib. The space was so small he nearly broke his ribs. His mistress had to get him out and take him to the house.

"My grandmother used to take me with her after dark when she'd go out to pray. She wouldn't go anywhere without me. One time when she was out praying, I touched her and said to her that I heard something in the corn crib. She cut her prayer off right now and went and told it to her old mistress, and to the young master, who was in the house just then telling the Negroes they were all going to be free. The Jayhawkers spied us and they got out and went on their way. My young master crawled out and went back to the Confederate army. He had to crawl out because he wanted to keep anybody from seeing him and capturing him.

- **Soldiers**

"I never seed but one or two soldiers. That was after the surrender. I suppose they were Union soldiers. They had on their blue jackets. There never was any fighting in Nashville, while I was living there.

"About all that I knew about the War was that the men went off to fight. None of the colored men went—just the white men. The colored men stayed back and worked in the field. Isabel Mitchell and her boys were bosses. What they said goed.

• Slave Houses

"The slaves lived in old log houses. Some of them were plank houses. Some of the slaves chinked 'em up with dirt. They had these big wooden windows in the houses. Sometimes they would be two, sometimes they would be three windows—one to each room. There would be two or three or four rooms to the house. That would be according to the family. My mother had three girls besides her own children. She had a four-room house. Her house was built right in the white folks' yard. My grandmother didn't work in the field. She tended to the children. She worked in the big house. My mother was boss of the whole thing. She would go and work in the field but grandmother would see after the children. She wouldn't let me go from her to the gate without her. I just had to follow her everywhere she went.

"Grandmother besides taking care of us used to make clothes. She cooked for the white folks. But she sure had to see after us children. I seed after myself. I was all the girl-child there and I just did what I wanted to.

"The country was kind of wild in those days. The deer used to come loping down and we would be scared and run and hide. Some people would set the dogs on them and some people would kill them no matter who they belonged.

You see, some people had them as pets.

- **Amusements**

"I never seed nothing in the way of amusements except people going to church and going to parties and all such as that. They believed in going to church. They would have parties at night. The white folks didn't care what they had. They would help prepare for it. They would let 'em have anything they wanted to have and let 'em go to church whenever they wanted to go.

And if they took a notion they would have a supper. When they would have a party they would do just like they do now. They would have dancing. I never seed any playing cards. When they danced, somebody would play the fiddle for them. When they had a supper, they would usually sell the things. Then the white folks would come and buy from them. There would be nice looking things on the table.

- **Church**

"They had meetings at Center Point, and at Arkadelphia. And they would let us go to them or anywhere else we wanted. We had to have passes, of course. They had colored preachers. Sometimes the slaves would go to the white people's church. They wouldn't go often, just every once in awhile. White ladies would get after the colored to come and go with them sometimes. Sometimes, too, when they would have a dinner or something, they would take Aunt Sue or mother to cook for them. They wouldn't let nobody meddle with them or bother them—none of the other white folks. And they would let them fix a table for their own friends that they would want to have along.

- **Personal Occupations**

"I used to work in the field or in the house or anything I could get to do. I would even go out and saw these big rails when my husband would have a job and couldn't get a chance to do it. It has been a good while since I have been able to do any good work. My husband has been dead fifteen years and I had to quit work long before he died.

- **Right after the War**

"Right after the War my folks worked in the field, washed, cooked, or anything they could do. They left the old place and came down about Washington, Arkansas. I don't know just how long they stayed in Washington. From Washington, my mother went to Prescott and settled there at a little place they called Sweet Home, just outside of Prescott. That is where my daughter was born and that is where my mother died. I came here about nine years ago.

- **Present Support**

I came here to stay with my daughter. But now she doesn't have any help herself. She has three small children and she's their only support now. She's not working either. She just come in from the Urban League looking for a job. They say that they don't have a thing and that the people don't want any women now. They just want these young girls because they make them work cheaper. We have both applied for help from the Welfare but neither of us has gotten anything yet."

Interviewer: Miss Irene Robertson
Person interviewed: Hattie Thompson, Widener, Arkansas
Age: 72

HATTIE THOMPSON

"I was born the second year after the surrender. I was born close to Arlington, Tennessee. My parents was Mariah Thermon and Johnson Mayo. They had eight children. They belong to different owners. I heard mama say in slavery time she'd clean her house good Saturday and clean up her children and start cooking dinner fore pa come. They looked forward to pa coming. Now that was at our own house.

"Mama was heired. She was the house woman and cook for her young mistress, Miss Sallie Thermon. She married Mr. John Thermon. She was Miss Sallie Royster till she married. I heard her say she raised Miss Sallie's children with her own. She was a wet nurse. I know Miss Sallie was good to her. I don't think she was sold but her mother was sold. She would spin and weave and the larger children did too. They made bed spreads in colors and solid white. They called the colored ones coverlets. They was pretty. Mama helped quilt. She was a good hand at that. They made awful close stitches and backstitched every now and then to make it hold. They would wax the thread to keep it from rolling up and tangling.

"Thread was in balls. They rolled it from skeins to

balls. They rolled it from shuck broches to the balls. Put shucks around the spindle to slip it off easy. I have seen big balls this big (2 ft. in diameter) down on the floor and mama, knitting off of it right on. When the feet wore out on socks and stockings, they would unravel them, save the good thread, and reknit the foot or toe or heel.

"When I was a child, patching and darning was stylish. Soon as the washing was brung in the clothes had to be sorted out and every snag place patched nice. Folks had better made clothes and had to take care of em. Clothes don't last no time now. White folks had fine clothes but they didn't have nigh as many as white folks do now.

"Mama was a pretty good hand at doing mighty nigh what she took a notion to do about the house. She never was no count in the field—jess couldn't hold out it seem like. She worked in the field lots. Pa was a shoemaker. He made all our shoes and had his tools, lasts, etc. He learned his trade in slavery. He farmed.

"It has been so long ago I tell you I don't recollect things straight. I don't know how they found out about freedom but they left I think. They got all they could take, their clothes and a little to eat. They started share cropping. They was out from Holly Springs when I come to knowledge. Mama was a nice hand at cooking and hand sewing. She said Miss Sallie learnt her. She never could read.

"I come to Arkansas fifty year ago this spring with one little girl—all the little girl I ever had. I never had no boys. I come here to get work. I always got work. It was a new country and it was being cleared out. In the spring we could get wild polk greens to cook. You can't get none now.

"Times is sider'bly changed since then. Hogs run wild. Plenty game here then. Something to eat was not hard to get then as it is now. We raise a hog in a pen nearly every year but it takes plenty to feed it that way.

"My husband have rheumatism and we get $12 and commodities. He works in the field and I wash and iron when I can get some to do. That is scarce. He works all he can."

United States. Work Projects Administration

Interviewer: Miss Irene Robertson
Person Interviewed: Mamie Thompson
Brinkley, Ark.
Age: 68

MAMIE THOMPSON

"I come here with my parents in 1887. Nothing much here in Brinkley then but woods and three stores. My mother was a mix-breed. She was mixed with Cherokee Indian and Negro. My father come from Virginia. He was black—so black he shined. My mother was born in Cairo, Illinois. My mother and father both died here in Brinkley. This town started from a big saw mill."

"Understand, all I knows was told to me by my parents. Grandma's master was Master Redman. He kept Aunt Emma and my mother. They never was sold. My mother was put on the block but her mistress come took her down. Master Redman had her in the field working. The overseer was a white man. He tried to take her down and carry on with her. She led him to the house. He wanted her whooped cause she had whooped him sort of. He was mad cause he couldn't overpower her. Master Redman got her in the kitchen to whoop her with a cow hide; she told him she would kill him; she got a stick. He let her out and they come to buy her—a Negro trader. Old Mistress—his wife—went out and led her down from there in the house and told Master Redman if he sold Mattie she would quit him—she meant leave him. Mistress Redman kept her with her and made a house girl out of her. She tended to the children and cleaned the house. Aunt Emma milked and churned.

"Grandma was a Molly Glaspy woman. She had straight wavy hair, small eyes. She was a small woman. Grandpa was a tall big man. He was a full blood Indian.

"My mother called whiskey 'jagger'—I don't know why.

"After Mr. Redman died, Miss Mary married Mr. Badgett. Me and George and Sissy all growed up together. My mother was married twice too. She had two of us by her first husband and eight children by her last husband.

"I heard them say they lived in Crittenden County, Arkansas during the Civil War. They lived in west Tennessee not far from Memphis when I was a child. Mrs. Badgett lived in Memphis after she got old. Mary's mother visited her long as she lived. I did too. She has been dead several years. She give me a sugar bowl when I was twelve years old—I still got it. I won't sell it. I'll give it to my girl.

"I don't know about the Ku Klux. I never heard a great deal about them.

"I don't vote—not interested.

"Well, I sewed till the very day I was 65 years old. The foreman said I was too old now, but sign up for the pension. I am crippled. I did. I get commodities, but no money.

"I washed, ironed, cooked. I worked at Mrs. Jim

Gunn's and I cooked nine years for Mrs. Dora Gregg. I work whenever I can get work to be done. I like to sew but they cut me off."

United States. Work Projects Administration

Interviewer: Miss Irene Robertson
Person interviewed: Mike Thompson, Widener, Arkansas
Age: 79

MIKE THOMPSON

"I was born near Honey Grove, Texas. I remember my grandparents on both sides—they were all Thompsons. They were cotton and corn farmers. I don't know where they come from. I was so small and as soon as the War was done a whole gang of us come from Texas to Dardanelle, Arkansas.

"The Bushwhackers was so bad we was guarded to the line and they went back. We come in wagons. Bushwhackers was robbers. I remember that. My grandparents and parents all come in the gang. Clem Thompson, my owner, died. He had a family. I don't know what become of none but Ed Thompson. We was the same age and growed up together. I worked for him at Dardanelle but I don't know how he come from Texas. He butchered and peddled meat and had a shop too. I don't think Ed owned land over at Dardanelle but my father owned eighty acres over there when he died. My father was Cubit Thompson. His father was Plato Thompson. My mother was Harriett Thompson.

"The Thompsons was fairly good to their niggers, I recken. Ed was good to me. He promised me I should never want but I don't know if he be dead or not. I wish I could hear from him.

"When I was about twenty-five years old I was coming in home from town one night. I seen his house on fire. I kept going fast as I could run, woke him up. He run out but his wife didn't. He said, 'My wife! my wife! my wife!' I run in where he run out. She was standing back in a corner the flames nearly all around her. I picked her up and run out and about that time the whole house fell in. They never got through thanking me. I come off over here and never hear a word from him. He always said I saved their lives and hers mostly.

"Times—young men can get work if they will go to the field and work. If you can't work, times is hard two ways. If you are used to work, you hard to get contentment and loss of the money too. Money don't buy much. Awful sight of cotton and you don't get much out of it. Young folks is got young notions.

"I come to Widener in 1908. I made a good living. I own this house. Now I got to quit working in bad weather. My rheumatism gets so bad. I'll be eighty years old 23rd of September this year (1938)."

Interviewer: Samuel S. Taylor
Person Interviewed: Laura Thornton
1215 W. Twenty-Fourth Street, Little Rock, Arkansas
Age: 105?

LAURA THORNTON

"My native home is Alabama. I was born not far from Midway, Alabama, about twelve miles from Clayton. Midway, Clayton, and Barber are all nearby towns. We used to go to all of them.

"My master was Tom Eford. When he died, I fell to Polly Eford. Polly Eford was the old lady. I don't know where they is and they don't know nothing about where I is. It's been so long. Because I done lef' Alabama fifty years. I don't know whether any of them is living or not. It's been so long.

"Their baby boy was named Giles Eford. His mother was Miami Eford and my father's name was Perry Eford. That is the name he went in. My mother went in that name too. My father died the second year of the surrender. My mother was a widow a long time. I was a grown-up woman and had children when my father died.

"I married during slavery time. I don't remember just how old I was then. My old man knows my age, but I can't remember it. But he's been dead this year makes thirteen years. I had one child before the surrender. I was just married to the one man. I was married after the surrender. I don't want to be married again. I never seed a man I would give a thought to since he died. Lord knows how long we'd been married before he died.

"We came here and stayed four years and we bought a home down on Arch Street Pike about ten miles from here. I lived there sixty years. I've got the tax receipts for sixty years back. I ain't never counted the ones I paid since he's been dead.

"I was the mother of three children and none of them are living. All of them dead but me.

"They made like they was goin' to give old slave folks a pension. They ain't gimme none yit. I'm just livin' on the mercy of the people. I can't keep up the taxes now. I wish I could git a pension. It would help keep me up till I died. They won't even as much as give me nothin' on the relief. They say these grandchildren ought to keep me up. I have to depend on them and they can't hardly keep up theirselves.

"When the Civil War broke out, my baby was about seven years old. My mother was here when the stars fell. She had one child then.

"I remember a war before the Civil War. I heard the white folks talking about it. They wouldn't tell colored folks nothing. They'd work them to death and beat them to death. They'd sell them just like you sell hogs. My mother was sold from me when I was little. Old lady Eford, she was my mistress and mammy too. If she ever slapped me, I don't know nothin' 'bout it.

"My daddy made his farm jus' like colored people do

now. White man would give him so much ground if he'd a mind to work it. He had a horse he used.

"We lived a heap better than the people live now. They fed you then. You ate three times a day. When twelve o'clock come, there dinner was, cooked and ready. Nothin' to do but eat it, and then set down and res' with the other people. There was them that was good.

"But them what was mean done the colored folks bad.

- **Early Days**

"I was little when my mother was sold from me. I was runnin' about though in the yard. I couldn't do nothing. But I was a smart girl. The first work I can remember doin' was goin' to the field ploughing. That is the first thing I remember. I was little. I just could come up to the plough. I cut logs when I was a little child like them children there (children about ten years old playing in the street). I used to clean up new ground—do anything.

"My mother and father both worked in the field. My father was sold away from me jus' like my mother was. Old lady Eford was my mother and father too. That was in Clayton, Alabama. Old Tom Eford had three boys—one named Tom, one named William, and there was the one named Giles what I told you about. William was the oldest, Tom was the second, and Giles was the youngest.

"I never learnt to read and write. In slave time, they didn't let you have no books. My brother though was a good reader. He could write as well as any of them because he would be with the white children and they would show him. That is the way my brother learnt. He would lay down all day Sunday and study. The good blessed Lord helped him.

• Marriage

"The man I married was on the plantation. They married in slave time just like they do these days. When I married, the justice of peace married me. That was after freedom, our folks would give big weddings just like they do now (just after the war). I ain't got my license now. Movin' 'round, it got lost. I was married right at home where me and my old man stayed. Wasn't nobody there but me and him and another man named Dr. Bryant. That wasn't far from Midway.

"I can't talk much since I had those strokes. Can't talk plain, just have to push it out, but I thank God I can do that much. The Lord let me stay here for some reason—I don't know what. I would rather go, but he ain't called me.

• How the Day Went

"We got up after daylight. Tom Eford didn't make his folks git up early. But after he was dead and gone, things changed up. The res' made 'em git up before daylight. He was a good man. The Lord knows. Yes Lord, way before day. You'd be in the field to work way before day and then work way into the night. The white folks called Eford's colored people poor white folks because he was so good to them. Old Tom Eford was the sheriff of Clayton.

"His folks came back to the house at noon and et their dinner at the house. He had a cook and dinner was prepared for them just like it was for the white folks. The colored woman that cooked for them had it ready when they came there for it. They had a great big kitchen and the hands ate there. They came back to the same place for supper. And they didn't have to work late either. Old Tom Eford never worked his hands extra. That is the reason they called his niggers poor-white folks. Folks lived at home them days and et in the same place. When my old man was living, I had plenty. Smokehouse was full of good meat. Now everything you git, you have to buy.

"Next morning, they all et their breakfast in the same kitchen. They et three meals a day every day. My mother never cooked except on Sunday. She didn't need to.

• Patrollers

"Me and old lady Eford would be out in the yard and I would hear her cuss the pateroles because they didn't want folks to 'buse their niggers. They had to git a pass from their masters when they would be out. If they didn't have a pass, the pateroles would whip them.

• Jayhawkers

"The jayhawkers would catch folks and carry them out in the woods and hang them up. They'd catch you and beat you to death.

• Runaways

"Colored folks what would run away, old lady Eford would call them 'rottenheads' and 'bloody bones.' We would hear the hounds baying after them and old lady Eford would stand out in the yard and cuss them—cuss the hounds I mean. Like that would do any good. Some slaves would kill theirselves before they would be caught. They would hear them dogs. I have seen old Tom Eford. He would have them dogs. He was sheriff and he had to do it. He carried them dogs. He would be gone two weeks before he would be back sometimes. Alden or Alton was the place they said they carried the runaways.

- **Slave Breeding**

"They never kept no slaves for breeding on any plantation I heard of. They would work them to death and breed them too. There was places where old massa kept one for hisself.

- **Amusements**

"Folks had heap more pleasure than they do now in slave time. They had parties and dances and they would bow 'round. They had fiddles and danced by them. Folks danced them days. They don't dance now, just mess around. My brother could scrape the fiddle and dance on, all at the same time. Folks would give big suppers and ask people out. They would feed nice times with one another. Folks ain't got no love in their hearts like they used to have.

"Folks would give quiltings. They don't think about quilting now. They would quilt out a quilt and dance the rest of the night. They would have a big supper at the quilting. Nice time too. They would kill a hog and barbecue it. They would cook chicken. Have plenty of whiskey too. Some folks would get drunk. That was whiskey them days. They ain't got no whiskey now—old poison stuff that will kill people.

My daddy was jus' drunk all the time. He had plenty of whiskey. That was what killed old Tom Eford. He kept it settin' on the dresser all the time. You couldn't walk in his house but what you would see it time you got in. Folks hide it now. I have drunk a many a glass of it. I would go and take a glass whenever I wanted to.

- ### How Freedom Came

"The old white folks told me I was free. They had me hired out. I wasn't staying with my owner. There wasn't nobody there with me but the white folks where I was staying. That morning I got up to get breakfast and there wasn't no fire and there wasn't so matches. I went to some neighbors to get a chunk of fire and they told me to go back to my folks because I was free. When I got back to the house they was mad and wanted to whip me. So I just put the fire down and never cooked no breakfast but jus' went on to my brother's. The reason they wanted to whip me was because I had gone outside of the house without their knowing it.

"When I went to my brother's, I had to walk twelve miles. My brother carried me to my mother and father. And then he took me back to old lady Eford, and she told me to go on to my mother, that I was free now. So he took me on back to my ma and pa. He said he'd do that so that I could stay with them.

- ### Slave Earnings

"Slaves had money in slave time. My daddy bought a horse. He made a crop every year. He made his bale of cotton. He made corn to feed his horse with. He belonged to his white folks but he had his house and lot right next to theirs. They would give him time you know. He didn't have to work in the heat of the day. He made his crop and bought his whiskey. The white folks fed 'im. He had no expenses 'cept tending to his crop. He didn't have to give Tom Eford anything he made. He just worked his crop in his extra time. Many folks too lazy to git theirselves somethin' when they have the chance to do it. But my daddy wasn't that kind. His old master gave him the ground and he made it give him the money.

"My daddy left me plenty but I ain't got it now. I didn't care what happened when he died. People made out like they was goin' to put my money in the bank for me and took it and destroyed it. Used it for theirselves I reckon. Now I need it and ain't got it—ain't got a penny. For five or six years at my home, I made good crops. We raised everything we needed at home. Didn't know what it was to come to town to buy anything. If anybody had told me twenty years ago I would be in this shape, I wouldn't have believed it because I had plenty.

- **What Slaves Got When Freed**

"They said they was gwine a give the slaves something, but they never did do it. Then the master made out like he was gwine a give the slaves so much if they stayed 'round and made his crops for him, but he didn't do it.

- **Come Again**

"If the Lord lets you git back tomorrow, try and come a little sooner in the day than you did today. I gits up about six in the morning. I don't believe in layin' in bed late. I go to bed directly after dark and I wake up early. The Lord never did mean for nobody to sleep all day."

- **Interviewer's Comment**

    A number of people testify to Laura Thornton's age. I am trying to check up on it. Results later. If she isn't a hundred [HW: and] five years old, she is "mighty nigh" it. She has feeble health, but a surprisingly alert mind, and a keen sharp memory. She has a tendency to confuse Reconstruction times with slavery times, but a little questioning always brings out the facts.

    She doesn't like to talk much about marriage in slavery. Evidently she dislikes the fact that one of her children ms born before emancipation. She was evidently married only once, as questioning brought out; but she will refer to the marriage before emancipation and the one afterward as though they were to different persons.

United States. Work Projects Administration

[HW: Curtis, Ark.
Emma (Bama?) Tidwell]

EMMA TIDWELL BAMA?

Ah'm one uv dem ole timers. Ah been here since way back yonder. Fust thing ah kin member is a bad storm an mah ma put us undah de baid. She wuz skeered hit would blow us away. Ah use tuh play till ah got bigger nuff tuh work. Ah member we use tuh play runnin. We'd play walkin tuh see which one uv us could walk de fastest tuh de field tuh carry dinner. We use tuh jump an we use tuh ride stick hosses an limbs offn trees.

Ole boss learnt mah pa how tuh make shoes an de way he done: Dey kilt a cow an a deer an take dey hides an tanned dem. De way he tanned hit wuz tuh take red oak bark an white oak bark an put in vats. Dese vats wuz somethin like troughs dat helt water an he put a layer uv oak ashes an or layer uv ashes an a layer uv leather till he got hit all in an covered wid water. Aftuh dat dey let hit soak till de hair come offn de hide den dey would take de hide oft an hit wuz ready fuh tannin. Den de hide wuz put tuh soak in wid de redoak bark. Hit stayed in de water till de hide turnt tan den pa took de hide out uv de redoak dye an hit would be a purty tan. Hit didn' have tuh soak so long. Den he would git his pattern an cut an make tan shoes outn dat tanned hide. We called dem brogans. We all wore shoes cause mah pa made em.

We planted indigo an hit growed jes like wheat. When hit got ripe we gathered hit an we would put hit in a barrel an let hit soak bout er week den we would take de indigo stems out an squeeze all de juice outn dem, put de juice back in de barrel an let hit stay dere bout nother week, den we jes stirred an stirred one whole day. We let hit set three or four days den drained de water offn hit an dat left de settlings an de settlings wuz blueing jes like we have dese days. We cut ours in little blocks. Den we dyed clothes wid hit. We had purty blue cloth. De way we set de color we put alumn in hit. Dat make de color stay right dere.

Ah'll tell yuh how tuh dye. Er little beech bark dyes slate color set wid copper. Hickory bark an bay leaves dyes yellow set wid chamber lye; bamboo dyes turkey red, set color wid copper. Pine straw an sweetgum dyes purple, set color wid chamber lye. Ifn yuh dont bleave hit try em all.

Mah ma made cloth while mah pa made shoes. Ah member jes as good when dey handcuff mah ma's two brothers tuh keep um from runnin off when dey got ready tuh sell em. Ah seed um handcuff as many as eight tugethuh when dey marched dem tuh de pen. Yuh know dey had uh pen kinder like de pond pen fer cows an hosses. Well dey would drive us niggers tuh de pond pen an dey had er big block in de pen an dey put one uv us niggers on hit at a time. Bid us off tuh de highest bidder. Mah ole boss wuz a gambler. People talk bout dis gamblin an drinkin bein a late thing—dem white fokes done hit way back yonder 90 years ergo, cause mah ole boss gambled me off, ah clare he did. Gambled me off one Sunday mornin'. Ole Boss made whiskey jes like dey do tuhday.

Black preachers couldn' preach tuh us. Ole boss would tie em tuh a tree an whoop em if dey caught us eben praying. We had er big black washpot an de way we prayed we'd go out an put our mouths to der groun an pray low an de sound wud go up under de pot an ole boss couldn' bear us. De white preacher would call us under a tree Sunday evenin tuh preach tuh us. Dis is whut his text would be: "Mind yo mistress." Den he would ceed tuh preach—"Don't steal der potatoes; don't lie bout nothin an don' talk back tuh yo boss; ifn yo does yo'll be tied tuh a tree an stripped neckid. When dey tell yuh tuh do somethin run an do it." Dat's de kind uv gospel we got.

We cooked on fiuhplaces in er iron pot; cooked bread in a ubben. We had ash cakes. We et purty good.

Ah didn go tuh school. Ah wuz awful sly. Ah wanted tuh learn tuh read so ah hung eroun ole mistess when she wuz teachin huh chillun tuh read. Ah listened an when she put de book down an went out ah got de book. Ah kep' hit up till ah learnt tuh read. Ah been teachin one Bible class in Curtis 42 years. Some uv em dare ask me how ah learnt tuh read so good an ah tole dem dat a person dat couldn' learn tuh read in a hunnert years ought tuh be daid.

Ah wuz twenty-two when de silver war broke. Ah know when hit started but ah don' know whut hit wuz erbout. All I know Jeff Davis an Abraham Lincoln wuz de two presidents. Lincoln wuz somethin like regular president an Jeff Davis wuz somethin like er confedric president or somethin. Ah didn' know jes how hit wuz. Jeff Davis ah think wuz er rebel and Lincoln republic. When de fight come up dey wuzn fightin tuh set de niggers free, ah don' think. At de time dey wuz fightin ovah de Union but aftuh de slave owners wuz gwianter take de innocent slaves an make dem fight on dey side. Den Lincoln said hit wouldn' be. So dat when he sot em free. Whoopee! Yo ought ter seed dem Yankees fightin. Aftuh de battle wuz ovah we would walk ovah de battle groun' an look at de daid bones, skellums ah think dey called em. Aftuh de white fokes tole us we wuz free dey didn' give us nothin. Turnt us out widout a place tuh stay, no clo'es but whut we had on our back an nuthin tuh eat. We jes slept undah trees an roun bout. Didn' have nuthin tuh eat cept parched corn. We stole dat. Had tuh do somethin. De nex year de white fokes let us make a crop wid den fuh somethin tuh eat an clo'es an de women could work fuh a few clo'es an somethin tuh eat. So in er year er two niggers went tuh tryin tuh duh somethin fuh demselves, an been tryin tuh help dey selfs evah since. Ah know all bout hit. Ah wuz tall an ah is now when dey cried "Free!" Ain't growed nairy nother inch.

Interviewer: Mrs. Bernice Bowden
Person interviewed: Joe Tillman
W. 10th and Highway No. 79
Pine Bluff, Arkansas
Age: 79

JOE TILLMAN

"I was born in 1859 down here at Walnut Lake. The man what owned us was Crum Holmes.

"All I can remember was the patrollers and the Ku Klux. I reckon I ought to, I seed 'em. I got skeered and run. I heered 'em talk 'bout how they'd do the folks and we chillun thought they'd do us the same way.

"I 'member hearin' 'em talk 'bout the Yankees—how they'd come through there and how they used to do.

"I guess we had plenty to eat. All I know was when I got ready to eat, I could eat.

"My parents was brought from Tennessee but all the place I know anything about is Walnut Lake.

"I know my mother said I was the cause of her gettin' a lot of whippin's. I'd run off and the boss man whipped her cause she wasn't keepin' me at home. If he didn't whip her, he'd pull her ears.

"When we was comin' up they didn't 'low the chillun to sit around where the old folks was talkin'. And at night when company come in, we chillun had to go to bed out the way. Sometimes I'm glad of it. See so many chillun now gettin' into trouble.

"I never been arrested in my life. Been a witness once or twice—that's the only way I ever been in court. If I'd a been like a lot of 'em, I might a been dead or in the pen.

"In them days, if we did something wrong, anybody could whip us and if we'd go tell our folks we get another whippin'.

"After freedom my parents stayed there and worked by the day. They didn't have no privilege of sellin' the cotton though.

"I didn't start to farm till I was 'bout twelve years old. They started me bustin' out the middles till I learnt how and then they put the plowin' in my hands.

"White people been pretty good to me 'cause I done what they told me.

"I went to school a little 'long about '70. I learnt how to read and kept on till I could write a little.

"I used to vote 'til they stopped us. I used to vote right along, but I stopped foolin' with it. 'Course we can vote in the president election but I got so I couldn't see what ticket I was votin', so I stopped foolin' with it.

"I farmed till 'bout '94, then I worked at the compress and brick work."

Interviewer: Samuel S. Taylor
Person interviewed: J.T. Tims
111 Mosaic Temple, Ninth and Broadway
Little Rock, Arkansas
Age: 86
Occupation: Cook, waiter, and farmer

J.T. TIMS

"I was born in Jefferson County, Mississippi in 1853. That would make me eighty-six years old. I was born six miles from Fayette—six miles east of Fayette. I was eighty-six years old the eleventh day of September.

"My father's name was Daniel Tims, and my mother's name was Ann Tims. My mother was born in Lexington, Kentucky. Ma's been dead years and years ago, and my father is gone too. My mother's name before she married was ----; she she told it to us all right but I just never can think of it.

"I don't know the name of my mother's master. But my father's master was named Blount Steward. Pa was born on Blount's plantation and Blount bought my ma because they brought her from Kentucky for sale. They had her for sale just like you would sell hogs and mules. Then my father saw her and liked her and married her. She was a slave too.

• Master

"Blount Steward was kinder good. He was very well till the war started—the Federal War. Miss Ann went to whip me for nothing.

• Whippings

"I was carrying her daughter to school every day except Saturdays and Sundays. One day, Miss Ann was off and I was at the back steps playing and she decided to whip me. I told her I hadn't done nothing but she put my head between her legs and started to beatin' me. And I bit her legs. She lemme loose and hollered. Then she called for William to come and beat me. William was one of the colored slaves. William come to do it. Ma had been peeping out from the kitchen watchin' the whole thing. When William come up to beat me, she came out with a big carving knife and told him, 'That's my child and if you hit him, I'll kill you.'

"Then she sent for Tully to come and whip me, I mean to whip my mother. Tully was my young master. Tully came and said to my mother, 'I know you ain't done nothin' nor your child neither, but I'll have to hit you a few light licks to satisfy ma.'

"Blount come the next day and went down to where pa was making shoes. He said, 'Daniel, you're looking mighty glum.'

"Pa said, 'You'd be lookin' glum too if your wife and chile had done been beat up for nothin'.'

"When he said that, Blount got mad. He snatched up a shoe hammer and hit pa up side the head with it.

"Pa said, 'By God, don't you try it again.'

"Blount didn't hit him again. Pa was ready to fight, and he wasn't sure that he could whip him. Pa said, 'You won't hit me no more.' The war was goin' on then.

- **Runaways**

"The following Sunday night, twelve head of 'em left there. My ma and pa and me and our whole family and some more besides was along. We went from the plantation to Rodney, Mississippi first, trying to get on a steamboat—gunboat. The gunboat wouldn't take us for fear we would get hurt. The war was goin' on then. So we just transferred down the river and went on to Natchez. We went there walking and wading. We was from Sunday night to Sunday night gettin' there. We didn't have no trouble 'sept that the hounds ms runnin' us. But they didn't catch us—they didn't catch none of us. My ma and my pa and my brothers and sisters besides me was all in the crowd; and we all got to Natchez.

"They are all dead and gone to Judgment now but me. I think that I got one sister in Chicago, Illinois. She is my baby sister. I ain't never heard nothing about her bein' dead.

- **Natchez**

"At Natchez, ma didn't do anything. We children didn't do nothin' either there. But pa joined the army. He joined it the next day after he got there. Then I went to work waiting on the sixty-fourth—lemme see—yes, it was the Sixty-Fourth Brass Epaulettes. I was waiting on one of the sergeants. He was a Yankee sergeant. The sergeant's name was Josephus, and the captain of the Company was Lieutenant Knowles. I was with them two years and six months. I never did get hurt. When they went to fight at New Orleans, the captain wouldn't lemme take part in it. He said that I was so brave he was a 'fraid I might get hurt.

"Me and my father were the only ones working in the family at that time. I stayed right in Natchez but my father didn't. My father's first stop was in Bullocks Bar right above Vidalia. That was where his company was stationed first. Lemme see, he went from there to Davis Bend. I wasn't with them. He was in a colored regiment. I was with a white regiment. He left Davis Bend and want to Vicksburg. His next trip was up the Sunflower River. His next trip he went from there up here to De Valls Bluff. That is where he come free. That was the end of the fighting there—right there.

"From there he come back to Rodney. We all want to Davis Bend while pa was there. When he left and went to De Valls Bluff, ma went to Rodney. I stayed with the soldiers two years and a half down there at Natchez. That's as far as I went with them. When they left I stayed.

"I went to Rodney with my mother and stayed with her and the rest of the children till she died. My ma died in 1874. My father died down here in Pine Bluff several years ago. After ma died, pa married another woman. He went back to Pine Bluff and was killed by a train when he was crossing a trestle.

- **Age and Other Masters**

"Blount Steward was the only master any of us

ever had, outside of my ma's first master—the one in Kentucky. I don't know anything about them. I was eight years old when the war began and twelve years old when it ended. I must have been older than that because I was twelve years old when I was serving them soldiers. And I had to come away from them before the war was over.

- **Slave Work**

"The first work I ever did in slave time was dining-room service. When I left the dining-room table, I left carrying my young mistress to school six miles from Fayette. They give me to Lela, my young mistress. She was the young girl I was carrying to school when I got the whipping. When ol' mis' was whippin' me, I asked her what she was whipping me for, and she said, 'Nothin', 'cause you're mine, and I can whip you if I want to.' She didn't think that I had done anything to the girl. She was just mad that day, and I was around; so she took it out on me. After that, I never did any more work as a slave, because the whole family ran away about that time. I don't reckon pa would ever have run off if ol' miss hadn't whipped me and if ol' massa hadn't struck him. They rats good till then; but it looked like the war made them mean.

- **Patrollers, Jayhawkers, Ku Klux, and Ku Klux Klan**

"They had pateroles going 'round watching the colored people to keep them from running off. That's all I know 'bout them. I don't remember hearin' anything about the jayhawkers.

"I heard lots 'bout the Ku Klux. They were terrible.

The white folks had one another goin' 'round watching and keeping them from runnin' off. The Ku Klux would whip people they caught out. They would whip them just because they could; because they called themselves bosses, because they was white and the colored people was niggers. They didn't do nothin' but just keep the slaves down. It was before the war that I knew 'bout the Ku Klux. There wasn't no difference between the pateroles and the Ku Klux that I knows of. If they'd ketch you, they all would whip you. I don't know nothin' about the Ku Klux Klan after the war. I know they broke them up.

- **Slave Houses, Furniture, Food, and Work**

"Before the war, we lived in a old log house. It had one window, one door, and one room. Colored people didn't have no two or three-room houses before the war. I'll tell you that right now. All the furniture we had was bed stools and quilts. 'Course we had them old stools that pa made. We kept food right there in the house where we was in one corner. We didn't have no drawers—nothing like that. The white folks fed us. They give us as much as they thought we ought to have. Every Saturday night you would go to the smokehouse and get your meat and meal and your molasses. Didn't get no flour, no coffee, no sugar. Pa was an ox driver and when he would go to Rodney to carry cotton, he would buy sugar and coffee for himself. You see, they would slip a little something and make a little money off it. Like they was goin' to Rodney tomorrow, they would slip and kill a couple of hogs and carry them along with them. That was the only way they could get a little money. My pa's main work was shoemaking, but he worked in the field too. He was a driver chiefly when he was out in the field. He hoed and plowed. He was the leader of the gang. He never got a chance to make no money for hisself before the war. Nope, the colored people didn't have no money 'tall lessen they slipped and got it.

• Slave Marriages

"Say I wanted this woman for my wife. We would just put down the broom and step over it and we would be married. That is all there was to it before emancipation. Didn't have no matrimony read nor nothing. You were married when you stepped over the broom handle. That was your wife.

• A Lincoln Story

"They say Abe Lincoln come down in this part of the country and asked for work. He had his little grip just like you got. The man said, 'Wait till I go to dinner.' Didn't say, 'Come to dinner,' and didn't say nothin' 'bout, 'Have dinner.' Just said, 'Wait till I go eat my dinner.' When he come back, Abe Lincoln was up there looking over his books. He'd done changed his clothes and everything. He had guards with him but they didn't see 'em. That is the story I heard them tell.

• What the Slaves Got

"When the slaves got freed, they wasn't expecting to get nothing that I knows of 'cept what they worked for. They weren't spectin' no forty acres and a mule. Who was goin' to give it to 'em? The Rebs? They didn't give 'em nothin' but what they could put on their backs—I mean lashes.

"Blount had stocks that he used to put them in. The stocks had hinges on one side and latches on the other. The nigger would put his head in one hole and his arms through the others, and the old man would eat on the other end. Your feet would be stretched out and you would be layin' on your belly.

"Blount whipped me once because I wouldn't go to the cow barns to get the milk to put in the coffee that morning. I didn't have time. They had given me to Lela, and I had to take her to school. I was 'sponsible if she was late. He had give me to Lela. Next morning with her, and we didn't come back till Friday evening. She went down to her Aunt Leona Harrison's and carried me with her. She was mad because they whipped me when I belonged to her.

"After slavery, we worked by the month on people's plantations. I did that kind of work till after a while the white people got so they rented the colored people land and selled them mules for their work. Then some worked on shares and some rented and worked for theirselves. Right after the war most of the farms were worked on shares. We were lucky to be able to get to work by the month.

• Schooling

"I went to school in Natchaz, Mississippi. My teacher came from the North, I suppose. But those I had in Rodney, I know they come from the North. Miss Mary—that's all the name I knowed—and Miss Emma were my teachers in Rodney. They come from Chicago; I never went to school here. I didn't get no farther than the second grade. I stopped school to go work when the teacher went back to Chicago. After that I went to work in the field and made me a living. I hadn't done but a little work in the field helping pa now and then before that.

• Marriages

"I married a long time ago in Rodney. Lord, it's been so long ago I couldn't tell you when. I been married four times. They all quit me for other men. I didn't quit none of them.

• Present Condition

"I get along tolerably now for an old man. The welfare gives me a little help. But I have to pay five dollars for these two rooms every month. What's more, I got to eat, and I got to have somethin' to wear. Washington won't allow me nothin' for my army service. They say I wasn't regular. I gets eight dollars from the Welfare.

• Opinions

"The young people's terrible. They rather go to the penitentiary or the county farm or get killed than to do what is right.

• Voting and Vocational Experiences

"I used to vote. I never had no trouble about it.

"They tried to whip me once since freedom, but not about votin'. A man tried to whip me down in Stoneville because another man give me a drink. He tried to cut me with his knife. I knocked him down. I told him I could kill him, but I just didn't want to. While I was swearing out a warrant to get him arrested, he went and got a gun somewheres. He came right on in with his pistol and struck me with it. I knocked him down again, and he was dead for twenty-five minutes. They didn't have to go nowheres to serve the warrant on him. Nobody did anything to me about it.

"I come to Little Rock fifty years ago or more. I farmed as long as I was able. Doctor stopped me when I began to fall out.

"I cooked for Dr. Stone and his wife for ten years in Greenville, Mississippi. Then I come to Pine Bluff on a vacation. The next time they give me a vacation, I stayed away for eleven years. I went to get some money Dr. Stone owed me for some work I had done for him once and he wanted me to come back and cook again. I didn't do that and he died without paying me for the work. He said it was his brother that owed me. But it was him that hired me. I 'tended to some mules for nine months at four dollars a week. I never got but one four dollars. The miles belonged to him and his brother both, but it was him that hired me. It wasn't Captain Stone, his brother. It was him, and I looked to the man that hired me for my money. I didn't have nothing to do with nobody but him. It was him promised to pay me."

- **Interviewer's Comment**

Throughout his story Tims carefully avoided using his first name. Never at any time did he let it slip.

The capture of New Orleans was effected in 1862. If the troop with which he worked took part in the capture, he must have been twelve years old by 1862, and his age must be at least eighty-eight. But this would be inconsistent with his statement that he served Sergeant Josephus for two years and a half. The detachment might have gone to New Orleans later than '62. At any rate, Tims is at least eighty-five, and possibly older. Here again we have a definite conviction of the use of the word Ku Klux before the War. The way he talks of it, the term might have been a colloquial term applied to a jayhawker or a patroller. He doesn't mean Ku Klux Klan when he says Ku Klux.

The Lincoln story is included on my part merely because it is at least legendary material. I don't know what basis of fact it could or might have.

United States. Work Projects Administration

Interviewer: S.S. Taylor
Person interviewed: Hannah Travis,
3219 W. Sixteenth,
Little Rock, Ark.
Age: 75
Occupation: Housewife

HANNAH TRAVIS

"The Jay Hawkers would travel at night. When they came to a cabin, they would go in and tell them that owned it they wanted something to eat and to get it ready quick. They stopped at one place and went in and ordered their dinner. They et the supper and went away and got sick after they left. They got up the next morning and examined the road and the horse tracks and went on. They all thought something had been given to them, but I don't guess there was. They caught my mother and brought her here and sold her. If they caught a nigger, they would carry him off and sell him. That's how my mother came to Arkansas.

"I don't know what year I was born in. I know the month and the day. It was February tenth. I have kinder kept up with my age. As near as I can figure, I am seventy-three years old. I was 18 in 1884 when I married. I must have been born about 1864, I was brought up under my step father; he was a very mean man. When he took a notion to he'd whip me and mother both.

"My mother was born somewheres in Missouri, but

whereabouts I don't know. One of her masters was John Goodet. His wife was named Eva Goodet. He was a very mean man and cruel, and his wife was too. My grandmother belonged to another slaveholder and they would allow her to go to see my mother. She was allowed to work and do things for which she was given old clothes and other little things. She would take em and bring em to my mother. As soon as she had gone, they would take them things away from my mother, and put em up in the attic and not allow her to wear them. They would let the clothes rot and mildew before they'd let my mother wear them. If my mother left a dish dirty—sometimes there would be butter or flour or something in the dish that would need to be soaked—they would wait till it was thoroughly soaked and then make her drink the old dirty dish water. They'd whip her if she didn't drink it.

"Her other master was named Harrison. He was tolerable but nothing to bragg on.

"After she was Jayhawked and brought down South, they sold her to John Kelly, a man in Arkansas somewhere. She belonged to John Kelly and his wife when freedom came. John Kelly and his wife kept her working for them without pay for two years after she was free. They didn't pay her anything at all. They hardly gave her anything to eat and wear. They didn't tell her she was free. She saw colored people going and coming in a way they wasn't used to, and then she heard her Mistress' youngest daughter tell her mother, 'You ought to pay Hannah something now because you know she is free as we are. And you ought to give her something to eat and wear.' The mother said, 'You know I can't do that hard work; I'm not used to it.' After hearing this my mother talked to the colored people that would pass by and she learned for shor enough she was free.

"There was a colored man there that they were keeping too. One Sunday, they were taking him to church and leaving my mother behind. She said to them, 'Well, I will be gone when you come back, so you better leave Bill here this morning.' Her old mistress said to her, 'Yes; and we'll come after you and whip you every step of the way back.' But she went while they were at church and they did not catch her either.

"The Saturday before that she made me a dress out of the tail of an old bonnet and a big red handkerchief. Made waist, sleeves and all out of that old bonnet and handkerchief. She left right after they left for church, and she dressed me up in my new dress. She put the dress on me and went down the road. She didn't know which way to go. She didn't know the way nor which direction to take. She walked and she walked and she walked. Then she would step aside and listen and ask the way.

"It was near night when she found a place to stay. The people out in the yard saw her pass and called to her. It was the youngest daughter of Mrs. Kelly, the one she had overheard telling her mother she ought to set her free and pay her. She stayed with John Kelly's daughter two or three days. I don't know what her name was, only she was a Kelly. Then she got out among the colored people and got to working and got some clothes for herself and me. From then on, she worked and taken care of me.

"From there she went to Pocahontas and worked and stayed there till I was about fifteen years old. Meanwhile, she married in Pocahontas. Then she moved to Newport.

When I was fifteen, I married in Newport. My mother supported herself by cooking and washing. Then she got a chance to work on a small boat cooking and doing the boat washing, and there would be weeks that some of the deck hands would have to help her because they would have such a crowd of raftsmen. Sometimes there would be twenty or thirty of them raftsmen—men who would cut the logs and raft them to go and bring them down the river. Then the deck hands would have to help her. I too would have to wash the dishes and help out.

"I went to school in Pocahontas and met my future husband (Travis). I brought many a waiter to serve when they had a crowd. I took Travis to the boat and he was hired to wait on the men. When they had just the crew—Captain, Clerk, Pilot, Engineer, Mate, and it seems there was another one—I waited on the table myself. I help peel the potatoes and turn the meat. When we had that big run, then Mr. Travis and some of the others would come down and help me. The boat carried freight, cotton, and nearly anything might neer that was shipped down to town. Pocahontas was a big shipping place.

"My mother said they used to jump over the broom stick and count that married. The only amusement my mother had was work. I don't know if she knowed there was such a thing as Christmas.

"Mother's little house was a log cabin like all the other slaves had.

"They didn't give her anything much to eat. They was farmers. They raised their own cattle and hogs. The niggers did the same—that is, the niggers raised everything and got a little to eat. They had one nigger man that was around the house and others for the field. They didn't allow the slaves to raise anything for themselves and they didn't give them much.

"The slaves made their own clothes and their own cloth. They would not let the slaves have anything much. To keep them from being stark naked, they'd give them a piece to wear.

"Mama got to see her mother in 1885. When I married she left and went to Missouri and found her sister and half-sister and her mother and brother or cousin. She found her sister's oldest daughter. She was a baby laying in the cradle when mama ran through the field to get away from a young man that wanted to talk to her.

"My grandmother was a full-blooded Indian. Her husband was a French Negro. Nancy Cheatham was her name.

"The Ku Klux never bothered us. They bothered some people about a mile from us. They took out the old man and whipped him. They made his wife get up and dance and she was in a delicate state. They made her get out of bed and dance, and after that they took her and whipped her and beat her, and she was in a delicate state too.

"There was a man there in Black Rock though that stopped them from bothering anybody. He killed one of them. They went to the train. They was raging around there then. He got off the train and they tried to take him to jail. The jail was way out through the woods. He hadn't done anything at all. They just took hold of him to take him to the jail because he had just come into the town. They had tugged him down the road and when they got to the woods, he took out his gun and killed one of them, and the rest left him alone. The man who was killed had a wife and four or five children. They sent the nigger to the penitentiary. He stayed there about a year and come out. That broke up the Ku Klux around Black Rock and Portia. They never seemed to get much enjoyment out of it after that.

"I heard from different ones' talk that a big hogshead full of money was given to the Negroes by the Queen, but they never did get it. I think they said the queen sent that money. I reckon it was Queen Victoria, but I don't know. But the white folks got it and kept it for themselves.

"Didn't nobody have any rights then. They would just put em up on a block and auction them off. The one that give the most he would take em. Didn't nobody have no schooling only white folks. The white children would go to school but they didn't allow her to go.

"Once there was a slave woman. They worked her day and night. She had a little log cabin of her own. The spirit used to come to her at night and tell her if she would follow them she wouldn't have to work all the rest of her life. At first she was scared. But finally, she got used to them and she listened to them. She got directions from them and followed them. She went up into the loft and found a whole lot of money hid there. She took it and built her a new house and used it. I heard my grandmother tell this. That was my step-grandmother named Dilsey.

"One of my bosses had a lot of money and he hid it in a cave. They tried to find it and to make my mother tell where it was hid, but she didn't know and couldn't tell. They came back several times and tried to find him at home but they couldn't catch him. That was in Missouri before freedom came.

"I hate my father. He was white. I never did have no use for him. I never seen him because Mama was jayhawked from the place. I never heard my mother say much about him either, except that he was red-headed. He was my mother's master. My mother was just forced. I hate him."

United States. Work Projects Administration

Interviewer: Miss Irene Robertson
Person interviewed: Mark C. Trotter, Edmondson, Arkansas
Age: 71

MARK C. TROTTER

"My owners was Miss Betty and Mr. Luke Trotter. I was born in Tunica County, Mississippi. I farmed all my whole life. I did like it. One thing they said about slavery, you couldn't get away. They had dogs and you get away and have no place to go, nothing to eat. Travel was hard through the rough wilderness. One owner would notify another about a runaway. They would take him back or send him word to come get the runaway. Some of 'em tried to stay in the woods. They said they never tried to get away. I wasn't born till after freedom. They said they felt sorry when somebody got beat but they couldn't help it. They had feeling for their color.

"I come to Arkansas in 1925. I jus' can make it. I'm sickly. I made my part, three bales cotton, last year and prices was so low and provisions so high it is all gone. I don't get no help from the Welfare.

"I heard old folks set around the fire and spit and talk about them very things but I got here too late to know well enough to tell it.

"I recollect when seed was a scarce thing. We had to

save all our seed. The women would swap around. Folks had to raise their own stock.

"The Ku Klux didn't bother us.

"I voted here in town. I don't bother the polls no more. I don't own nothing.

"Times and folks both been changing all my life. Some things is better and some people as good as they always been."

Slave Narratives

El Dorado District
FOLKLORE SUBJECTS
Name of Interviewer: Pernella Anderson (Colored)
Subject: NEGRO FOLKLORE—Uncle James Tubbs
Story:—Information

PERNELLA ANDERSON

"Well ah wuz born second year after surrender. Some say dat makes me 72 years old. Mah maw only had two boys. Ah am de baby. My pa wuz name Manger Tubbs. I wuz a purty bad boy. When ah wuz one. Ah use ter hunt. Use ter catch six and eight possums in one night. Ah use ter love ter fish. Spunt er many a nite campin and fishin. An playin marbles wuz a wonderful game in mah days yo knows. Fokes wuzen so wile den.

"Ah recollect one night we went coon huntin and de boys wuz wanderin roun and got lost. Some of de boys wuz wanderin roun tryin to git out and couldn' so ah said: "Dar de seben star yo all jes wait and let me fine de way out and dey say all right," "We gwina trus yo to fine out a way out." Went on bout 200 yards and struck our fiel'. We crawled under fence and went on, struck our coan (corn) fiel'. Den dey all reconcile wha dey is and ah had a big laff. When ah wuz a boy ah use to drink a little whiskey. Finally ah said that would be mah ruin. Aftah ah got oldah ah jess decided ah'd quit. Ah nevah did do no hahm tho. Parents didn't raise me ter drink, ah jes taken up the habit mahself. Ah use ter steal Grandma's aigs, He! He! She use ter go ter church and tell us not to bother anything and fore she got out er sight we'd done gone in de hen house. We boys git dem eggs and git on out in our play thicket and roast em and eat em and you know grandma found out where we roast dem aigs at, and whooe if she didn' whup us. He! He! You know the wurst race ah evah had in mah life ah wuz comin on fum Spearsville and two coach whipper wuz layin side de road and you know dem things run me ooo-eee till ah got tuh a stream and you know ifn hit had not bee fer dat watah dem things woulder caught me.

"Coase mah grandma and me had had some putty good races. She tryin' ter cotch me but ah loves her terday fer dose races we had. Mah ma died when ah wuz one munt ole. Mah pa married agin and mah step-ma wuz mean to me so mah grandma come an got me and raised me. Ah hant nevah been in jail. Haint nevah been rested er nothin. Ah wish the chilluns of terday wuz like dey wuz when ah wuz a boy. We lived in er two room log house. Our house had a double chimney and we cooked on dat. You know we'd put a big back stick uv wood on. Mah pa loved his big back sticks of wood to hold the fire. Wudden no stoves at that time. We cooked on chimney fires. We et ash cakes. Hit sho wuz good too. Granma say ash cake wuz healthy. Ah bleve fokes ought ter eat a few of dem now. We had a putty good school house made outn logs. Ah stop school when ah wuz in the third grade. Ah learnt purty fair. We uster have ter take rocks an beat corn ter make meal. We wud have ter go sometime fifty mile to git ter a griss mill. An when we couldn't git coan mashed inter meal we wud make hominy and hit sho wuz good too.

"Ah use ter card fer granma while she wuz spinnin. We made our socks, gloves, and thread. We didn' have dat ter buy. When ah wuz a boy everybody farmed and we had a plenty. Didn' have drouth in does days.

"Any kine of lan' would produce. Ah use ter get a many lashin bout pickin cotton. Ah couldn' pick until ah got dem lashins. Some fokes say lashin don' help but ah clare dey do.

"Ah use ter pick cotton and sing. Ah can recollect so well de song. Hit went lak dis:

> Me an' mah wife had a fallin out
> She wanted me ter work on de railroad track
> Etc. (See enclosed song)

"Ah jes love ter talk bout when ah wuz a boy. We had a lop cabin fuh a church house. In dem days on meetin' Sunday fokes would go ter church and carry de chillun but now not neither the chillun nor dey ma's go either.

"Fokes would serve the Lord. Dey would git happy in de fiel' and fall out choppin, choppin cotton. No sich times as hit wuz now. Aftah all er mah youth and hardship and goodship the Lord called me ter preach and when he called me ah answered. Ah wuz comin cross de fiel about 12 er'clock. Ah tole him ah couldn' preach. Den ah heard a voice above mah haid. Ah stopped and wondahed and pondered wid mahself knowin' de condition uv mahself. Ah said, "Lord yo knows ah caint preach." Den ah made a vow and ah stuck to hit but ah heard nother voice say, "Go and preach" again. And ah heerd ah nother voice say "Yo go in de mawnin and pray befo sunrise." Ah goes thar and gits on mah knees and tried ter pray an ah heard dogs a barkin and chains rattlin an cats mewin and everthing. Ah had heard ole fokes talk bout when yo go ter pray chains and things would track yer tenshun. The same happen ter me. Ah want on and ended mah prayer and yo know ah wuz a glad soul. Ah felt lak ah cud go an then an do whut the Lawd said. Ah gone on an stahted preachin. Hit seemed the church wuz so crowded wid so many local preachers ah couldn' do whut de Lawd wanted me ter so ah ask the pastor ifn ah could run prayer meetin and he said, "Why chile yes," and ah went on wid de prayer meetin till ever'body quit his church and come to mah prayer meetin so den he called mah han', got jealous and made me move mah prayer meetin. So som good white fokes let me come ovah neah them and start a prayer meetin so de people followed me and we built a church and hit is yet dare terday."

Interviewer: Mrs. Bernice Bowden
Person interviewed: Mandy Tucker
1021 E. 11th Street, Pine Bluff, Arkansas
Age: 80?

MANDY TUCKER

"I was here in slavery times but I don't know what year I was born. War? I was in it!

"I member old master and old mistis too. I member I didn't know nothin' bout my mother and father cause it was night when they went to work and night when they come in and we chilluns would be under the bed asleep.

"I know the white folks had a kitchen full of we chilluns. We went over to the kitchen to eat.

"My mother belonged to the Cockrills and my father belonged to the Armstrongs. They were cousins and their plantations joined.

"I was large enough to know when they took my parents to Texas, but I didn't know how serious it was till they was gone. I member peepin' through the crack of the fence but I didn't know they was takin' em off.

"They left me with the old doctor woman. She doctored both white and colored. I stayed there till I was fourteen years old.

"I know we had our meals off a big wooden tray but we had wooden spoons to eat with.

"I member when they was fightin' here at Pine Bluff. I was standin' at the overseer's bell house waitin' for a doll dress a girl had promised me and the guns was goin' just like pop guns. We didn't know what it was to take off our shoes and clothes for six months. We was ready to run if they broke in on us.

"The Yankees had their headquarters at the big house near the river. All this was in woods till I growed up. We used to have our picnic here.

"I was standin' right at the post when they rung the bell in the bell house when peace declared. I heered the old folks sayin, 'We is free, we is free!'

"I know before freedom they wouldn't let us burn a speck of light at night. Had these little iron lamps. They'd twist wicks and put em in tallow. I don't know whether it was beef or sheep tallow but they had plenty of sheeps on the place.

"Colonel Cockrill would have us come up to the big house every Sunday mornin' and he'd give us a apple or a stick of candy. But them that was big enough to work wouldn't get any. They worked on Sunday too—did the washin' every Sunday evenin'.

"Oh lord, they had a big plantation.

"After the War I went to school some. We had white teachers from the North. I didn't get to go much except on rainy days. Other times I had to work. I got so I could read print but I can't read writin'. I used to could but since I been sick seems like my mind just hops off.

"After freedom my parents rented land and farmed. I stayed with the old doctor woman till I was fourteen then I went to my parents.

"I married when I was eighteen and had five chillun. When I worked for my father he'd let us quit when we got tired and sit under the shade bushes. But when I married I had to work harder than ever. My husband was just a run-around. He'd put in a crop and then go and leave it. Sometimes he was a constable. Finally he went off and took up with another woman.

"I been here in Arkansas all my life except eight months I lived in St. Louis, but I didn't like it. When I was in St. Louis I know it started to snow. I thought it was somebody pickin' geese. I said, 'What is that?' and my granddaughter said, 'Gal, that's snow.'

"I don't know what to think of the younger generation. I think they is just goin' out to nothin'. They say they are gettin' weaker and wiser but I think they are weaker and foolish—they are not wise in the right way. Some are very good to their parents and some are not.

"Honey, I don't know how things is goin'—all I know is they is mighty tight right now."

Interviewer: Mrs. Bernice Bowden
Person interviewed: Emma Turner
330 W. Sixth Avenue, Pine Bluff, Arkansas
Age: 83

EMMA TURNER

"Yes ma'am, I was born in slavery days. They never did tell me when I was born but I was ten the seventh day of August the same year we was freed.

"No ma'am, I wasn't born in Arkansas. I was born in Georgia. I sent there and got my license to show my age. I was twenty years old when I married.

"George Jones was my old master. But, Lawd, them folks is all dead now. Old master and old missis, yes ma'am, all of 'em dead.

"Fight 'round us? No, they didn't fight there but they come through there. Yes ma'am, they come through there. Oh, chile, they got horses and mules.

"Used to give us the Confederate money. Wasn't no good though. They got the silver and gold. Confederate money was white on one side and green on the other. Yes'm, they was Yankees.

"Oh, yes'am, old master was good to us. He didn't never marry. My grandmother was the cook.

"My mother was born in Virginia. I heerd her talk of the Nat Turner Rebellion but I never did see him.

"Our folks stayed right on after freedom and hired by the month. And hired us children for our victuals and clothes.

"I stayed there till I was married. Then I come to Vicksburg, Mississippi. Had nine children and all dead but two.

"Me? Oh, I done washin' and ironin' mostly, cooked and most anything I could get to do. I'm all worked down now though.

"We emigrated from Georgia to Mississippi. All my children born there.

"I 'member the soldiers had guns and we was scared of 'em. We looked for 'em to come up the road but they come out of the woods and was around us right now. They didn't mind creeks or nothin', ridin' horseback or walkin'. I know they said, 'We ain't gwine hurt you.'

"Old master's mother and father was named Sally and Billy. 'Member 'em? 'Co'se I do—many times as I waited on that table. But they all dead 'fore I even thought about bein' grown.

"Oh, yes ma'am, we had a plenty to eat. That's the reason I misses it now.

"I went to school one year but I had to work so hard I done forgot nearly everything I learned. I can read a little but my eyes ain't no good.

"Dem Ku Klux—you dassent be out after dark. You

better not be out on the street after dark. But Sunday night they didn't bother you when you went to church.

"I was raised up with two white girls and their mother didn't 'low us to get out of the yard.

"I used to pick peas and cotton. Yes ma'am, that was when we was with the same old man, George Jones. I used to huddle (herd) cows for miles and miles. My mother was the milk woman. I don't know how many she milked but she milked a heap of 'em.

"Used to climb up in trees and tear our clothes. Then they'd whip us. Old master say, 'Don't you tell me no lie.' Then old Miss Sally would get a stick and make out she gwine kill us, but she wouldn't touch us a lick.

"Younger generation? Now you done asked me too soon. I set here and look at 'em. Sometimes I don't know what gwine come of 'em. When we was young we didn't do nothin' like they doin' now. Why we dassent raise our dresses. If we see a man comin' we pull down our skirts. Yes, Lawd."

United States. Work Projects Administration

FOLKLORE SUBJECTS
Name of interviewer: Watt McKinney
Subject:
Ex-Slave and Confederate Soldiers Story:—Information

This information given by: "Uncle" Henry Turner (c)
Place of residence: Turner, Phillips County, Arkansas
Occupation: Plantation hand
Age: 93
[TR: Information moved from bottom of first page.]

HENRY TURNER

I'm gettin' old and feeble now and cannot walk no more
And I've laid the rusty-bladed hoe to rest.

Ole marster and ole missus are sleeping side by side
And their spirits are a-roamin' with the blest.

The above lines, had they been composed today, might well have been written with reference to "Uncle" Henry Turner, ninety-three years of age, of Turner, Arkansas, in Phillips County, and among the very few remaining ex-slaves, especially of those who were old enough at the time of their emancipation to have now a clear recollection of conditions, customs, events, and life during those days long past immediately proceeding and following the Civil War. "Uncle" Henry's eyes have now grown dim and he totters slightly as, supported by his cane, he slowly shuffles along the path over a short distance between the clean, white-washed cabin where he lives with a daughter and the small, combination store and post office, on the porch of which he is accustomed to sit in an old cane-bottomed chair for a few hours each day and the white folks in passing stop to speak a few words and to buy for him candy, cold drinks, and tobacco.

Though "Uncle" Henry is approaching the century mark in age, his mind is remarkably clear and his recollection is unusually keen. He was born a slave in northern Mississippi near the small towns of Red Banks and Byhalia, was the property of his owner. Edmond Turner, and was brought to Phillips County by "his white folks" some months before the war. Turner, who owned some fifty other slaves besides Henry, settled with his family on a large acreage of land that he had purchased about fifteen miles west of Helena near Trenton. Both Turner and his wife died soon after taking up residence in Arkansas leaving their estate to their two sons, Bart and Nat, who were by that time grown young men, and being very capable and industrious soon developed their property into one of the most valuable plantations in the County.

As "Uncle" Henry recalls, the Turner place was, it might be said, a world within itself, in the confines of which was produced practically everything essential in the life of its inhabitants and the proper and successful conduct of its operations. Large herds of cattle, hogs, sheep, and goats provided a bountiful supply of both fresh and salt meats and fats. Cotton and wool was carded, spun and woven into cloth for clothes, fast colored dyes were made by boiling different kinds of roots and barks, various colored berries were also used for this purpose. Medicine was prepared from roots, herbs, flowers, and leaves. Stake and rider fences enclosed the fields and pastures and while most of the houses, barns and cribs were constructed of logs, some lumber was manufactured in crude sawmills in which was used what was known as a "slash saw". This was something like the crosscut saws of today and was operated by a crank that gave the saw an alternating up and down motion. Wheat was ground into flour and corn into meal in mills with stone burrs similar to those used in the rural districts today, and power for this operation was obtained through the use of a treadmill that was given its motion by horses or mules walking on an inclined, endless belt constructed of heavy wooden slats.

Candles for lighting purposes were made of animal fats combined with beeswax. Plows, harrows and cultivating implements were made on the plantation by those Negroes who had been trained in carpentry and blacksmithing. Plows for breaking the land were sometimes constructed with a metal point and a wooden moldboard and harrows made of heavy timbers with large, sharpened wooden pegs for teeth. Hats of straw and corn shucks were woven by hand.

Small, crude cotton gins were powered by horses or mules hitched to a beam fastened to an upright shaft around which they traveled in a circle and to which was attached large cogwheels that multiplied the animal's power enormously and transmitted it by means of belt to the separating machinery where the lint was torn from the seed. No metal ties were available during this period and ropes of cotton were used to bind the bales of lint. About three bales was the daily capacity of a horse-powered plantation gin.

It was often difficult to obtain the services of a competent doctor and except in cases of serious illness home remedies were administered.

Churches were established in different communities throughout the County and the Negro slaves were allowed the privilege of attending the services, certain pews being set apart for them, and the same minister that attended the spiritual needs of the master and his family rendered like assistant to his slaves.

No undertaking establishments existed here at this time and on the death of a person burial was made in crude caskets built of rough cypress planks unless the deceased was a member of a family financially able to afford the expensive metal caskets that were available no nearer than Memphis. "Uncle" Henry Turner recalls the death of Dan Wilborn's little six-year-old boy, Abby, who was accidentally killed when crushed by a heavy gate on which he was playing, and his burial in what "Uncle" Henry described as a casket made of the same material as an old-fashioned door knob; and while I have no other authority than this on the subject, it is possible that in that day caskets were made of some vitrified substance, perhaps clay, and resembling the present day tile.

The planters and slaveowners of this period obtained the greater share of their recreation in attendance at political rallies, horse races, and cock fights. Jobe Dean and Gus Abington who came to Trenton from their home near La Grange, Tennessee were responsible for the popularity of these sports in Phillips County and it was they who promoted the most spectacular of these sporting events and in which large sums of money were wagered on the horses and the game cocks. It is said that Marve Carruth once owned an Irish Grey Cock on which he bet and won more than five thousand dollars one afternoon at Trenton.

No Negro slave was allowed to go beyond the confines of his owner's plantation without written permission. This was described by "Uncle" Henry Turner as a "pass"; and on this "pass" was written the name of the Negro, the place he was permitted to visit, and the time beyond which he must not fail to return. It seems that numbers of men were employed by the County or perhaps by the slaveowners themselves whose duty it was to patrol the community and be on constant watch for such Negroes who attempted to escape their bondage or overstayed the time limit noted on their "pass". Such men were known then as "Paddy Rolls" by the Negroes and in the Southern states are still referred to by this name. Punishment was often administered by them, and the very mention of the name was sufficient to cause stark terror and fear in the hearts of fugitive slaves.

At some time during that period when slavery was a legal institution in this country, the following verse was composed by some unknown author and set to a tune that some of the older darkies can yet sing:

> Run nigger run, the Paddy Roll will get you
> Run nigger run, it's almost day.
> That nigger run, that nigger flew
> That nigger tore his shirt into.
> Run nigger run, the Paddy Roll will get you

Run nigger run, it's almost day.

Both Bart Turner and his brother Nat enlisted in the services of the Confederacy. Nat Turner was a member of the First Arkansas Volunteers, a regiment organized at Helena and of which Patrick R. Cleburne was colonel. Dick Berry and Milt Wiseman, friends and neighbors of the Turners, also volunteered and enlisted in Cleburne's command. These three stalwart young men from Phillips County followed Cleburne and fought under his battle flag on those bloody fields at Shiloh, Murfreesboro, Ringgold gap, and Atlanta; and they were with him that day in November in front of the old gin house at Franklin as the regiment formed for another and what was to be their last charge. The dead lay in heaps in front of them and almost filled the ditch around the breastworks, but the command though terribly cut to pieces was forming as cooly as if on dress parade. Above them floated a peculiar flag, a field of deep blue on which was a crescent moon and stars. It was Cleburne's battle flag and well the enemy knew it; they had seen it so often before. "I tip my hat to that flag" said the Federal General Sherman years after the war. "Whenever my men saw it they knew it meant fight." As the regiment rushed on the Federal breastworks a gray clad figure on a chestnut horse rode across the front of the moving column and toward the enemy's guns. The horse went down within fifty yards of the breastworks. The rider arose, waved his sword, and led his men on foot to the very ramparts. Then he staggered and fell, pierced with a dozen balls. It was Cleburne, the peerless field-marshal of Confederate brigade commanders. The Southern cause suffered a crushing defeat at Franklin and the casualty list recorded the names of Nat Turner, Dick Berry, and Milt Wiseman, who like their beloved commander had given their life for their country. There is an inscription on the stone base of the magnificent bronze statue of General N. B. Forrest astride his war horse in Forrest Park in Memphis that could well be placed above the graves of Cleburne, Turner, Berry, and Wiseman, those brave, heroic soldiers from Phillips County. The inscription in verse is as follows:

> Those hoof beats die not on fame's crimson sod
> But will live on in song and in story.
> He fought like a Trojan and struck like a god
> His dust is our ashes of glory.

United States. Work Projects Administration

Interviewer: Zillah Cross Peel
Information given by: Seabe Tuttle
Residence: Washington County, seven miles east of Fayetteville.

SEABE TUTTLE

Seabe Tuttle who was born in slavery in 1859, belonged to James Middleton Tuttle of Richland, which was about seven miles east of Fayetteville.

"I was just a baby when the war was but I do recollect a lot of things that my ma told me about the War. Our folks all come from Tennessee. My mother was named Esther, she belonged to Ole Man Tom Smith who gived her to Miss Evaline, who was Mister Mid Tuttle's wife. The Tuttles and Smiths lived joining farms."

"You see, Mister Tuttle was a colonel in the Confederate army and when he went off with the army he left all his slaves and stock in care of Mr. Lafe Boone. Miss Mollie and Miss Nannie, and Miss Jim and another daughter I disrecolect her her name, all went in carriages and wagons down south following the Confederate army. They took my pa, Mark, and other servants, my mother's sister, Americus and Barbary. They told them they would bring them back home after the War. Then my mother and me and the other darkies, men and women and children, followed them with the cattle and horses and food. But us didn't get no further than Dardanelle when the Federals captured us and took us back to the Federal garrison at Ft. Smith, where they kept us six months. Yes'm they were good to us there. We would get our food at the com'sary. But one day my ma and my sister, Mandy, found a white man that said he would bring us back to Fayetteville. No'm, I disremember his name."

"We found us a cabin to live in here. Didn't have to pay rent then likes they do now. We lived here but after a while my mother died. They had two battles 'round here, the Battle of Prairie Grave and one was the Battle of Pea Ridge, after we comed back but no soldiers bothered us. I remember that back from where the Christian church is now, down to the Town Branch, there was a whole lot of Federal soldiers staying, they called it then Cato Branch, cause a man by the name of Cato owned all that land."

"Yes'm, I guess we had a purty good master and missus. We never did get treated much rough."

"After the War, Miss Evaline brought back all the colored people that she took with her, but my father. He got married down there and didn't come back for a long time. Then he did and died here. Two of Miss Eveline's daughters married down there. They didn't have no boys 'tall, just four girls."

"When Peace was made the slaves all scattered. We none was givin' nothin' for as I know. I worked on a farm for $13. a month and my board, for a man down at Oxford's Bend, then I went down to Van Buren where I worked as a porter in a hotel then I went to Morrilton and I married. We come back here and I worked all the time as a carpenter. I worked for Mister A.M. Byrnes. I helped build a lot of fine houses round here and I helped put a roof on the Main Building at the University."

"Yes'm, I own my home down by the school, I can't make much money these days. It kinda worries me. My folks all dead but three of my brothers children. One of these is blind. He lives on the old home my mother had. The county gives him a little food and a little money."

"Yes'm, my white folks were all good to us. Purty good to us."

"After Peace was made though, we all jes' scattered, somehow."

www.ingramcontent.com/pod-product-compliance
Lightning Source LLC
Chambersburg PA
CBHW071618170426
43195CB00038B/1342